All Expenses Paid

John Launer

Pocol Press
Punxsutawney, PA

POCOL PRESS
Published in the United States of America
by Pocol Press
320 Sutton Street
Punxsutawney, PA 15767
www.pocolpress.com

© 2019 by John Launer

All rights reserved. No part of this book may be reproduced in any form whatsoever without the express written consent of Pocol Press. Exceptions are made for brief quotations for criticism and reviews.

Publisher's Cataloguing-in-Publication

Names: Launer, John, 1943-, author.
Title: All expenses paid / John Launer.
Description: Punxsutawney, PA : Pocol Press, 2020.
Identifiers: LCCN 2019955602 | ISBN 978-1-929763-92-4
Subjects: LCSH Launer, John, 1943-. | Vietnam War, 1961-1975--Personal narratives, American. | Vietnam War, 1961-1975--Veterans--Mental health. | Veterans--United States--Psychology. | Press--United States--Influence. | War in mass media. | BISAC BIOGRAPHY & AUTOBIOGRAPHY / Military | BIOGRAPHY & AUTOBIOGRAPHY / Personal Memoirs
Classification: LCC DS559.5 .L378 2020 | DDC 959.704/3/092--dc23

Library of Congress Control Number: 2019955602

Front Cover: The author.

DEDICATION

To the three loves of my life

My Wife
JAN

My Daughter
LISA

My Mother
EMILY

FOR THOSE VIETNAM VETERANS WHO SERVED IN THE COMBAT INFANTRY

Youths, Pawns, Victims

Stand tall, young man, be proud.
And listen to a Greeting from me.
I give to you this duty,
To help me keep people free.

You'll have to leave your loved ones.
Give up your youth, your plans.
But in return a Combat Badge,
I'll put into your hands.

I won't look back in years to come,
Or hear the tales you tell.
But I know you'll go to Heaven,
'Cause you've served your time in hell.

J.L.

Preface

This book is non-fiction. All names have been changed to protect and respect the individuals' privacy.

I feel qualified to say that public opinion of the American Combat Infantrymen in Vietnam has been, and still is, generally incorrect, and has resulted in faulty and unfair judgement. Most of this has been caused by movies and books that contain drugs, sex, and many other untruths, but claim they are telling the facts as they were, "Vietnam – the way it really was." Another part was caused by biased news media. This constant negative barrage has resulted in what I feel is the greatest atrocity of the war; sending America's young people to courageously fight that dirty war, not giving them the support they needed and deserved, labeling them drug users, or murderers for the unfortunate tragedies of war which only combat soldiers had witnessed before this television war. It seems that the Infantry is accused of these things more than any other part of the Armed Forces.

It has become an automatic response when someone finds out you served in Vietnam, you were immediately labeled as an offender of these problems, especially drugs. When it happened to me, I was not only very insulted, but I was also very disappointed that having been to Vietnam was the only qualification needed.

I decided it was way past time for someone to say something in defense of the soldiers. America still doesn't know much about the Infantry because no one has told them.

This easy-to-read book is to speak up and set the record straight, since no one else has bothered to do so. It's a day to day recount of the Infantryman's life; danger, environment, circumstances, stress, and much more. The story about how the boy next door became a combat soldier, then a pawn, and finally a target for society's ill-conceived disgust with the soldiers it sent.

It is written in the first person because it's my story. I have compared my experiences with other Infantry Vets and have found that our tours were very similar. It also helps to draw the reader "into" the events rather than looking at them from the outside. It covers all facets of daily life in the Infantry but focuses on the human interest aspect as opposed to the military and political.

I have recalled most of the book from memory. An experience like this is not forgotten, having been burned into your memory, nor does it even fade much. A small part was supplied by letters home, which were kept by my parents.

Table of Contents

Chapter 1	1
Section I: The Truth	21
Chapter 2	22
How it Began	23
Section II: Developing "The" Attitude	24
Chapter 3	25
Section III: Conditions	32
Chapter 4	33
Chapter 5	39
Chapter 6	45
Chapter 7	50
Chapter 8	55
Chapter 9	67
Chapter 10	74
Chapter 11	127
Section IV: Circumstances	138
Chapter 12	139
Chapter 13	150
Chapter 14	156
Chapter 15	166
Chapter 16	172
Chapter 17	179
Chapter 18	185
Section V: Physical and Emotional Effects	189
Chapter 19	190
Section VI: Looking Back	196
Chapter 20	197

1

Just as it started getting light, rain began falling. The long night was almost over. I sat listening to the rain hitting my helmet, and the few leaves left on the destroyed vegetation, wondering what would happen today, wondering what was happening at home, and knowing we had nothing more to look forward to but another day of the same thing.

I waited quietly for the sun to rise. I was covered with mosquito bites and dirt, getting soaked from the rain, my guts hurt, I was starving, and I stunk. Like everyone else, I needed sleep. But, I was happy. I survived the night. I was alive and one day closer to home.

The sunrises and sunsets during the monsoon season are very nice. Today's sunrise was spectacular, the most beautiful yet. The clouds were an iridescent orange, purple, red and yellow. Big, fluffy clouds that seemed to defy gravity by staying up in the air. The peaceful sunrise that follows a terrible night.

I slowly looked around. It didn't seem like the same place I saw yesterday. The area was slightly rolling and very green. To my front, the stand of bamboo was hacked and shredded. I stared at that for quite a while, remembering the shrapnel and bullets that had passed above me and hit the bamboo. It made my stomach feel like a lump. To my left, the rubber trees were bleeding white latex sap heavily down their trunks. Splintered branches hung loosely. To my right, trees were leaning against each other, lying on the ground, and some were still smoldering, victims of the artillery barrages and air strikes. The scenic area had become a wasteland.

In the center of our perimeter, near the CP, gear was scattered all around; ammo boxes, fatigues, bandages, and some items left by the wounded that were MEDEVACed. Several wounded were being attended to by a Medic. Shirtless and covered with blood and bandages, they were quiet and motionless, waiting for another DUSTOFF. Next to them were poncho-covered bodies, men whose luck had run out. I thought about Ski and Dean. I wanted to know who the casualties were but I didn't look, thinking I'd be better off not knowing.

Craters dotted the area, inside the perimeter, and outside. There was no telling how many twisted bodies littered the surrounding brush.

I walked around my immediate area and looked over the destruction. You can't believe it until you see it; even then you may not believe it. The number of shells, bullets, and bombs flying around must have been unbelievable.

I looked at the men working around the CP. They were dirty, blood spattered, and exhausted. And their eyes, always the eyes; sad, hollow, and aged. Eyes are the window of the soul.

Sgt. Bauer came over from the CP. "You OK, John?"

"Yeah, Sarge," I answered. "What all happened?"

"Well, we had two ground attacks. Centered on the other side. The second one weakened the perimeter. Had a little hand-to-hand. They didn't hit your side directly. But, right over there in the rubber trees, four VC came walking down the trail. Captured all of 'em.

First Sergeant got some shrapnel in his back, below the flak jacket, cuz he was going from position to position making sure everyone had plenty ammo, and to see if he needed to shift some men around. DUSTOFF took a load of dead and wounded in. Several more going in soon. We didn't lose many, but Charlie lost a bunch.

"They'll be back. You can bet on it.

We're going to shift the perimeter, but you go out on OP. Fill in your hole and go down the trail the VC came in on. By yourself, no backup, we need everybody else to dig in for tonight. You can come in about noon and maybe catch some shut-eye. You'll need it because you won't get any tonight either."

I looked once more at the wounded. One was propped against some ammo crates. He had a bandage around his chest and blood was running down his abdomen. Another had a bandage around his head, over his eyes, and blood was smeared all over his chest. The three others had a bandaged leg, hand, and arm. Here and there around the perimeter, the stark white of a fresh bandage marked those not wounded seriously enough to be sent in. Being short of men meant walking wounded would have to stay and fight.

I filled in my hole, filled my magazines and stacked unnecessary gear under a tree. After yelling "OP going out", so I wouldn't get shot, I went down the trail about 80 meters and sat on top of a berm made by the rubber workers to stop soil erosion of the rolling land.

It was cool and scenic under the trees, and I dropped my guard. Sitting on top of the berm was not a good idea and it almost cost me my life. I laid my rifle down, took off my helmet and opened a can of rations. Behind me, in the perimeter, DUSTOFF and resupply helicopters came and went. To my front, the trail disappeared in the trees. All seemed quiet for now.

About 30 minutes later, I heard the familiar AK-47 POP to my left. A green tracer sizzled by my head, less than six inches from my nose. If I had still been eating rations, I would have lost my hand. The quickness of a bullet is slower than the quickness of your thoughts but much faster than your reflexes. It makes you appreciate the fact that you have to be careful because after a shot is fired, it's too late.

I slid down the berm, putting on my helmet and grabbing my rifle as I slid down – "hatting up." I signaled to the perimeter that I was all right.

Shaken, but alert, I scanned the trees for my sniper friend. This one was going to be mine, just mine. I looked and waited for almost an hour but he never showed. He must have run right after he fired – "*didi mau.*"

Exhausted, I had to concentrate on keeping myself alert, and awake. I watched and waited, half expecting another shot from the sniper.

The warm air and sleepless night made it very difficult to stay awake.

About noon, I was relieved on OP. I dragged myself to the perimeter, anticipating that nap. First things first, though. Sgt. Bauer assigned me to a position with Wesley. I helped him finish digging the hole and fill sandbags. Tonight we'd be in the rubber trees, behind a berm, facing that dirt road. I'll be waiting for my sniper friend. Then we cleaned our weapons and set out trip flares and claymore mines.

On the other side of the perimeter, small details of men had been gathering enemy dead and their gear, including weapons. We wanted to go over and take a look, but we had orders to keep busy and stay at our positions. From what I could see, there was a grisly collection of bodies and pieces being accumulated. This many was a good sign because the VC always took the dead and wounded with them when they retreated. This would deny us information about their numbers, condition and other information. If there were enemy bodies left behind, then we know the enemy had been hurt badly. I didn't envy the GI's who had to carry those remnants, but I didn't realize that after several times you become very calloused, even gloating, toward such a thing. It doesn't become fun, but it does become a satisfied vengeance to know you made it and they didn't.

While this was going on, choppers were flying in and out of the perimeter, dropping off rations, ammo and a water trailer. It looked like we were going to be here for a while. We never got much information about plans and played it mostly by ear. If you happened to be one of those people who need to know what's going to happen in the next few minutes, hours, or even days, you'd never make it here. No one knows much for sure, and anyone who does know something doesn't tend to share it with grunts. You just have to wait and see, hang in there.

One of the choppers circling the area landed and out climbed the Commanding General himself, General Westmoreland, followed by three newsmen with a TV camera. The General met a few officers and looked around while the newsmen filmed. The newsmen followed closely behind the General, never venturing more than a few yards from him. In less than 30 minutes, they were gone, long before dark. I never heard what was reported from their visit but it seemed to me that if they wanted to report the full story, they should spend some time with the grunts. It seemed they would be showing bits and pieces, probably only parts of their own choosing. If they stayed the night, they could report what happened from beginning to end and not show an edited war.

It was late afternoon and I happily stretched out on the dirt for a nap, oblivious to all the noise and activity. The VC must have been waiting for just this moment because in a few minutes the camp was mortared. As exhausted as we were, we found plenty of strength to jump into our holes. The mortar attack didn't last long and I quickly dozed off again, lulled to sleep by distant sounds of helicopters, jets and artillery, and nearby explosions of DEFCON's the FO was setting for the action we expected after dark.

After a nap of about three hours, Chief and Blue woke me to give me some mail that came in one of the choppers. In the distance, I could still hear the sounds of war. We BS'ed for a few minutes in the twilight, relaxing before the night's onslaught.

"Wish we had a full moon tonight so we could see them little bastards," Blue said.

"Yeah," Chief said. "Least there's no damn rain. Clear so you can see them stars. And these are the same stars you see at home. There ain't but one moon and there it is through the trees." Blue and I laughed at the unexpected response to yesterday's riddle, "Are they the same stars as at home"? We enjoyed having a little diversion provided by the riddles. It helped keep us from dwelling on the war and the emptiness of being so far from home. Chief continued, "I got one for you. What percent of grunts get killed or wounded? There's something to think about."

We drifted back to our positions to prepare for Charlie's visit tonight.

"See you in the morning. Get a good night's rest."

"You take care of your shit. I got mine together."

"If you need help with the heavy stuff, let me know."

Sgt. Bauer was just walking by to the CP and he added to our remarks, "If you hear something behind you during the night, don't shoot. It might be me crashing over the berm to get up to the line."

It was too dark to reread my mail, so I folded it and stuffed it into a pocket, wondering if I would survive the night and could read it in the morning. Staring out into the night, I too wished there was a full moon.

The seasons seemed to be changing. Rain fell less frequently, and the sky was clear more often. The wet season seemed to be trying to give way to the dry season, sort of like our daily mood change I noticed around camp. Everybody was happy in the morning, sleep or not. They were alive. As the day wore on, we became tight, pensive. After dark, everyone became quiet, alert, and tense.

Here we were again, in the dark, watching, and waiting. It seemed as though night came earlier each day and lasted longer. So we waited, wondering when and where Charlie would hit, and what else we could do to get ready; rifle in hand, magazines laid out, grenades placed within reach, Claymore detonators lined up-left, middle, right. Ready to shoot, to kill. In the dark, you needed everything in place so you didn't have to waste precious time searching.

There was no marijuana here, or drugs. No one wanted to be in a stupor at a time like this. Nor did anyone want to put their life in the hands of someone whose brain was mush. Since we never knew when Charlie would hit us, nor have any free time, marijuana and drugs were not found in this unit, during my tour anyway.

Wait. Listen. They're out, somewhere. Watch. Look out into the dark. Keep alert. They will hit us. Since we didn't move our perimeter from last night's location, they knew exactly where we were.

During Advanced Combat training, one of the instructors told us, "Ninety ten. Remember that. For an Infantryman, life is ninety percent pure boredom, and ten percent sheer, stark terror. But, that ten percent will be ninety percent of your memories." I guess he was right about the ten percent. The ninety percent boredom was never from a lack of something to do, but from doing the same things over and over, every day, and waiting; waiting for chow, waiting for immunizations, wait for pay, and now we're waiting for someone to shoot at us.

Wait. Listen. Watch.

My stomach groaned, and I realized I had time to eat only once today. I hadn't shaved, read any mail or done anything for myself, for me, except take care of the trots. Nothing new about that.

In the distance were those sounds; helicopters, artillery, machine guns. All around us, in every direction.

Our bunker was set between two rows of rubber trees, so we had a clear lane of fire, like a bowling alley. Zipper was in the position to our left, and Chief had a 75mm recoilless rifle to our right, each between his own rows of trees. Good old Chief. He was tall and skinny, but strong. His Indian heritage gave him his nickname. He was a good man to have on your side.

Sgt. Bauer came by and said, "They're out there. Several positions have reported seeing cigarettes glowing, getting all screwed up on marijuana. Makes 'em do crazy shit. Crazy." Then he moved on, checking on his men.

Wesley and I had agreed on guard hours on the slim chance we would get some sleep. It was about 8 P.M. I was anticipating a little snooze when we heard that distinctive POOP of a mortar. All our senses immediately became tuned in. Muscles and stomachs tightened. Adrenalin started pumping. Breathing quickened. Eyes widened. Sweat trickled. Hearts pounded. POOP. POOP.

We jumped for our bunker at the same time. Wesley said, "Oh shit. Gimme my shootin' iron. They'll be here right after the mortars."

WHAM. The mortar rounds hit inside our perimeter. Then everything broke loose.

Going into combat, you feel numb. Your mouth is dry. It's very noisy. The volume of noise, activity and explosions is scary, confusing. The air becomes electrified. Bright flashes of light stab the darkness for a split second, then shrapnel searches for you. You can't move fast enough, but you don't know what you'll need to do next. You remain focused out front and you are ready to shoot at anything that moves, shoots or is suspicious.

Rockets and mortars exploded all around us. We ducked lower in our holes and waited for an occasional pause to stick our head out and see if the VC were moving in. We had nothing to shoot at until then. WHAM. WHAM. Mortar shells hammered the ground. Every round felt as though it missed us by a few feet. The ground was jarred again and again. Sweat rolled down our faces as we hunkered down in our holes, hiding from the shrapnel. Dirt from the explosions showered down on us and stuck to our sweat soaked skin and fatigues. The mortars continued to pound us, trying to soften the perimeter for the ground attack that was sure to come next.

After about an hour, the shells eased up and green tracers started coming in. The VC hit the perimeter from two sides; ours and the side to our left. We grabbed our rifles and peered over the berm. Artillery explosions briefly lit enemy figures moving toward us. My skin crawled and my hair stood on end. Shadowy figures were everywhere, and they were suicidal enemy. Somewhere out there may be a bullet with my name on it. Maybe more than one.

We opened fire on the advancing, shadowy figures. Some of them crumpled. Their green tracers hit all around us. An RPG spewed just overhead and hit somewhere behind us. Artillery crunched in the trees outside the perimeter. An artillery flare popped. Light. Bless those flares. Zipper opened up with his machine gun. There was a steady stream of tracers from his position that ricocheted off trees and rocks, bouncing off in many different directions. Chief was firing recoilless rounds that exploded heavily (a great weapon we called a stovepipe).

We fired, ducked below the berm to reload, then fired some more. A grenade exploded on the other side of the berm. Another RPG spewed by. We ducked lower. Wes yelled, "My helmet. Where's my damn helmet?" He couldn't find it in the dark. Wes fired into the green tracers. Artillery shells exploded. Machine guns fired. Grenades and Claymores went off. The VC were at the perimeter. We felt like we may be overrun. We fired as fast as we could.

If you could verbalize the sounds of combat, it would be something like
WHAMPOPPOPTAKATAKAPOWWHAMWHAMCRASHTAKATA KATAKA[POPPOPBOOMWHAMBOOMTAKATAKATATTATTAT TATPOWPOWPOPBOOMWHAMTAKATAKATAKA, all spoken in just a few seconds. The Fourth of July would be green with envy.

Load another magazine and fire. Green tracers hit leaves and branches just above our heads and the ground around us. Some ricocheted off crazily. They knew exactly where we were. It was going to be a bloody one.

We depended on artillery explosions and occasional flares for light to find targets. I fired into the dark. Artillery flashed. I adjusted and fired at two advancing figures, crouching as they moved toward us. I hit one. The other kept coming and threw a grenade. I fingered the Claymore detonator. No, save it in case they mass attack. Don't waste it. I threw a grenade and yelled at Wesley. He eased to the top of the berm after the explosion and stood to fire down the other side. He fired a whole magazine, slid back down, and yelled, "Wonder who that was?"

The entire perimeter was lit up, firing. It sounded as though the whole war had been condensed and placed right here. Zipper's gun spewed tracers all over, searching for the enemy. Wesley yelled right next to my ear, "We're going to run low on ammo. Who's going back for more before it gets rough?" Would I rather leave the safety of our hole and leave the line, or stay here and fight it alone?

We looked out into the trees, the darkness, and an artillery flare exposed two figures. Wesley yelled, "Look." Two VC were running straight toward our position. The man in front had a Claymore type mine strapped to his chest, and apparently the man behind him had the detonator in one hand and a rifle in the other. They were getting close. If the flare hadn't popped when it did, we wouldn't have seen them until it was too late. Wesley dove for our detonator and I fired at number two, the man with their detonator. BOOM. Number two was blown backward by the impact of our mine, along with dirt and tree branches, and was pinned to a tree trunk by the steel shot. Number one disintegrated. In the blink of an eye, he just disappeared, vaporized. Poof, and a human being was no longer there, MIA forever.

The blast set off our trip flares. We had two Claymores left and no trip flares.

I yelled, "You go after the ammo. Get anything you can carry. See what's happening." He gave me his last full magazine and took off in a crouch.

The flare burned out and it was dark again. No light. No moon. I imagined all sorts of VC coming at me in the dark. I'm sure everyone had doubts about making it through this night.

BOOM. Chief fired his recoilless rifle. He'd do that only if he had a serious target, close.

WHAM. More mortar rounds hit all around us. One exploded behind me, about where Wesley should be. A picture flashed through my mind of Wesley on the ground in the morning, a poncho draped over his motionless body. Then TAPS, and then the flag. Just hang on, maybe he made it. Maybe Sgt. Bauer will come by soon. WHAM. WHAM. More rounds fell around me. I ducked lower in my hole. CRASH. A tree limb fell over my hole. Magazines fell around me. I felt in the dirt for what I could find and scrambled to the top of the berm.

Wesley came stumbling back, cursing. "Son of a bitching,..." WHAM. "...ing VC bastards."

"I thought you were a goner," I yelled.

"YOU did? Damn mortar round hit the other side of a tree from me and knocked my young ass down. 'Bout broke my head. Sgt. Bauer was coming the other way and I took everything he had; ammo, LAW's, grenades. We're ready....."

"Help me get this damn limb off our hole," I interrupted. "You OK?"

"Yeah, if I can get my heart thumping again."

Another flare popped and exposed us. We immediately dove for cover. Neither one of us had any use for a Purple Heart. A blizzard of green tracers passed overhead. The realization that they were meant for us personally, left me with a very insecure feeling. Training can prepare you for a lot of things but not the other half of combat – getting shot at, just waiting for the bullet that hits you. The tree limb stayed.

We crawled back to the top of the berm in time to see several VC in Chief's alley of trees. The recoilless fired. One VC was cut in half, the top half flying backwards. Two more VC were spun around, then fell. The remaining VC panicked and ran into our alley. They were close and well-lit by a low flare. I saw black pajamas, crossed bandoliers, and at least one that appeared to be a female. That upset me. Not because I was going to shoot a female, but because during the day she would use her gender to hide in public and all the while she would be planning to kill more Americans. I never hesitated shooting a female after today. We opened fire, knocking four down. The few left continued running down Zipper's alley and he finished them off. It was like a shooting gallery, a game, where humans became nothing more than targets. But, if you miss the targets, you may not get a second chance.

The whole intention of combat is death, either yours or the VC's. I was beginning to realize I wasn't intimidated for shooting a human. They were merely targets. Anxious or nervous – maybe. But, not horrified. There was no enjoyment, but no regrets, either.

The shooting here stopped for a while, we waited, reloading magazines. I glanced behind us, and through the rubber trees I could see tracers all around the perimeter. Screams, yells, and gunfire. The flares stopped, but shooting continued. Green tracers streamed in along our side of the perimeter. We fired in response, hoping for another flare soon.

This made the third attack in twenty four hours. Surely the VC will run out of ammo and men soon.

I didn't know how long we had been fighting but I was beginning to feel dehydrated, tired, hollow and long overdue for a break. I was totally exhausted; physically, mentally, and emotionally.

Where's Puff tonight? We could sure use those big flares and guns.

Another artillery flare popped. Bless those flares. I quickly scanned the area out front before the flare burned out, and was surprised to see only one body and one live VC. The bodies that had littered had disappeared during the dark interval between flares. I felt cheated. Our rewards of victory had disappeared, our measure of accomplishment.

The lone VC, dragging the last body away, was immediately joined by two others. Evidently, they came out to provide cover for the first VC because they turned toward us, almost face to face, and returned our fire. Our two lines of tracers converged on one VC. His arm flew off, the grenade in his hand dropped and exploded, killing him and the second VC. It was just like a John Wayne movie. It couldn't happen except by sheer luck.

The flare flickered out. In seconds, another popped, and another. We fired, emptying our magazines. More VC came. Damn. Where are they coming from? How many will we kill before they get to us?

The flare burned out. Green tracers started coming in heavily. We fired and my rifle jammed. No flares to see by. I felt around in the dark, trying to find my cleaning rod. We had been trained to clean and maintain our rifles in the dark. I found a grenade and threw it in case the VC were sneaking up on us in the darkness. Our position was a mess. Wesley yelled, "Come on, they're gonna get closer." Oh, shit. What can I do? I can't find anything. I can't see anything. I can't do anything. My hand hit a LAW. That'll buy us some time. I fumbled with it in the dark, and fired. WHOOSHBLAM. The green tracers stopped for a while, long enough to let me find my rod and unjam my rifle.

Then it started over again. Mortars hit. Tracers streaked in. The VC must have regrouped for a last attempt.

WHAMBAMBLAM. Our artillery was screaming in, tight against the perimeter. We had to get low in our hole because of shrapnel and concussion. The explosions rattled our brains and bounced us in the air. I felt as though I was in a barrel and giants were hitting the barrel with tree trunks. It literally rained artillery. The heaving earth bounced us around in our holes. Showers of rock and dirt fell on is. I pushed my fingers into my ears until I thought they might meet in the middle of my head. I wondered which would happen first; dirt would cover me; a shell would land on us; I would be thrown out of the hole by the heaving earth; or I would lose my mind and run through the trees holding my head, and screaming. The barrage continued for about an hour, shifting here and there around the perimeter, searching. The FO was bringing hurt on Charlie; he was good. But yet, I could fully understand how there could be casualties from "Friendly Fire."

The explosions stopped and flares popped again. I pictured heads slowly poking out of holes, faces smeared with dirt and blood, sunken eyes looking for movement, ears listening for any enemy activity clues. No sound, just eye movement.

Dawn is close, maybe an hour or so. Just wait it out.

A few red tracers went out, nothing came back. Quiet, deathlike silence, hung over the perimeter, punctuated by occasional moans from wounded, and the burning of a nearby flare which sounded like bacon frying.

We reloaded magazines while we waited and listened. Nothing happened.

Exhausted, hungry and thirsty, the perimeter gradually stirred to life. Medics were busy, going from position to position. GI's not wounded stood to work the stiffness out of their legs, and check on friends.

You can't tell much of what is happening during the night. So much happens so fast that you're too busy to think about it. You search your memory for events you can remember. They're slow to return. It doesn't matter anyway. You made it through the night and you're happy for that. That's all that's important right now. Three hundred days to go, half a million minutes. Just take each day one minute at a time.

Dawn came and I looked around, dreading what I was going to see. Green clad GI's, tired and homesick, were busy trying to help tend to wounded, cleaning and repairing positions, and cleaning weapons. What are these young men doing here? Why us? We're no different than anyone else back in the States. Same needs, same wants. We might even be protesting the war if we hadn't been sent here. We didn't want this but we have adapted and fought very well, for Country, and for survival.

As the daylight got brighter, we got a better look at the perimeter, and the area just outside the perimeter.

Wesley looked over the berm and said, "There's my helmet. It rolled down the other side and that's what I shot. Damn thing's full of holes." He held it up. The helmet had three holes shot through the top. "Have to get another one off a KIA," he continued, sticking his finders through the holes. "Makes you wonder how much protection they really are."

I dug some bullets and shrapnel out of the sandbags on the front of our bunker. Nice souvenirs, reminders of what almost was. The sandbags were shredded, dirt trickling out like sand in an hour glass.

The rubber trees were bleeding white sap where they were hit during all the firing. Some trees were leaning against others, blasted by the artillery. Craters of all sizes pocked the area.

I saw our Medic at Chief's position and went over. He had been hit in the shoulder. His fatigue jacket had been cut off, and blood all over his position. He was moaning from pain and exhaustion.

Everyone had aged overnight, old age older. The eyes, always the eyes, reflected their tiredness of it all. They were not the same people as before last night; it was a night that changed lives, and ended lives. You can't go through that and be the same. You can't know there are many more days of this ahead and not change. To survive, you must fight back emotionally, become angry, and develop a mean streak, maybe even hatred. With each death-filled night, with each day of stink and fear, the bitterness, frustration, resentment, anger and hatred become more ingrained. When this happens, you quickly learn how cheap life can be, how easy to kill without regret, without guilt. Deep inside there is something trying to remind you that you should feel guilty. But, it's kept down inside, to be dealt with later, because if you let it surface now it'll kill you. You have to become calloused. It's necessary for your own wellbeing. War is harsh and cruel and, to survive, you must be also.

I held a cigarette for Chief to smoke while the Medic worked on his wounds. Through clenched teeth, he asked for a drink of water. I held his head up so he could swallow. The Medic said Chief would probably go to a hospital in Japan and be back in a month, maybe two.

Chief said, "Screw you. I'm going home. This is my ticket home."

The Medic responded, "Never happen. You'll be back. DUSTOFF'll be here in a few minutes. Better di di to the LZ."

I said, "Come on, I'll get you there." I helped him stand, his good arm across my shoulders for support. After another drink of water, we stumbled off to the LZ. As we moved, he said "I don't want to come back to this son of a bitch. If they take me to Japan, it'll take a lot of big MP's to get me back."

Occasional moans came from other wounded being moved toward the LZ. Chief said, "You can have the sodas in my pack. Shit, you can have anything you want in my pack. I don't intend to come back even if I have to get VD. Get VD, avoid VC." He was feeling punchy and tried to laugh at his own joke until it made him hurt. "Besides, I got to count the percent killed, and the wounded, in the hospitals."

What do you say to somebody that's been shot, in pain and oozing blood? "You're going to be all right"? He knows whether or not he'll be ok. "You look good?" "You look bad?"

The chopper arrived shortly. I helped Chief aboard, and then helped carry others, some of them friends. Both wounded and dead. Some cried out in pain from being moved. I was afraid one died during movement because he stopped breathing. The dead look back at you with glassy eyes. The wounded look back at you with eyes that ask for help, pain filled eyes. Pain that's soul deep. You want to reach out, to help, but you can't do any more than you're doing right now.

One man lost a leg, another his arm, another his life. It's difficult to get the memory of dead friends out of your head, but it's impossible to erase the picture of someone in pain, suffering, dying.

I wondered if I had been in one of their foxholes, and one of them in mine, wouldn't they be helping me aboard right now? Wouldn't that same bullet or shrapnel have hit me? Isn't it all just a matter of being in the wrong place at the wrong time? It's very strange carrying a casualty off the battlefield, almost like saying, "You didn't make it. You go back. A replacement will be sent to try his luck. We made it, so our reward is to stay for more. We'll try to hold out until our year is over."

As we loaded the last body on the floor of the chopper, and the whine of the turbine engine got louder, I gave my friend a thumbs up and said, "If I see you again, I hope it's back in the world." Then they were gone.

Walking back to my position, I clearly realized the feeling of isolation was beginning to nag at me. We were isolated from everything that we knew and trusted, but the strongest feeling came from having to deal with your own possible death, alone. Twenty four hours a day, you have a fear that any time, any second, you could get killed. It wears you down mentally and makes you feel very alone. No one at home can help you. Your buddies here can't help you. They have to deal with the same problem themselves. Here you are, born a free person, trapped in a world that deals solely in earth, and nowhere to turn for help. You share food with your buddies, cigarettes, laughs, even your blood, but your death is yours to face alone.

An artillery shell hit outside the perimeter and I instinctively hit the ground. I got up as quickly when I realized it was not near enough to hit me. Anxiety, from loud sudden noises, and sudden movement, had developed a reflex reaction to dive for cover that would stay with us for many years after we returned home. As I returned to the perimeter, I tried to remember the night's events. Just what did I do? How much of it had I learned during training? Did training really help me?

When I got back, Wesley said, "Grab your rifle. We're supposed to sweep out front, see what we can find."

He continued, "Man shit, Chief got it. Somebody in Zipper's position was killed. We were right in the middle and didn't get hit. Down that way, VC broke through the perimeter. What did we do right?"

We took off, over the berm, and entered last night's never-land along with a handful of other guys from our Company. A morbid curiosity had set in. I wanted to see dead enemy as a sort of assurance that we had fought well, and that they paid for our dead and wounded. I wanted to see that they had been hurt. I couldn't believe I was thinking these things. I had never felt anything like this before in my life. War does change people, now I knew. The real question in my mind was if it's temporary or permanent.

First, I saw the VC pinned to the tree. He was just hanging there, like a rag doll, a pool of blood on the ground. Leaves and branches were everywhere, scattered by the explosions. As we moved, we found pieces of gear the VC had dropped in the dark; canteens, magazines, grenades, a little clothing. A little further were craters, trees blown over, drag marks where the VC dragged their dead away, plenty of blood, and bandages.

Then came bodies, as if the VC had gotten this far and had to abandon the effort to retrieve bodies, or join them. Twisted, mangled, bloody, mutilated human bodies, some just young kids, had already started to draw flies; intestines hanging out, legs and arms missing, heads half gone, clothes shredded to rags, face missing, a stray leg, half a body. You can't believe these things until you see them for yourself. This is why we were here, though. This was our mark of accomplishment.

Revolting. Victorious. Nauseating. Proud. Disgusting. Successful. I wasn't sure what I felt. Or, maybe I did, but couldn't believe it. This is what we were supposed to be doing, right? We did it well, right? Why shouldn't we be proud? This was not to be the end, though. Or even the middle, but the beginning of an unforgettable year. We would see these things many more times.

The way the bodies had been dragged and then abandoned, I felt sure the artillery put a stop to their activities. I also realized that retrieving bodies must be a high priority thing for the VC, just as it was for us, and that I had personal doubts that our body counts were inflated, as I would read in future years.

One of our Company officers came out and told us to gather the bodies and gear for the official count. We dragged the bodies to a nearby artillery crater, which would become their grave. An OP was set out to watch for snipers. Somebody said, "Be careful moving the bodies. If the VC had time, they may have booby trapped some." What an inglorious end for a soldier, to be dragged like a sack of potatoes, guts hanging out. There were NVA uniforms, black pajamas, that female, and some kids. Some of the bodies were getting stiff and starting to stink. Every one of them could easily hide, disguised as a friendly villager. Just because they aren't armed doesn't mean they aren't the enemy.

Life had no meaning here and now, no value. People were checked off like numbers on a pad; alive, dead, wounded. Cold bodies, warm bodies. I promised myself that if I made it back home, I was going to enjoy living, appreciate every day, and accomplish something for me. I felt I have earned it.

We rolled the bodies into the crater, after carefully moving them first to make sure a booby trap was not triggered, covered them with dirt, and went back to the perimeter. We were covered with more dirt, blood and stink. There is no place to clean up out here, no clean clothes to change into, so we went about our business, eating, reading mail, cleaning our weapons, and whatever. I opened a can of rations, dug yesterday's wadded up mail from home out of my pocket, and let my mind wander half a world away for just a few minutes. I have got to write a note home, let them know I'm ok. I found a small scrap of paper and pencil stub I'd been saving.

Nov. 7 (I think)
Dear Mom, Dad, Janice and David.
How are you guys doing? I hope everyone is well. I'm doing fine. Keeping busy. Still in the field. I'm not sure what day it is, but I think it's a Sunday in November. Days change back and forth from

rainy and coolish, to dry and hot. I haven't decided which are worse. Thanks for the cookies, Mom. Can't tell you how much they mean. You should start getting my paychecks soon. Just put them in the bank for me. Don't really know much but I need to get back to work. No more room on this paper anyway. Keep those letters coming - they mean a lot. 307 (?) days to go.
Love, John

No need to tell them more than that. No need.

Sgt. Bauer came over and sat down. "No rest yet. We've got the honor of a 10 click (10,000 meters) sweep to look for Charlie. See if he's still around or what. We hurt him bad, so he probably is leaving the area, knowing we will come looking.

"Delta found a dead Chinese advisor and a lot of NVA uniforms. They are up to something big. The airstrip's been hit hard, too. And the town. VC killed a bunch of villagers; women, kids, and old people. Real nasty bastards."

"How many did we lose, Sarge?" Wesley asked.

"Don't know for sure yet. Still finding things. One guy was hit and thrown over the berm and didn't realize it. He tried to crawl away from the berm. Instead of going to the CP, he crawled the wrong way, farther outside the perimeter.

"Found some dog tags in the bushes. One bunker collapsed and they're digging it out. So, we lost about ten. But, it's not over yet." Even though he was talking about lives, he seemed removed, emotionally detached. He wasn't, but he didn't want it to eat on him.

"Get ready to move. Bring extra ammo, water and C's in case we hit some shit."

I went to the water trailer to fill my canteens. Several guys were there pouring Kool-Aid into their canteens to cover the lousy taste of the treated water. I considered writing home to ask someone to send Kool-Aid but I kept thinking about getting cavities in my teeth. Of all the things to worry about in a combat zone, cavities were the least hazardous. I was probably one of only a few Infantrymen in Vietnam to worry about getting cavities. I was sure I had seen very few brush their teeth in the field.

The water tank was almost empty. It didn't matter though. We'd probably leave in a day or so. We don't want this piece of ground. We successfully defended it, but we'd move on and maybe fight for it again someday. You'd think it would be our territory now, but that's not the way it works in this war. It's more like a boxing match than a football game. In football, you fight to gain ground, but in boxing, the ring is secondary and the opponent is the objective.

On my way back to the perimeter, I went by the CP to get some rations and ammo. That's when I saw my first serious case of combat stress. The poor guy was just sitting on an ammo box, staring straight ahead. Tears were running down his cheeks and he was trembling. He didn't utter a sound or seem to hear anything going on around him. I couldn't imagine what it must be like for your mind to just give up, to throw up a wall and shut out the world. I supposed it could happen to anyone but for some reason I thought a new guy in country would be the most likely candidate. This guy wasn't new. His scuffed boots and worn helmet cover told of many weeks in the bush. The endless days of stress and exhaustion finally took their toll. When you operate 24 hours a day, seven days a week, knowing you can be killed any second, humping your guts out in the boonies, constantly living in the elements, seeing your friends die, and getting very little sleep or rest, you get worn thin mentally and emotionally. Eventually, it'll get to you. A lesson I learned quickly was to divide everything into two groups; things involving survival, the things you need to worry about; and everything else, which you make yourself forget about, or as the saying goes, "Don't sweat the small stuff." The less cluttered the first group, the larger the second group, the better off you'll be.

 We took off on our 10K patrol, toward the border with Cambodia; back to the grind. It was all still there, waiting; heat, sweat, bugs, stink, exhaustion, senses on high alert, eyes always moving, and always looking for booby traps and snipers. Moving through the trees was easy but we were ideal targets for snipers. I felt it in my bones that we were going to get hit. I could feel foreign eyes watching us. Certainly, we were meant to be bait, but if someone didn't go look for the enemy how would we ever find them?

 Wesley and I drew flank. The terrain was rolling and in a few places was very steep. At the bottom of these rolls and steeps was always a stream wide enough, and lined with enough brush, to cause problems getting across.

 After a couple of hours of over hill and dale, we stopped for a break. No one had sighted the enemy. In fact, there hadn't been anything moving; no rubber tree workers, no villagers, and no animals. I didn't know where the Vietnamese were, but I was sure all the animals had been killed, eaten, or had to run for their lives.

 We took off again, bone tired from lack of sleep, but able to find the strength to keep pushing. We moved hoping to find a sign that we were going in the right direction. It finally came, unexpectedly. After hours of looking up in the trees and scanning the distance, we stumbled upon a nest of fighting holes. There were hundreds of them, a few feet deep and about eighteen inches across. Most of them had a small cache of food and gear; gas masks, grenades, rice balls, and cooking utensils. They were obviously meant to be returned to by a sizable fighting force which had its mind changed. It was a good sign because we were not only in the right area, but it meant that Charlie was hurt badly. The main force must have retreated over the nearby Cambodian border so we couldn't follow. We collected the explosive material, smashed the gear, scattered the rice and continued patrolling. We passed a small village surrounded by dense brush. There was no sign of life, nobody in sight. The CO radioed Battalion to see if we were to search and was denied. We moved a short distance from the village and all hell broke loose. We must have spoiled an ambush set around the village. AK's POP POPPed and Wesley and I took cover, cut off from the file. The firefight was short and intense. Grenades punctuated the exchange of rifle fire, and then everything sputtered out. I doubt if any of us even saw a VC. They just disappeared, poof, like magic. We moved ahead through the brushy area cautiously, but found nothing. Neither side had any kills. It seemed as though we were back to the cat and mouse game.

We dragged ourselves through the rest of the 10 K somehow, moving our exhausted limbs with monumental effort. It was late in the day and we were in no condition to fight again all night, not without some rest. Almost everyone from the patrol immediately lay down, right on the dirt, sticks and rocks, gear still on, hungry, thirsty, and slept about three hours until dark.

The night was curiously and gratefully uneventful, compared to the previous two nights. Only sporadic sniper fire interrupted the otherwise quiet of the night, probably intended to keep us from sleeping; harassment. But, guarding one hour on and two off, we managed maybe five hours sleep. As usual, it was a sleep of exhaustion, waking in the same position as when we fell asleep, not bothered by the mosquitos or ants, rifle still in hand.

The next day, a different Company drew patrol and we stayed in. We didn't get to sleep, though. Somebody always found something for us to do; replace torn sand bags, repair fighting holes, clean weapons, bury trash, improve lanes of fire, set out more trip flares and Claymores.

About two in the afternoon, the OP on our side of the perimeter was hit by a sniper. He didn't respond to communication so a squad of us went out to check on him. He had a chest wound. His lung was hit and he was drowning in his own blood. He kept saying, "Die ... Die ...," over and over. He knew he wouldn't make it. He looked at us with pleading eyes as we bandaged his chest and tried to gently move him to the LZ for a DUSTOFF. A sucking chest wound is one of the ugliest wounds you'll ever see a person suffer with, fighting for his life. The wound drains foamy, red blood. The wounded fights to breathe, to stay alive. His life keeps oozing out of him. You cover it with a nonporous material like plastic or rubber so the lung can inflate. But, it's hopeless out here. We left him with the Medic. You can stay around a dead body and not get too involved emotionally, but someone dying a painful death is a different story. We did what little we could, but he didn't live.

The patrol returned and reported light contact.

We got ready for the night. All we could do is wait, listen, wonder and stay loose; that ninety percent boredom. Just be ready.

The night was uneventful, with only a few visits from a sniper. The next day we drew patrol again. Rumor had it that we would move if we didn't hit sustained contact. Back to the grind. It never changed much. Always a struggle, a fight. This patrol seemed to be as routine as yesterday's. Charlie was nowhere in sight. He seemed to have called it quits and left us looking for him. We stopped about midday to eat and we set out a two-man OP. They disappeared into the thick brush to set up on the edge of a nearby dirt road. In about thirty minutes, we heard an RPG explode in the OP's direction, but no return small arms fire. Sgt. Bauer told five of us to grab our weapons and go with him to check it out. We moved cautiously through the brush. Wesley and I went out onto the road and looked around. The only thing we saw was a Non La, a conical coolie hat, with a female's ribbon chin strap, lying in the road. Voices came from the edge of the road a few meters away. We went over and saw what was left of the men on OP. The RPG hit a small tree next to one of the men. He lost his face and half his chest. The other man's arm and side looked like hamburger but he was still alive. He was telling Sgt. Bauer that two females were walking along the road, and one had a bundle on her shoulder. They called out to stop the females, to check the bundle. The one turned the bundle toward them and fired. It was an RPG. He said he should have known better that to trust females instead of shooting them. A DUSTOFF landed on the road shortly, and we put the two aboard. Charlie scored again. This was getting old; carrying bloody mangled bodies; watching our numbers slowly dwindle. These two had not been in-country long enough to become desensitized and callous enough to suspect the two Vietnamese, female or not.

We returned to our perimeter, a little sadder, a little wiser, and a lot angrier.

It was late in the afternoon and a resupply helicopter was coming soon, bringing rations, ammo, water, and mail. We were short on food and morale so we waited patiently. When the chopper just came into view, about a mile away, all heads turned and watched silently as the just-visible sling broke and fell to the ground. Since it was late, and the sling was far away, Charlie would not only get resupplied with our food and ammo, but he'll get our mail, too. I mentally pictured some VC son of a bitch eating my cookies from home and reading my mail.

We cursed the luck and shared the rations we had left. Infantrymen are more generous to each other than to friends. We looked after each other because each other is all we had. We drew no lines of distinction by race, religion, or anything else. We were brothers, family.

After another uneventful night, we were told to destroy our perimeter because we were moving out. We scored another battle victory, but didn't claim the ground. We just folded up and moved on. Hours later, soaked in sweat, hungry and tired, we waited for choppers to take us somewhere else. We didn't know where we were going, and didn't care. We did know that, wherever we would be, we had more of the same thing waiting for us.

I wanted to write a letter home but I didn't have any paper and probably not enough time. I'd just have to wait until we returned to Dau Tieng, between operations. Writing letters in the field was nearly impossible. Short notes were tough, but possible. In fact, I still had a note in my pocket that I hadn't been able to mail. Probably a moisture-soaked wad by now.

We flew back to the airstrip at Loc Ninh, where we landed in the C-130 aircraft when we first arrived, but it didn't look like the same place. The first time we landed, the rubber trees were growing right up to the edge of the runway. Now, the big trees were leveled for over a hundred meters. Lacking the manpower that we had to repulse the attack of a large force, artillery was airlifted in and fired point blank, directly at the approaching enemy, level with the ground, like giant shotguns. So many rounds were fired that the forest of trees was turned into a complete wasteland.

The battle at Loc Ninh was called Operation Shenandoah Number Two, for my Battalion. Officially, a different Division would get the credit for anything that we did because we were under their OpCon (Operational Control). In history books, where it might receive a line or two, it would be called one of the three Border Battles of 1967 (Loc Ninh, Dak To, and Con Thien). At the time, the attacks were thought to be a plan of the VC to disrupt the election and inauguration of the Republic of South Vietnam's new President and Vice President, Thieu and Ky. Later, it was recognized as part of the strategy leading up to Tet '68, to draw U.S. troops away from the cities, especially Saigon, leaving them more vulnerable to attacks. In reality, Tet '68 had begun.

I kept asking myself, "How did I get here? How is it that, only eight months ago, I was a happy kid from next door, and now I'm in the middle of a nightmare I can't conceive as being a part of my life, and there's no way out. A life of shooting people I have never known, them shooting at me, and living like an animal."

While waiting for our next flight to somewhere, my memory drifted back those eight months and I tried to understand how it all happened. It started just eight months ago, when I ……

I

The Truth

2

At first it was irritating, and tugged only lightly at my attention. The various movies and books about the Vietnam War were passed off as just entertainment. A few were somewhat characteristic, but were not true, and were very misleading.

As years passed, the irritation disappeared and insult developed. More years passed and insult became frustration, even anger, as more of this nonsense hit the market. Someone was profiting from pure hype at the expense of the Vietnam Veterans, who were being depicted as drug freaks, neurotic murderers, racists, and long-haired rag-heads with flashbacks causing twisted behavior. The American public was being fed crap, and believing it because they didn't know any better.

The scenarios always seem to be; kill a few people 8 to 5, go back to camp to get drunk at any convenient bar, trip out on drugs, sleep 8 or 10 hours, fight and argue with fellow GI's, and maybe go out again tomorrow. Or we may go to the beach instead, then to a restaurant for lunch and maybe buy a few souvenirs at the stores. And, oh yes, don't forget sex. No particular obligations, cares, anguish, morals, values, or discipline.

Who were these stories about? They certainly weren't about the Veterans I knew, during the war or after. And they certainly didn't take place in the same Vietnam I was in. I am mortified by the stereotype the stories promote.

How do you right such a wrong? How do you convince people that your story is the truth, and not what they have been bombarded with? How do you convince people that our soldiers were not a bunch of renegades, and that they lived and fought honorably under conditions very different than can be imagined? Ironically, decades after the war, America is still struggling with the effect of Agent Orange, but Americans still do not have a clear picture of their sons in the role of Combat Infantrymen in that war, and don't realize it.

Vietnam Veterans were brave soldiers, and are good citizens, and deserve better that to be cast as failures and misfits. It's time we take a look at what they really did endure, day after day, and how they handled it.

I think you too expect, and are due, the truth.

How it Began

II

Developing "The" Attitude

3

My draft notice arrived in March, 1967. I knew it was coming because I had been working full-time to pay for college and it was impossible to juggle available classes to fit work hours every semester, so I lost my Student Deferment. My friends joked that I would be taking Army 101 and that I'd get to see the Orient, "All Expenses Paid." I reported for duty knowing that I would probably be sent to Vietnam because I had this duty to fulfill to …. , whatever. It seemed that every generation has its military action to be part of, and this was mine. There was never any question in my mind whether or not I would serve my country when asked. It wouldn't matter if I thought we were right or wrong. I'd help my country with immediate needs and work on the long term needs later. If I disagreed with the current administration's policies, I'd express myself at the next election, not desert my country and hide in Canada. At my young age, I was for Democracy, Freedom, but I didn't fully appreciate exactly how it comes about, or is kept. I'd always taken it for granted, that it had always been here. I learned, and was an active participant in the lesson, that Freedom is not free. You must fight to gain it, fight to keep it, and you don't appreciate it fully unless you're a part of that fight. I felt as though I was going to go through my own little military journey, with my own personal experiences.

I didn't know that I was about to begin a passage that was repeated many times over, the same story with the same steps, but different faces; a story that begins with the fuzz-faced youngster next door that builds in intensity as it leads to a hell that can't be imagined.

When we arrived at the Military Reception Station, we were greeted by our official Army greeter, our Drill Sergeant;

"All right, scum, get in a row facing me. See if you can finish this today. MOVE, MOVE, MOVE. When I tell you to do something, I want to see nothing but assholes and elbows. In a blur.

"You, hippie with the beads, just tripped over your feet and fell. Get up. Were you taking a break, or do I have to teach you to walk, too?

"C'mere, lard ass. Yeah, you. You're going to have to lose those knobs you got under your shirt before we let you wear our uniform. Only girls and sissies have'm.

"You're lower than whale shit, Trainees, but before you leave here, you'll be men. I'm going to make you or break you, and you have no say so. You will do what I say, when I say, how I say. When I say move you will move so fast that you will leave a vacuum.

"You will address me as Drill Sergeant, Sir. You will not speak unless I give you permission. If you screw up, you will see my face so much, you'll see it in your sleep. You will stand at Attention, you will sleep at Attention, you will shit at Attention, and..."

I asked myself, "Where do they get these guys? Someone needs to throw him a chunk of raw meat."

We would soon affectionately nickname all of our new friends, not to their faces of course, and our Drill Sergeant came to be known as Mom.

After we became better acquainted with Mom, we were processed for training. First came the traditional head shave. Then we received our olive drab military wardrobe from the same two sizes they have had in previous wars, too small or too big. Next came immunizations, arm numbing in number. Then life insurance, notification of pay at $98 per month, and assignment of the rank of Private. Private is exactly what you aren't. Everything on you, in you and concerning you is poked, exposed and verified. Public is definitely a better title, Public Property.

After a battery of tests, a portion of my group and I were taken aside and told we were qualified for OCS (Officer Candidate School), but we had to enlist for four and a half years instead of the two we had as draftees. After looking at inspiring posters of Officers leading their men into battle and yelling "Follow me", we all decided one tour in Vietnam as a follower was better than the two tours likely for the four-year enlistment as an officer, the man in front. Our qualified group was then told about Warrant Officer Flight Training (WOFT), or, becoming a helicopter pilot. For similar reasons, no one accepted. It seemed as though the Army was determined to get us killed just because we made high scores. So, our highly qualified group of college students and graduates was assigned to the Infantry.

The philosophy of Basic Training is pretty much the same in any branch of the Armed Forces. You are suddenly cut off from family and society. Your freedom and independence are cancelled. Your world shrinks in size and number. Everything you have learned in life is now useless. Everything you do is wrong. The change from civilian to military life, from the boy next door to a soldier, requires many changes in you in a very short period of time; about one minute. The first step is to strip you of your individuality. "You are no longer you. You are now Joe (from GI Joe), a member of a team. The team functions as a unit. You dress exactly the same; you eat, sleep, train, and act together; if one of you makes a mistake, the whole team is disciplined." We were told when to eat and to sleep. We didn't have to make any decisions for ourselves, they were made for us. We learned to perform as a team, instead of like a mob.

The next steps are discipline and physical training. We started receiving commands from day one, and they never stopped. Discipline was reinforced with physical training (PT), and that never stopped either. This reinforcement, better known as Attitude Adjustment, was usually pushups; "You. Dummy. Double time up here and knock out fifty", or the front leaning rest position, the up position of a pushup; "Assume the front leaning rest position until I get tired." We were pushed to our physical limits by calisthenics, running, crawling, and jumping. Everywhere we went, we ran; "Double time, ho." When we got there, we always had to wait in line, "Hurry up and wait."

Finally, we received basic military training, the "Hup. Tup. Hreep. Haw. Yo leff" school of learning how to march, fire, and maintain a rifle and pistol; "Lock the safety, load a round in the chamber. All ready on the firing line." Throw hand grenades, apply first-aid to a sucking chest wound, and use hand-to-hand combat, all sprinkled very liberally with PT. Further training included combat assault, infiltration, land navigation, CBR (chemical-biological-radiological) warfare, and bayonet training;

"What's the spirit of the bayonet?"
"To kill."
"I CAN'T HEAR YOU."
"TO KILL, TO KILL."

These things and more, most of which we were not too interested in. However, we decided we better go with the flow, because, as we had been told by Mom, "You better give your heart to God, because your ass is mine."

We trained from before sunrise until late at night. At the end of the day there was no free time, and there was very little time to even write a letter home on weekends.

As intense as the training was, occasional humor did creep in. During an outdoor class in first-aid, a trainee gave a wrong answer. The instructor told the trainee, "Go yell at that tree 'I'm a dumbass,' and keep yelling until I tell you to stop. I want you to sound-off so I can hear you all the way to next week." Inevitably, a second trainee made a mistake and was told to join the first, following his yell with "Why am I like this?" Finally, a third mistake sent another trainee to follow the second yell with "I don't know." So, our class continued to background shouts of;

"I am a dumbass."
"Why am I like this?"
"I don't know."
"I am a dumbass."
"..."

Step-by-step, your Drill Sergeant teaches you his way of life, often by putting his face up to yours and yelling at the top of his lungs:

"Before you leave here, you're going to hate me. When you get to 'Nam, you're going to love me."

"Keep your head lower than your butt, Joe. We can patch a hole in your butt, but not in your head."

"Stay alert, stay alive."

"Move across open areas fast, close areas slow. If you're being fired at directly, zig-zag. Otherwise, move in a crouch, weapon at the ready. You're not looking for your girlfriend here, you're looking for the enemy. He wants to kill you. Find him before he finds you."

"Don't think, react."

"Do you understand, Joe?"

"Yes, Drill Sergeant, sir."

"SOUND OFF LIKE YOU HAVE A PAIR, SON."

"YES, DRILL SERGEANT, SIR."

Your reaction is to take all the yelling and reprimands personally. But then you realize that to your DI, you're not you. You're a fellow American and he's trying to teach you what he knows from experience so you have a chance to survive. He's wearing a CIB (Combat Infantry Badge) so he's been in combat. He knows what he's talking about. We had more hardcore Sergeants and Officers, but they were dedicated, professional soldiers.

After a couple of months of intense training, we graduated to Advanced Combat Training, Grunt school. During the Vietnam War, this meant more physical training and more weapon firing. We were greeted by a sign in our new Company area which said, "The mission of Delta Company is to train Combat Infantry soldiers to close and destroy the enemy by means of fire, maneuver, and close combat." We knew this before we arrived, but we had not heard it stated so bluntly. It definitely put everything into perspective.

Our days still started long before sunrise, training and sweating non-stop, all day and into the night. We were pushed to the edge of physical exhaustion, learning to put out just a little more effort than we thought we ever could. And then, a little more. We didn't get much sleep because of nightly activities like guard duty and maneuvers. We had no free time. We thought to ourselves, "I'll be glad when I finish training so I can get some sleep." We didn't know that we hadn't seen anything yet. We were about to spend a year of sleepless nights, a year of days all worse than our worst day of training. The Army was getting its $98 per month out of us.

Training became more oriented to Vietnam. It included jungle warfare, ambush, counter ambush, survival, night compass courses, escape and evasion, radio communications, camouflage, preparation of fighting positions, mines, booby traps, trip flares, thirty and fifty caliber machine guns, quick-kill reactions, and attacking and searching mock-up Vietnamese villages, complete with tunnels and punji stakes.

We also received specialized combat training which was determined by our Military Occupational Specialty (MOS). The MOS seems to be assigned to new troops based on some loose combination of the Army's current needs and a flip of the coin.

My MOS was 11C. The eleven means Infantry and the C means Indirect Fire Weapons, or mortars. I thought this meant that I wouldn't be in direct combat, but behind it. What it really meant was that my troubles were doubled.

The eighty-one millimeter mortar has three main parts; the bipod legs (40 lbs.), the tube, or barrel (30 lbs.), and the base plate (50 lbs.), which rests on the ground and absorbs the recoil shock when a round is fired. A favorite disciplinary measure of the DI's was to make a trainee hold that 50 pound base plate out at full arm's length, chest high, until further notice. We usually didn't last very long but it straightened out our act pretty quick.

A mortar can be set up, fired, dismantled, and carried away in a very short period of time, even before the shells hit. This makes it a good weapon for an Infantry unit which must move fast in anti-guerilla warfare, as well as an effective guerilla weapon against you. Another desirable characteristic of the mortar is the steep, almost vertical, trajectory of the fired round. This means that the round can penetrate the jungle canopy better than artillery, which has a flatter, more horizontal trajectory.

A disadvantage of this indirect fire weapon is its inherent inaccuracy. In the movies, heroes fire one or two rounds and score a direct hit. In reality, the mortar is not accurate enough for pin point targets such as a tank or a bunker. You may fire many rounds and not score a direct hit. Consequently, any hit within 20 meters of the target is considered a direct hit. Its area bursts also make the mortar an ideal weapon against personnel. The shrapnel can wipe out a Company of men with just a few rounds.

We trained for weeks with the mortar. In daylight and darkness, we disassembled and reassembled, fired, and cleaned until we could do it in our sleep. We had to learn how to remove a live round hung in the tube after a misfire, because we wouldn't have time to take it to an Ordnance section if we were in the jungle, and they sure would not come to us. We also learned how to construct a protected gun pit, when to use white phosphorus shells, how to use the flare projectiles at night, and many more procedures.

All these weeks of training taught us necessary skills. More importantly, it changed us so that we would do things we wouldn't otherwise have done. "The Attitude" was instilled in us, in our lives, and was even reflected in cadence calls while marching.

> "We're on our way to Vietnam.
> We're gonna' kill the Viet Cong.
> Got to be. Infantry.
> Motivated. Dedicated.
> Lean and mean. Green machine.
> Rough and ready. Rock steady.
> Eleven C. Infantry.
> 'I'M A KILLER. I'M A KILLER."

If you were sent to the war without this attitude, this realization, you'd never be able to handle it.

During our last week of training, we were given lectures and demonstrations of America's firepower. We were told about bombers dropping thousands of tons of bombs, helicopter gunships and jet fighters giving the Infantry direct support, Armed Personnel Carriers, artillery, and more. It was all very impressive but, at the time, we didn't know enough to ask why the war seemed to be dragging on.

All through training, we were a close-knit group. Morale was high, attitudes positive. There was that nag in the backs of our minds about what the future held. There was also the resentment about being overqualified for our MOS, that we should be doing something more important. Since all this was for our country, the Red, White, and Blue, we accepted things as they were.

Finally, after all this training, we were Infantry soldiers, ready for combat. We were the best trained soldiers America had ever sent to any war. We could use a variety of weapons from our hands to an 81 mm mortar. The U.S. had trained us in every aspect of conventional combat. We were in great physical condition. It was a very proud moment for us. We had stood up to the rigors of training. We had met the challenge. Then, we realized we were just another ounce of cannon fodder, another warm body, for the war effort. We were going halfway around the world to fight, and maybe die. The fun and games were over.

We were honed to a sharp fighting edge, but one essential ingredient was missing. An ingredient you can't pick up in training; emotional preparedness. It is difficult enough to cope with the sudden, drastic physical transition from the civilized, rational world at home to the savage, unforgiving horror of combat. But, it's impossible to fully prepare yourself for the emotional trauma you'll face every day. Either you can handle it or you can't.

Good advice for anyone entering the military service, specifically combat arms during time of war, is: develop strong self-control and emotional stability and don't lose your sense of humor. These are some of the essential things for self-preservation. Although you are about to experience a deadly serious time in your life, you can't allow yourself to take everything to heart. If you do, you probably won't survive emotionally, and maybe not physically. There will be things you'll have to do which are against your sense of morality. There will be things that happen that you can't accept. There will be the constant presence of terror and death. Nothing will be fair. You can't dwell on these things though, because you will go to pieces. This is a very difficult thing to do, especially for the young who don't have maturity and a fully developed sense-of-self. The average of the U.S. combat soldier in Vietnam was very young, about nineteen years old. Fortunately for me, I was several years older. I saw young men become emotionally scarred because they couldn't "not dwell on it." They couldn't develop that protective callousness.

III

Conditions

4

I received the usual thirty day leave after training. One month sounds like a long time, but it isn't if, when it's over, you are to report to an Army depot for shipment to a combat zone.

It was almost exciting that a few months ago I was slaving away at work and school and now I was on an airplane full of GI's on the way to the other side of the world, something I probably would never be able to afford, or do, on my own.

During the 24-hour long flight overseas, I had a lot of time to think about things. Vietnam is many centuries old and has been the scene of war almost constantly. The country hasn't changed much with the passage of all those years but, we were told, we were on our way to help the Vietnamese build a democratic heritage, through freedom. We weren't told how we were going to do this, but it did sound a little presumptuous to me. Whatever this war was all about, it must be very important because Uncle Sam just spent a lot of money on me, and millions of other guys, and is going to spend a lot more. For all of us, he is going to buy all our clothes and food. He is going to move us around the world and entrust us with millions of dollars of equipment. He paid military personnel to train us, and others to provide support. He'll bury us if we are killed. In short, we are going to live with "All Expenses Paid." Add to all this millions of dollars in aid going directly to the South Vietnamese government and you quickly realize that freedom is not free, but has a very high price.

The strange part about the last few months is not what we had been told, but what we hadn't been told. We were never really told that we were being trained to kill. We knew we were, of course, but we were trained to go through some motions without being told we were supposed to become killers. Yes, our boys were killers, but not murderers. The U.S. Government never officially told us to "go kill." Yet, we were about to be put in a position where we had no choice; somebody was going to be trying to kill us.

All our lives we had heard about man's law; if you kill you go to the electric chair. Most of us, maybe all of us, knew about God's law; Thou shalt not kill. Now, for God and Country, all that was being set aside for 365 days. I guess we were supposed to receive a blanket pardon somewhere along the way. We had to forget how we had been taught to live our lives. We had to turn our lives round, 180 degrees. Then, one year later after using weapons to kill, overnight, turn them back again.

That's not only strange, but it is a recipe for trouble placed on the innocent boy next door.

I wondered what the difference was between a mercenary and a soldier, and decided that a soldier receives pay while killing to defend his country, and a mercenary is paid to kill, no matter which country he's helping. Isn't someone who kills for money a murderer? Then, is the only thing that keeps soldiers from being murderers the fact that their own government is paying them? It can't be that simple, yet...

I wondered how many of the guys on this plane would be killed or wounded. Some were married, probably most were drafted. We were just the boys next door, from all over America, hanging on to life, following wherever it led.

The reality of our destination was temporarily forgotten until the pilot spoke on the plane's intercom. "Gentlemen, please fasten your seat belts. We'll begin our descent in about ten minutes, which will be fairly steep to avoid possible sniper fire. The temperature at Cam Ranh Bay is about 100, and so is the humidity. It's been our pleasure to serve you and we'll be back in one year to take you home." You could almost hear everyone's silent plea; "God, let me be here, too."

Vietnam is a beautiful country from the air. Looking out the plane's window, I saw what countless other GI's saw; the deep blue water of the South China Sea washing up on a beach of golden sand. Beyond the beach was the greenest foliage anyone could imagine. The monsoon rains had spawned a lush jungle, nurtured by the organic decay from many past years' growth. Green hills in the background framed this picture of tropical beauty. So this is where all the fighting and dying is happening, I thought to myself. It looks harmless enough from here, picturesque, even inviting.

It was Friday, September 8, 1967, when the plane touched down, taxied, and came to a stop. During the landing, everyone stared out the window for a hint of what to expect. I think we all expected to see some kind of war activities when we landed. Some explosions, gunfire, screaming jets... All we could see was the runway, a few people around the plane, and some buses full of GIs. No buildings in sight, no tanks, nothing. We didn't realize that, since this wasn't a conventional war, we wouldn't see large, smoke and dust covered battlefields which ultimately covered the entire country. Instead, this was a guerilla war, made mostly of small skirmishes here and there. There was no front line, behind which was a secure area. It wouldn't look like the movies.

When the door was opened and I stepped out, the beauty of the country was completely blocked out by the smell. It was the most disgusting smell you'll ever experience, and it stays with you for the entire year of your tour. It permeates your clothes and clings to your skin. No matter how many times you blow your nose, it won't go away. The smell is a mixture of burning human excrement, rotting plants, rotting garbage, mold, mildew, diesel engine exhaust, burned gunpowder and, occasionally, decaying bodies. The smell hangs on you because of the extremely high humidity. It's a smell you'll never forget.

As my group of green troops left the plane, there was another line of troops coming from the buses. They were going home on our plane. Their year was over and most definitely looked the worse for wear. They looked very tired, burned out.

They must have been happy to be going home, but it seemed like they couldn't believe it yet. Their faces were drained of their youth. Their eyes looked at you as if looking far away, at nothing; an empty stare. But, that empty stare told you a lot. They had been taken somewhere they didn't want to go, to do something they didn't want to do. Now they can't get back, they can't forget.

A new guy asked, "Hey, Sarge, how was it?" The Sergeant replied, "Man, you can't know the half of it."

It seemed as though America's young were being brought here for a year, turned into numb, hollow shells, then shipped back home. I asked myself, "Are you ready for this?"

By this time we were soaking wet with sweat and there was a cloud of flies, mosquitoes, and other bugs buzzing around us. We boarded a well-used military bus with screen wire over the open window. The screen was to prevent hand grenades from being thrown into the bus when full of GI's and becoming a coffin. The sun was beating down on the bus and the heat was stifling. I sat on a dusty, ragged seat and looked out the window. This beat-up old bus contrasted sharply with the first-class trip on the commercial jet airplane; it was almost anticlimactic.

I could see dark clouds up in the hills, where a tropical rain storm was forming. A hot breeze blew dust in my eyes. Everyone on the bus was quiet as we lurched through a quaint little village near the edge of the airfield. In the village I saw mamasans, old papasans and very young children. There were no young men around because they were all in the military service, or hiding so they wouldn't have to serve.

The mamasans and papasans squatted in the shade in their peculiar Oriental style. The children were chasing the bus with their open hands extended, yelling "GI give cigarette. GI give gum. GI numbah one, VC numbah ten. Hey, wha' chew nam? My nam Le." I couldn't help feeling sorry for them, young and old alike. Generation after generation had been born, lived, and died in a country at war. They were born into a life with no chance of being truly happy or free.

On the far side of the village, we entered our military camp and a thought quickly passed through my mind. I assumed the village was friendly, but, if the bus needed a screen wire over the windows to drive through it, then either the village was enemy territory or was frequented by the enemy. Maybe I didn't feel sorry for the villagers because they may have been the enemy.

There was no mistaking the camp at Cam Ranh Bay for anything but a military installation. The buildings were rather crude, but in very straight lines. The activity was also unmistakably military; organized confusion and frustration. We got off the buses and stood around for about fifteen minutes. A Sergeant appeared out of somewhere and rattled off in a hurried monotone, "Grab a bunk in building D-4 mess hall is the last building in that row report to the canopy at 0800 for processing," then disappeared.

"Must have a hot date," said a voice nearby.

I turned and saw a familiar face from Advanced training. Jim was an easy-going Italian from Pittsburgh and we would become very good friends.

There was no grass in the area, just deep, fine sand. As we shouldered our duffel bags, and moved toward D-4, we knew our boots, bags, and barracks floor would be filled with sand. In less than a week, most of us would be happy to trade and have this sandy ground again.

The building we bunked in had no doors, wire-screen for walls, and bunk beds, jammed together, with worn out pads and no sheets. None of the comforts of home but more luxurious than anything we'd see during the next year.

The first night in country was restless. Between slapping at mosquitoes and wiping sweat out of my eyes, I wondered where I would be assigned and what it would be like. Maybe I'd be sent to the Mekong Delta where the terrain is marshy low-lands and most of the movement will be on River Patrol Boats. No, thanks; sounds like I'd be a sitting duck in narrow waterways, and with that much water around I'm bound to get malaria. Maybe I'll be assigned as security at an airbase next to the coast and go to the beach once in a while. Maybe it'll be some tiny camp where the war hasn't gone yet. Fat chance.

There was a lot of chatter in the barracks. Everybody was tired from the twenty-four long flight over, but nobody could sleep because we were in a state of Military limbo; giving up roots and security for we didn't know what. Morale was high, attitudes positive, but you could read between the lines.

In the distance I heard occasional artillery rounds. A little later I heard helicopters. The night was so dark it almost pressed against my eyes. What the heck is a chopper doing flying around if you can't see? Then I heard small arms firing. There is a pattern to these sounds but I don't recognize it yet because I'm new in-country, green. I wondered why the fighting was so close to us. I almost felt offended that it was allowed nearby when we didn't even have a rifle. It soon sputtered and stopped.

Early in the morning the sea breeze stopped. The rain storm I saw forming in the mountains was getting close. Mosquitoes closed in, the humidity climbed. A feeling of loneliness passed through my mind. We should be back home. I felt like talking to someone but sudden torrents of rain lashing the tin roof made the effort futile.

Vietnam. Ports of entry; Cam Ranh, Da Nang, Tan Son Nhut, Qui Nhon. At each were lines of young Americans streaming in, fewer leaving. Like a sideshow at a carnival, or a rite, a passage to manhood; "Step right up, try your luck! Buy a ticket, get a rifle. See if you live to be a man! Test your skill against Sir Charles, the jungle fighter. Last twelve months, earn a CIB. This way, this way. Step right up."

At dawn, those that didn't sleep, and those that woke up early for chow, fumbled in their duffel bags for shaving gear and towel. Living out of a duffel bag requires a special patience. Since the bag is long and narrow with the opening on one end, you have to keep the items you'll need at the top, or unpack and repack the bag several times each day. Since you can't anticipate all your needs, you learn to unpack and repack in your sleep. It's no joy but will also soon become something wished for, instead of living out of a small backpack in the jungle. I've never heard one good reason why duffel bags are made the way they are instead of maybe having a zipper running the full length of the bag.

Everyone had slept in their clothes and there were no thoughts of changing into a clean set. This would be part of daily life, beginning today, for the Infantry. Many of the things you take for granted back home are no longer available. Many adjustments in life would have to be made.

Jim and I were assigned to the 25th Division, headquartered in a place called Cu Chi. After filling out a stack of forms, we caught a flight and landed in what we thought would be our home base camp. A truck met us at the airstrip and took us through the camp to Division HQ to sign in. The base camp was large and looked like good duty. Some of the buildings were not as crude as the ones in Cam Ranh Bay, some of the streets were even topped with oil to keep down the dust. A base like this promised a well-stocked PX, and movies.

Our spirits were pretty high as we entered a small, open auditorium for our official welcome by no less than a General. However, after the reception, our spirits sunk. We were to spend only a few days here for booby trap school and then be reassigned to the 2nd Battalion, 12th Infantry, 3rd Brigade at Dau Tieng, Binh Duong Province.

Coming into Vietnam was a strange experience. It was as though we were following some Army Orders with our names on them to fulfill the warm-body quota they represented, instead of the Orders accompanying us to make our presence official. The feeling of inverted priorities, of property being used, never went away.

5

Like everything else from now on, the booby trap school was held outdoors. The first day, Jim and I got acquainted with some of the other new guys while we waited for our instructor.

"Seems like we wouldn't be here if we were trained right in the States. What do you think we'll be doing?" asked Jim.

A Master Sergeant nearby answered, "This is my second trip and, believe me, things are not what you'd expect. This school is put on by Division, and you'll be hearing stuff from guys who've been humpin' the boonies. Could save your life."

"Second tour? How'd you get so lucky?" Jim asked.

"They're hurting for bodies. Everybody goes home after a year. Takes a lot of guys to keep sendin' replacements, and escalate the numbers. So, us lifers get a second tour. Some have gotten three."

"Hey, Sarge." It was my turn to ask a question. "Do you know where the Second of the Twelfth is? What they're doing?"

"Let's see. Two twelve. Yeah. They used to be part of the Fourth Division. Third of the Twenty Fifth was up by Pleiku. The Fourth and Twenty Fifth swapped Brigades. Didn't move the men, just swapped names. They're over by the Cambodian border in the Michelin Rubber Plantation, about twenty miles from here. Heard they were part of some big operations lately. The Ho Chi Minh trail filters through that area, then on to Saigon. Seems the VC have lots of small camps around there, and miles of tunnels. There was a big operation back in February, I think. Supposed to destroy tunnels and trails in the Iron Triangle. Never happen. The VC will be back the next day. Lots goin' on around there."

"Around Dau Tieng?" I asked.

"Yeah, that's the place. You two going there?" asked the Sergeant.

"Yeah. Doesn't sound too good," I answered.

"No place is good. Just that some places are worse than others. Some places are real bad. VC everywhere. Base camp warriors got it pretty good. They get rocket attacks once in a while, but they have showers, hot food, movies, clubs with cold beer and drinks, TV's, PX's..."

An Officer walked to the front of the group and started talking.

"I'm Captain Lebow. I'll be your instructor for the next couple of days. Gentlemen, if you don't listen to anyone else during the next year that's your business. But, you will listen to me because what I have to say, and show you, will save your life.

"First, the red tape. We are here at the request of the government of South Vietnam. We are guests here. Reread the card you received with the Nine Rules of Conduct for Vietnam. You are to treat the people, the customs, and their property with respect.

Unfortunately, you can't always tell the VC from the friendlies. That's the number one advantage the VC have and they use it well. They look like everyone else so they move around freely. The VC can be men, women, or children; either sex, any age. This makes those Nine Rules worth spit if you can't tell who's on your side and who isn't. Just stay alert at all times and do the best you can.

"Write home often. Your family doesn't know what you're doing so let them know you're all right. Just a few lines are OK. Remember, there's no postage. Just write FREE where the stamp goes. While we're talking about mail, don't carry letters with you in the boonies. The VC have been known to pick up lost mail and write bad news letters to families back home.

"Climate. There are two seasons here; Hot and wet, hotter and dry. Don't be a heat casualty. Take your salt tablets daily.

"Mosquitoes here carry malaria. Take your Atabrine tablets. Once you get malaria, you may have it the rest of your life, recurring again and again.

"Women. After several months here, they're all beautiful, if you see one. Stay away from them. Here in Vietnam, you can get three diseases for a dollar and not know the names of two of them. They may also be incurable.

"Now for the main course. The U. S. has years of experience over here, and we've learned a lot. Based on this, I now say to you, FORGET ALL THAT CRAP YOU WERE TAUGHT IN THE STATES ABOUT GUERILLA WARFARE. You were trained for conventional warfare. This is not a conventional war. The hill you fight for today is forgotten tomorrow. We're not here to battle with an enemy and conquer his country. We're fighting political ideals.

"You probably trained in a Pine forest under ideal conditions. Here you have rice paddies and jungles. You're going to have to bend, to adjust, and fast. Unlike conventional warfare, a guerilla war is made up mostly of ambushes and small unexpected fire fights. VC could stand for Very Crafty. (In radio phonetics, VC became Victor Charles from the Army alphabet, and this was shortened to Charlie for everyday use.) He is not worried about massive battles. He will happily pick you off one at a time, choosing the time and place to suit him so he can hit, run, and hide. You won't find him unless he wants you to, at which time he will have his act together. If you come back from a patrol without making contact, don't think you were never in his sights during the whole patrol. You probably were, but he just wasn't satisfied with the situation. He's very patient. There is no front line here, so no area is secure. The sooner you learn that the more likely you are to survive. Obviously, most of the fighting takes place away from large base camps. So, you'll learn to anticipate. In a rice paddy you have no cover. On a jungle trail you'll encounter punji pits, snipers, booby traps, and ambushes. Elephant grass (dense, stiff grass six to eight feet high, with razor sharp edges) means ambush.

"When you do run into an ambush, you don't turn and charge. Forget that. You hit the deck and get cover. Don't underestimate the VC. He will not ambush you unless he has you right where he wants you. If you try any John Wayne tactics, you will not have to worry about malaria tablets and letters from home. This isn't the movies where you can do anything you want and death only happens to someone else. We're fighting the enemy on his own turf, and he is jungle-wise. It's his home. He was born and raised here. He is comfortable here. He knows how to use terrain and the people to his advantage. He fights dirty. He doesn't care how he does it; booby traps, punji stakes, using kids or women, and he has many years of experience.

"When you encounter local VC units, you'll be in a strange area, but they won't. These units usually have a small, defined AO (areas of operation) and rarely leave it. They become very knowledgeable of their area and use this against you for concealment, maneuvering and ambush.

"When it hits the fan, you won't have time to make plans. You won't have time to choose a field of fire. You won't have time for hand signals; you probably won't even be able to remember them. You get cover wherever you can; a log, a rice paddy dike, or a termite hill. If you're not alive, you can't return fire, So GET COVER, and then return fire, if you can.

"Before we get into booby traps, let's talk about you and your gear in the field. You will need to clean your ammo every day, especially during the rainy season. Wading through rice paddies and crawling through the mud will get you and your ammo dirty. Don't worry about you, but do worry about your ammo and rifle. Take every round out of your magazines, and clean both. Your M-16 will jam if you don't, and then you won't have to worry about malaria tablets or letters from home. Speaking of ammo, practice fire discipline. You can empty a 20 round magazine in 2 or 3 seconds. If you have a target, bring smoke. If you don't have a target, conserve your ammo, firing in short bursts. When you're out of ammo, you're out of beer. The game is over.

"When you leave a laager site, or night defensive position, clean up behind you. The VC use everything you leave behind, so destroy or bury everything. Americans are very wasteful. Don't supply the enemy with your refuse. That's as important in guerilla warfare as all these other points. If you're through with sandbags, tear them up or burn them. If you open a can of C's, flatten the can and bury it. Do not leave any food or ammo behind. The VC will use it against you. He'll live on your food, shoot you with your ammo, and make booby traps from almost anything, including cans. Don't leave bunkers or foxholes without filling them up. They provide cover.

"When you shave or shower, do not use any kind of smell-good if you are going out to the boonies. The VC will smell you coming.

"We're fighting the enemy on his ground, so we have to adapt to his way of doing things. Don't set any patterns. Don't do the same things at the same times or places. Don't come and go by the same route. If you do, the VC will pick up on it and make use of it. Be alert at ALL times. Your eyes must keep moving at all times in the boonies. Learn what's normal, and what's not normal. Stay loose, don't assume. There's nothing that's a one hundred percent certainty in war. Be ready to react to anything, anytime, anywhere. If you drop your guard, chances are you won't get a second chance.

"Never let yourself think you're too tired to perform any job, no matter how small or unimportant it may seem. Always be ready to put out a little more effort. It just may save your life, again and again.

"The remainder of this school will cover booby traps, punji pits, and mines. We'll also review the areas just covered." The next couple of days we were shown how booby traps were made and where to watch for them. About the only defense for them is to not follow the path of least resistance through the jungle and rice paddies. Cross streams at a difficult spot, not the easy places to navigate. The VC realize that it's a natural thing to find the easiest route and that's where he will get you. I've never forgotten the lesson I learned in a demonstration. I was told to move through an area in one of the school's displays, and that there were two booby traps set up. I figured it would be pretty easy. As I carefully moved through, I spotted a trip wire about ankle high. I moved to a spot where the wire was most visible and carefully stepped over it. As I did, I brushed a limb at shoulder height and set off a booby trap by tripping a second wire at another level. A double triggered trap. I continued through the area, now wary of everything. I went around a stand of banana trees and stepped on a dead leaf just lying innocently on the ground, so I thought. Under the leaf, two bare wires touched and completed a battery charged electrical circuit which set off the second trap. I was told there were two and I missed them both. One was on a trail and the other was in a clear area chosen to avoid fighting the brush. How am I going to survive in the jungle if I can't make it here in class? Since you probably won't be able to spot the booby traps, you have to avoid the areas where they would most likely be found. I avoided the paths of least resistance for the next year.

After school hours, Jim and I walked around part of Cu Chi base camp to see what we could learn. Army tents and barracks were as far as we could see in every direction. Large green tents, some with the sides rolled up and some with sides made of wire screen. There were very few trees scattered around. Dirt roads ran in all directions. Tanks, jeeps, and APC's were moving up and down the roads making dust clouds so thick it was difficult to breathe. GI's were walking along the sides of the roads, rifles slung over their shoulders. They looked dirty, wrinkled and unconcerned. It was hard to believe these guys were marching in straight lines, not long ago, at training centers all over the U.S. We decided we could tell the base camp warriors from field troops. Field troops looked more tired, and maybe even a little guilty for being in camp for a short rest. Base personnel were hurrying around, getting their work done. Their fatigues were cleaner and fit better, and they were less tired looking.

The last night at school, we didn't have much to say to each other. When we did talk, we tried to avoid the insecure feeling brought on by what we had heard and seen in the last few days. Booby traps, punji pits'; are they part of the war, or are they attempts to frustrate your efforts of carrying the war to the enemy? Jammed M-16 rifles, malaria; part of war or just more frustrations? Where does circumstance end and war begin? Worries begin to nag you, attitudes begin to change, thoughts turn to home, insecurity makes itself felt. Home, that's where we should be. How am I going to remember all the stuff I heard in the school? What happens if I forget one of the points? Is that what kills GI's, or is it just the war? Am I supposed to memorize all those things?

The night brought more rain, and with it came more mud, more humidity, and more mosquitoes.

I kept thinking about what we had learned at school in the last few days and it seemed we should have learned them during training in the States. Now, we would have to learn while in the field, On the Job Training (OJT). Some of us would no doubt get wounded or killed because we hadn't had a chance to practice these things. I felt far short of ready for the next year.

Somewhere in the distance was the sound of small arms firing from the camp perimeter. You never know if it's just a handful of VC taking potshots or the beginning of something big. The BOOM of outgoing artillery brought me to the door of our hooch. There were sounds and lights of war in the distance in any given direction; flares floating down gently, red tracers, red-orange explosions, helicopters. Just like in the movies.

A year of this, "All Expenses Paid." Once again I asked myself "Are you ready for this?"

6

Finally, after 4 days in-country, thoroughly intimidated by the lessons learned at the school, homesick, and feeling entirely out of place, Jim and I arrived at our base camp. Dau Tieng was a Forward Base Camp, which basically meant that the area was not secure, and no permanent structures had been built. There were existing permanent structures nearby which were the Headquarters, and home in Vietnam, of the rubber plantation owner, Michelin, of Michelin tires. The camp adopted the name of the nearby village where rubber tree workers, and some rice farmers, lived.

The camp was located among the rubber trees which are grown in straight, measured rows and columns for miles, just like a fruit orchard back home. These were old trees, very tall, and their foliage made a tight canopy which allowed only a few sunbeams to filter through to the ground. The mass of trunks didn't let you see very far. The overall effect was eerie.

The hooches, or barracks, were the standard for a non-permanent base camp. They had wooden floors about one foot above the ground, waist high wooden sides with sandbags, and screen-wire from there up to the canvas tent used as a roof. The sides of the tent were rolled up to the top of the screen to let in light and air. Inside, there was a crowded row of cots along each side and a narrow aisle through the center. The tent floor space was about 50 feet by 15 feet. As we transferred closer and closer to our final duty camp, the more primitive the camps became. We started in Cam Ranh Bay with wooden buildings and indoor latrines. Cu Chi had some wooden buildings and outdoor latrines. Dau Tieng had rotting tents and boards over a half barrel. Be it ever so humble. As it turned out, none of this mattered anyway because we would be here only a few scattered days during the year, actually living in the jungles and rice paddies. Of course, out there we had no buildings or tents, and not even the luxury of something to sit on for BM's.

The hooches of each Company area were in straight rows and columns. A dirt road ran between the rubber trees from one Company area to another, and finally to the airstrip and helipad.

Jim and I were assigned to Company B, Badass Bravo. We signed in at the Orderly Room and were told to go to Battalion Supply. There we got our jungle fatigues, wool blankets (just what you need in the tropics), and combat gear which consisted of steel helmet, poncho and poncho liner, flak jacket, backpack, four canteens, jungle boots, socks (wool, of course), entrenching tool, gas mask, bayonet, web gear, and first aid pouch. Back in the Company supply room, we were issued salt tablets, M-16 rifles, ammunition, and hand grenades. It felt very strange, almost illegal, to be walking around with so much live ammo and explosives. During training, we were issued a measured supply of these items, at the training site, and we were supervised very closely. Any leftover was accounted for and turned in at the training site. Here you could get all the ammo you could carry, and do with it almost as you pleased. Instruments made for death and destruction with you day and night.

Jim was Lucky. He was made Company Armorer, so he would stay in camp. I was assigned to a mortar squad in the Weapons Platoon, so I would be spending my time in the boonies. I was assigned a cot that had been used by a guy killed during the last operation. Not a good place for a superstitious person. The Company was out on an operation at the time, and the cots of the killed or wounded hadn't been vacated yet. I was told I could switch to one of those later if I wanted. Since we spent very little time in camp, it really didn't matter. On the wall of my hooch was a hand painted sign that said, "Rules of the house. If it's on the floor, step over it. If it moves, step on it." Further along the wall hung another sign that said, "Yea, though I walk through the valley of the shadow of death, I fear no evil, for I am the evilest son of a bitch in the valley."

There were flak jackets, like bulletproof vests, hanging here and there. On the backs of some of them were claims like "Tiger", "The evilest son of a bitch", and "Killer." Interestingly, these labels disappeared after a short time in country.

The rest of the evening we were lucky enough to have time free of duty because the duty roster had been made before we arrived. We expected to have to police the area or something, but nothing was said so we wandered around the base camp to see what we didn't know. The Company area was right on the camp perimeter, which was the usual barbed concertina wire. In the wire there were trip flares, Claymore mines and Phou gas bombs (fifty five gallon drums of Napalm). If the VC tried to sneak through the wire, he would trip the flares and we would blow the mines and bombs.

Every hundred feet or so were sand-bagged bunkers with rifle ports in the front and side walls. During the day, there was one man in every other bunker, but at night there were two or more in each. The men in the bunkers were usually base camp personnel and walking wounded not fit enough to go back to the field yet. As we walked around, we could hear the sounds of war. Artillery was being fired from the other side of the camp, maybe half a mile away. From another direction we heard small arms and machine guns firing. Helicopters flew nearby, and then artillery shells exploded in another direction. A collection of sounds we had only heard in the movies. It was strange to be walking along with this going on around us. We felt like we should be participating, shooting, or something.

We found a small group exchanging war stories. We listened in and tried to get acquainted. Suddenly, there was a loud explosion, followed by a fading SWOOSHISHISH. Jim and I dove for cover which gave the group a good laugh. One of them caught his breath long enough to say, "That was out-going. Don't worry; after you've been here for a while you'll call'em in your sleep." After we dusted ourselves off, we joined in the bull session and learned about American GI's here. These guys were no different from anyone else, just the boys next door joined together by circumstances. One was a college graduate, one was a pole-climber for a power company, one was a carpenter, and another was a hippie. They had stopped for a few minutes before going to night perimeter guard duty to talk about home, how they wished they were back in the world. They had been in-country for a while and one was getting short, only eighteen days left to go. They had lost a lot of buddies and heard many VC had been killed, but the war kept escalating; it kept going on and on and on. They had had enough and just wanted to go home.

We went back to our hooch to try and get some sleep. It was the last night for a long time that I would sleep with my boots and shirt off.

All night long we heard the sounds of war; an exchange of rifle fire from somewhere on the perimeter, artillery barrages, an air strike with jets swooping in and bombs exploding, and even Puff, the Magic Dragon, firing its Vulcan cannon. About 2 A.M., I stepped out of the hooch to see what little I could make out in the dark, and maybe see where the air strike was happening. It must have been several miles away but I could see Puff working out, "bringing smoke on Charlie." First they dropped two huge, very bright flares. Then they circled back and opened fire. It was the most impressive display of light from a firearm I had ever seen, made all the more awesome by the contrast of the fire with the dark night. Even at this distance, I could see the stream of tracers, a solid line of hot-orange light, reaching from the dark sky all the way to the ground. At one hundred rounds per second, per gun, the continuous stream acted like water from a moving garden hose, snaking around and down. A few seconds later, I heard the guns. They sounded like the sky was being ripped open, like a giant canvas sheet. How could the VC face these weapons and keep coming back for more?

All these sights and sounds were so alien back home that they were almost alien to me. Nothing like this anywhere in my background.

Then it started raining again. This was the rainy season, the monsoon. Monsoon rains fall like they are the vengeance of an irate god.

I wondered if my tent roof was going to collapse under the strain of the sudden weight of so much water. The sound was deafening. Those poor guys out there; first they get shot at, and now they are lying in mud and water, and no way to keep dry or change into dry clothes. Soaked to the bone. Just guys like Jim and me; never did anything to anybody. I realized that soon it would be me out there in the mud. I wondered if there was a giant plug we could pull and sink this place, get rid of it and its hostile environment. I was covered with welts from mosquito bites, silent mosquitoes, I never heard them. What AM I doing here? And I haven't even been out in the field yet. I covered my head and chest with my shirt and tried to get at least a little sleep.

BOOM. BAM. BAM. The Company area was being mortared in the rain storm.

The movies have it all wrong. Mortars are called silent death because you don't hear the rounds coming in. They suddenly explode as if they had been there all the time, just waiting. You might hear them leaving the tube, making their distinctive POOP sound. If you don't, then you can't know if another round is on its way. This causes panicky terror after the first shell explodes. It reaches into the little space where you've been thinking of home, or trying to escape in sleep. If the shrapnel doesn't get you, the sudden explosion tears at your guts and exposes the raw edges to the ice-cold hand of fear and panic. Your blood pressure shoots sky high and makes your head feel like a balloon. Adrenalin makes you react like a coiled spring, your legs and arms move faster than your body and mind can keep up with. Before I realized what I was doing, I was running out the hooch doorway toward the nearby bunker that I had seen earlier, and yelling to Jim to run. No need for that, he was right behind me. It was pitch black and I couldn't see the rubber trees or the other hooches but my legs kept pumping my bootless feet. Water was splashing waist high and the ground was slick mud. Only seconds had passed since I was on the cot, but another round could fall at any time. Two did, close by. WHAM. WHAM. One to my left and the other to my right. My hair stood on end when I realized the next one could land right in the middle, right on top of me. The night exploded around me. Shrapnel whizzed by and THUNKED into tree trunks. The flashes from the explosions seemed to be searching for me. Mud, rocks, and tree branches rained all around me. It seemed like I had been running for hours. "Maybe I'm running the wrong way", I thought to myself. Can't stop and look around; too dark anyway. My heart was pumping so hard I didn't know why it didn't burst. A year of this and I'd go home with either a very strong heart or a very worn out heart.

I came to a shadowy, square shape in the darkness; the bunker. As I made a flying leap for what I hoped was the door, more rounds fell and I heard shrapnel hit the bunker wall and trees. I half rolled and was half pushed through the open doorway. More rounds fell. The floor was ankle deep mud and water. If the mortars fired all night, we'd be sitting in the mud trying to sleep. There were no lights in the bunker so I had no idea who else was in there.

The firing stopped shortly, and so did the rain. We waited about ten minutes, then splashed away into the darkness, going back to the business of trying to get some sleep. There were no lights anywhere. The VC knew where the camp was but you do not advertise yourself with any kind of light. I found a hooch I thought was mine and sat on a cot. I didn't really care if it was mine or not, or even if I was in the right hooch. In fact, I didn't care about anything except wondering if it was a good idea to be outside the bunker. I had no idea what happened to my shirt I had over me before the attack. With my feet on the floor, I laid back. My head hit a lump; a gas mask. Not my bunk, but the gas mask became my pillow.

7

It seemed like I had just closed my eyes when a head poked in the door and said, "I've been looking everywhere for you. First Sergeant says get your gear in order and be ready to go to the field. The Company will be at Nui Ba Den this morning and you'll go out on a small chopper. Be at the Orderly Room at zero eight, pick up a couple bags of mail and I'll take you to the helipad."

My fatigue pants and socks were soaking wet and muddy from last night, and now the cot was too. I was covered with welts from mosquito bites.

I walked through the mud and water in my socks, slipping and sliding, back to my hooch. On the way, I noticed one hooch that looked like slaw, and several others that looked like Swiss cheese, heavy on the Swiss. The rubber trees were bleeding white sap where they had been hit by shrapnel in the trunks, and branches littered the ground. Shrapnel was thick last night, and I felt very lucky to be alive and unhurt.

I found my hooch, got all my gear ready and pulled some family pictures out of my duffel bag. I put the pictures in my wallet, my wallet in a watertight plastic bag, and then into my pocket. If you don't, the whole thing will rot because it'll be wet for a year; wet from sweat, rain, and wading in rice paddies. Don't really need a wallet here except it's a good way to bring pictures with you. Then the duffel bag went under my cot and stayed there untouched for a year.

Jim and I found the Mess Hall and said our goodbye's over cold powdered eggs, cold toast, and a slice of Army coffee. Jim took off to start his new duties and I had some time to kill so I wrote a letter home, giving them my address. After last night, the letter probably didn't sound very cheery.

I arrived at the Orderly Room a little early so I visited with the Company Clerk. I asked, "Wayne, what's Nui Ba Den?"

"Step out the door and look to the right. See that mountain? That's it. The Black Virgin Mountain. You're lucky. Duty there is not too bad. It's security for the rock crusher that makes gravel for the roadbeds. You'll probably stay a few days; run a few ambushes, no big deal. When you're not on ambush you'll probably fire mortars, harass Charlie, and fire support for the ambushes.

"C.O. said to send some new fatigues out so you'll have three bags to take with you. The Battalion's been out almost four weeks. Fatigues don't last that long in the bush. They get torn, cut, ripped, rotten,... You name it. We're always sending fatigues out with ammo and mail."

Wayne was a college graduate caught up in the draft. He'd spent time in the field, so as Company Clerk he did anything he could for the guys; he knew what it was like out there. His personal philosophy was simple – to heck with all this, let's just get the guys home.

The Sergeant drove up in a jeep and yelled out, "OK, saddle up." Wayne gave me a thumbs up, but I could see it was more hope than promise.

The ride out in the helicopter was great. It was cool up there, almost clean. That smell was gone. For a minute I decided I'd made a big mistake by not going to Warrant Officer Flight School. When I get out at the mountain, these guys will probably go back to hot meals and clean sheets.

In the air, the country seemed benign again. The rubber plantation was a picturesque checkerboard, made by dirt roads crossing each other every kilometer, making green squares for miles and miles. Vietnamese farmers were working with water buffalo in their paddies. Uncleared land was lush with plant life. There were large, round bomb craters filled with stagnant water; remnants of forgotten air strikes. I felt as though I was in a mechanical intruder in a gentle, scenic land. It was still difficult to believe there was a war going on amid the quaint little hamlets and small, seemingly gentle people.

I wondered what I was supposed to do if we were fired at in the air because standard procedure was you unload your weapon when boarding a chopper (except on combat assault into a hot LZ, where there is active shooting going on) and hold it so that the muzzle is pointing down. If it fired while pointing up, you might shoot the chopper down because you might hit the engine or blade mechanism. I wasn't told to fire from the air, but to load up only when preparing to dismount. Many choppers had door gunners, manning 60 caliber machine guns but those on courier flights, like this one, didn't have any guns.

Nui Ba Den was a strange sight. It rose suddenly, the only mountain for many miles, from a flat plain to over three thousand feet. Its height, and the fact that it was the only high spot around, made it seem taller than it really was. The sides were fairly steep making it difficult to climb. The small camp was at the base of the mountain on the southwestern side. Directly above the camp, near the top, was a large rock, the only break in the green color of the mountain. The rock had a curious crack-like opening which appeared to be a cave entrance.

We landed just outside a typical defensive perimeter, or, temporary encampment. There were three-man positions about every forty meters in a rough circle. The circle was smallish, a few hundred meters across, for a company sized unit. In the center were the mortars and

Headquarters. The perimeter positions would be closer in the sight limiting thick foliage of the jungle or brush, so they can protect the area between them and not allow the enemy to sneak through. Perimeters like this one, being spread out and not very large, don't give any sense of security but do allow you to protect yourself.

I was met by a shirtless GI who could have been a PFC or an Officer. With no shirt bearing his rank, I couldn't tell. He swung the mail bags over his shoulders and we took off toward the mortars, amid a swirl of dust stirred up by the departing chopper.

The shirtless GI introduced himself as Dean, a Specialist Fourth Class (also called SP4 or Spec 4) in the Weapons Platoon. We dropped the mail and new fatigues at the C.O.'s hooch and continued to a separate area which had three mortar pits. Dean introduced me to the Platoon; Wes, Blue, Redford, Ski, Chief, Dave, George, Roy, and Sgt. Bauer, the Platoon Sergeant. They were a dirty and tired looking bunch. Their fatigues were ripped and smelled sour from being wet for a long time. They were caked with dirt and smelled bad. And their eyes, always the eyes; tired, sunken, sad, distant; old before their time. But, a new face drew smiles all around.

"Where're you from back in the World?" asked Ski.

"Texas," I answered.

"Hey, you been to the Astrodome?"

"What part? I know somebody from Texas."

"All right, listen up," Sgt. Bauer spoke up. "You guys can BS later. John, you'll be assistant gunner in Redford's squad, along with Wesley. We're short on bodies; never have been up to full strength. Too many casualties and not enough replacements. The whole Company is under strength. This means you will have extra work details. It means you'll go out on ambushes. It also means you fire the mortars at night and hump the boonies all day. (The term hump comes from the hump in a Grunt's back when he is carrying the usual heavy load of gear.) We're a Weapons Platoon at night and leg Infantry Platoon by day. Only consolation is you don't have to walk point much, except to an ambush site, but we do walk flank for Company movement. If you walk flank, you won't have to carry the mortars or ammo. You'll also have to go out on LP (listening post).

"Tonight we go out on ambush. Third squad stays back to fire the mortars for our support. No artillery to cover us. John, you go out tonight. You can't ease into anything here. You'll be pace man, make sure we set up at the right spot so the mortars can support you if needed. The ambush is about three klicks almost due west, on a trail running toward Tay Ninh. MI (Military Intelligence) thinks VC use it at night for supplies from Tay

Ninh. Leave here thirty minutes before sunset, set up after dark, register the mortars and hit anything that moves down the trail.

"Get your mail and get some rest before you go."

After the ambush briefing, the Platoon stayed in a group and the BS started again. Most of the guys were in-country only a few months but to them it was forever. They asked me all sorts of questions so they could catch up on home. They were a good group of guys, close knit. The same feeling of togetherness was apparent in them as it was in my buddies back home. Some showed more resentment and bitterness toward the war than others, but they were careful not to take it out on friends or duty.

Somebody brought our mail and a few guys drifted off to be alone while they read, being a very special moment.

My family didn't know my address yet so I had no mail. I grabbed my gear, found a spot with the shallowest mud and made sure everything was ready. For an ambush, you travel light; rifle, twelve or more magazines, grenades, Claymores, and one canteen. After I oiled my rifle, I tried to get a little rest. My stomach was knotted from anxiety, so I didn't eat anything.

There was a light drizzle falling so I wrapped up in my poncho and lay on some wooden crates. I heard artillery crash somewhere out there, as if to remind me I couldn't escape from the war. I closed my eyes but sleep never came. The mosquitoes did, and flies. Sweat drips from you all day and when you sleep in a poncho you wake up in a very wet sweat. I wondered how long it took to adjust your nose and personal hygiene to accept sour, muddy clothes and sticky skin; how many days until you didn't notice your own odor.

A flight of helicopters passed nearby and I wondered if they were carrying troops out, or wounded in. Then a flight of jets going west, toward Cambodia.

Our mortar fired, and a distant crunch of artillery seemed to be answering. Sounds; always the sounds of war. The sounds of killing and destruction. You hear them when you walk, when you talk, in your thoughts, and even in your sleep.

Thoughts inevitably turn to home. What are they doing now? Is it really thirteen hours earlier there? Three in the morning today? If I am killed on ambush at 2 A.M. Wednesday here, do they tell my family on Tuesday, that I died tomorrow?

Loud thunder and heavy rain brought me back to Vietnam. It was the loudest and strongest thunder I had ever heard. It rolled from one horizon, over our heads, and continued to the other horizon, shaking the ground all the way. It was eerie, as if the gods were trying to tell us something. We'll have to go out on the ambush in the rain and mud, and set up in it, and sit in it all night.

I still felt very much in limbo. I didn't know where I'd be the next day, didn't really know anyone yet, didn't know what I was supposed to be doing or what to expect for the next year. I also didn't know that this was pretty much how I would feel for the entire year.

Dean, Ski, and Wes came over to get better acquainted. They were nice guys, friendly and easy to talk with.

It's almost time to get ready for my first trip to the field. The minutes are flying by because I wanted them to drag on and on so I won't have to go out. Do the other guys feel like this, even though they have been in firefights before? I really didn't want to kill anybody. You will be in a physical position where you have no choice – it's you or them.

Maybe they will postpone the ambush because of the weather. Maybe the war will be cancelled. Maybe…

"SADDLE UP!

Time for "This isn't the movies."

8

Hi ho, hi ho. Time to start earning my "All Expenses Paid" keep. First time on the job.

Weapons Platoon, less third squad, moved slowly out to the mortar pits carrying gear. We squished and sloshed slowly through the mud and drizzle. The drizzle became rain as if to express our feelings. The big, heavy raindrops drummed on my helmet and whapped against my soaked fatigues. Thunder rumbled overhead, and then the wind picked up and pelted the raindrops against my face, stinging my eyes, and then ran down to drip on my fatigues. I turned my back against the wind and began to shiver; soaked to the bone, chilled and just plain miserable. This for a year? I was already tired of it and it's only the first day. What a miserable time to be out in the elements, as if fighting the war wasn't enough.

As we put our gear on, Lt. Young, our Platoon Leader, walked toward us for the final briefing. I looked around at this routine, but to me unfamiliar, activity. These guys are to be my family for a while so I studied them. I tried to look into their eyes in vain because everyone was looking down, fidgeting with a piece of gear. Nobody spoke, their thoughts definitely half a world away. The only hint of individuality would be found on the camouflage covers of their helmets. New guys have bright green covers; those almost ready to go home, getting short, have dirty, faded covers with a curious ragged-edged hole worn through the highest point of their helmet. The longer you were in-country, the more faded and dirty your cover, and the bigger the hole. Almost every cover had personalized graffiti, expressions of the soul; "Ho Chi Minh sucks fish heads", "LBJ uses a night light," "The draft is the shaft", "Relax, want to die all tensed up?"

I was also very aware of my individuality; my boots were still black, theirs were very scuffed and scraped; my fatigues were green and new, theirs were mud-brown and sour smelling.

I tied on my last piece of equipment, a boot lace, to a belt loop. The pace man counts the number of paces he's traveled because you need to know exactly where you are, and in the dark you don't dare use a light to see landmarks or a map. You also can't see pencil and paper so you tie a knot for every one hundred fifty paces which for this terrain is one hundred meters. Ten knots make a kilometer. When you travel in the dark, fighting mud and mosquitoes, concentrating on silence and not losing contact with the file, and hoping you don't walk into an ambush, it's very easy to lose count – one forty nine, one fifty. Is that seven hundred meters, or eight hundred? Just count the knots.

Lt. Young sat on the sandbags ringing the mortar pit and began. "All right, here it is. Sgt. Rice is patrol leader. Ambush site is 3100 meters at 260 degrees. Almost due West, on a trail running Northeast to Southwest. Leave at 1630 hours and begin your return at 0600. Sgt. Rice will F.O. (Forward Observer) DEFCON's with our mortars. No special equipment but First Platoon will send one M-60 and crew. Platoon radio will go and we'll ask for SITREP's (situation reports) every hour on the hour. Your radio call is Four Alpha, the mortars call is Bravo Support. There will be no artillery or air support, we stand alone. No change expected in weather; rain, heavy clouds. No moonlight so you don't need camo paint.

"One poncho – for the F.O. - emergency only – in case a major screw up requires a light to see the map. Sgt. Rice has map, light, and compass.

"Any questions?"

Nobody said anything.

"All right. Pick up the M-60 team at the perimeter. Check safeties frequently. An L.P. (listening post) will follow you and drop off about four hundred meters out.

"No cigarettes past the perimeter, so you better light up now. Brown, make a commo check at the perimeter and at halfway to site. Make your last-minute gear checks now. See you guys in the morning. Happy hunting."

Magazines were checked, rounds were chambered and safeties pushed on. Sleeves were rolled down to help protect against mosquitoes. Bug juice was rubbed on faces. Canteens gurgled. Cigarettes lit.

I glanced at faces again and found only distant stares, a blank look.

Dean came over to see if I had any questions, or if I needed any help.

Sgt. Rice said, "Order of march; Redford, point; Chief, slack; myself, Brown, radio; John, pace. Then First Squad, gun; Second, and Fourth is tail, security. When we hit the site trail, First, you leap frog me, and we close parallel to the trail. First and Fourth set out Claymores turned slightly inward, toward the kill zone. I fire the first round, if we spring the ambush.

"Return order, about face and move out.

"We're a little early, but let's move to the perimeter."

We moved single file, quietly, like a funeral procession, except for the squish and slosh. At the perimeter, the M-60 and L.P. were waiting. The gunner's nickname was Zipper, a big guy who handled the clumsy 60 like a toy.

We stood and waited, looking out into the darkening distance, out into the soggy, marshy terrain we had to pass through.

Here we were, a bunch of guys that really didn't know each other outside of their own squad, from different cities around the U.S., but who may have to depend on each other for their life.

We'd have to work as a team, no matter who was next to you or what the situation was – a mutual survival effort.

The rain let up a little and mosquitoes came back. I seemed to be the only one swatting. I guessed they had become used to the bites, or just gave up. Maybe it had been so long since they had a chance to shower that they didn't feel any mosquitoes trying to bite through the caked mud and crud on their skin.

I tried to mentally review my training, searching for anything that might help me in a situation like this:

Carry your weapon at the ready.

Stay alert.

Keep your eyes moving.

Learn what's normal, what's not.

Discipline, patience, stealth, concealment, teamwork.

Noise and light discipline.

Sgt. Rice checked his watch, motioned to Redford and said, "Move out." Indian country. Anything that moves out here gets it. If they see you first, you can hang it up. One step puts you outside the perimeter, over the imaginary line you like to think marks an area of security. I looked back as we moved – security was receding, a couple of GI's sat calmly on their bunker, smoking and watching us fade into the distance, no doubt happy that they didn't have to go.

The file had automatically spread to five-meter intervals between men so any unfriendly fire would inflict minimal casualties. Walking into the setting sun, glary behind clouds and the humid air, it was scenic but could be deadly because you can't see very well.

The terrain was slightly rolling and treeless for about the first kilometer, and the ground was very soupy in low spots. Mosquitoes hung in the air in clouds of thousands after point stirred them up, and they seemed to be waiting for the next man in line. When you hit the cloud, the mosquitoes are sucked into your mouth when you inhale, and some don't come out when you exhale.

There was no breeze, and the rain started again and dripped off our helmets in constant rivulets, down the shirt collar, mixed with sweat and ran all the way down to our boots, soaking us even more from head to foot.

Occasional rocks caused turned ankles and silent curses.

I counted paces and tried to adjust for short steps over the uncertain terrain. Plastic rifle stocks, like the M-16, are slick when wet. Rifle barrels point below horizontal to avoid the danger of filling the barrels with rain water.

Squish, slosh, squish. Noise discipline, no talking; no noise except boots hitting and sinking in the mud, and occasional sucking sounds of boots being pulled out of the mud. We crossed a trail, but it's not the one we want, too close to camp.

I tied another knot – fifteen knots. I caught up to Brown and whispered "Halfway." He made his commo check on the move. "Bravo Support, Four Alpha, over."

"Alpha, Support. Go."

"Support, Alpha. Halfway. How do you read? Over."

"Lima Charlie (loud and clear), Alpha. How me, over?"

"Same, same. Out."

The last half of the trip would be slower, trickier. It was dark now, very limited visibility, making it easier to make noise and easier to walk into an ambush. My breathing seems loud, loud enough to scare you into trying to stop breathing.

The clouds had gotten thick and heavy again, blocking out any moon light and star light. There was no reflection of city lights because most cities, and all villages, have no electricity. I have never felt the absence of all light like this. I don't know how the point man moved us along so well. He had to literally feel his way in unfamiliar territory. To avoid the danger of booby traps and mines, we stayed off any trails and cut through bush when there was some. We moved through rice paddies, staying along the edge of the mud dikes. The dikes were narrow and we frequently slipped and almost fell. Walking through paddy water and mud is noisy and slow. Point gambled there were no mines on or near the dikes. Since the night was so dark, the extra height of the dike would not cause our profiles to be seen against the sky.

Squish, slosh. Stay alert, at the ready. Squish, suck. Keep your eyes moving. Sweat dripped from our chins and noses. In the distance, artillery shells made their crunching sounds. Squish, squish.

I felt the safety on my M-16. It was pointing to "FIRE." I felt it again to make sure and my rifle was definitely set to fire. I flipped the selector to Safe. I had checked the safety at the briefing, and again at the perimeter, so it must have been jostled just wrong during the first kilometer. Every few steps, we either slid on some mud or jumped over something and at those times automatically tightened our grip on our rifles. If my finger had hit the trigger, I would almost certainly have hit somebody. I wondered how many other safeties had been bumped and if

I would have been hit. Every one of us was carrying a loaded weapon and any one of them could go off at any time; rifles, shotguns, grenade launchers.

You tune your ears to pick up any sound that's out of place; you strain your eyes to pick out anything that's not right, any piece of information.

A helicopter passed nearby: DUSTOFF?, Wounded coming in? If we suffer wounds, will they come get us in the dark? Will they be able to find us? We crossed another footpath but we're still not far enough out to be at our destination trail. Lots of paths out here make you realize there is a lot of traffic, and possibly some that you will run into unexpectedly.

We moved into scattered trees and heavy brush. We were closer than 5 meters apart now so we wouldn't lose contact. Branches and leaves brushed against us. As you pass them, you have to let them back slowly so they don't make noise and so they don't whap the guy behind you. We're moving along very quietly for three squads, only the squish, squish and sucking mud sounds.

I wondered what the base camp warriors were doing; movies, beer, sleep, hot food, shower, while thinking another dreaded day at work in an office. I could use some of that.

The mosquitoes were having an ambush of their own.

There wasn't a dry spot on any of us. I could feel that my feet were tightly wrinkled, like they are after a day in the surf.

We crossed another rice paddy, zigzagging alongside the dikes. If the sky was clear, there's a full moon tonight and we'd be dandy silhouette targets. Pickem' up and putem' down, push on. "Follow me. Onward." Gotta' keep those dominoes from falling.

I really don't know what the hell I'm doing here. This is the sort of thing you see in the movies, it doesn't actually happen.

My boots had been collecting layer upon layer of gummy mud on the bottoms. Each step collects another layer as the mud gets thicker and heavier. Your feet feel like they have gained 10 pounds. About every ten steps, the mud builds to several inches. It might fall off by itself, too heavy to stick, or it might fall off only one boot, making you walk like a drunkard with one foot on the curb and one in the gutter. Or, you might do the muddy boot two-step and kick the mud off; step-kick-step-kick. When it does come off, your feet feel light as a feather. But, then it starts all over again with the first step. Squish, squish, suck, step-kick-step-kick. I couldn't remember any of this in the movies or in the inspiring military posters.

One forty nine, one fifty. I tied another knot in the wet noodle hanging from my belt loop and counted twenty eight knots. Another knot and I whispered to Brown to tell Rice we were about three hundred meters away. We moved into more trees and brush. Some of the bushes had thorns and they raked our faces, arms and legs, and tore our fatigues. Nicknamed wait-a-minute bushes, they have long tentacle-like hanging branches covered with strong thorns that curve back up the branch. When you push the branch out of you path, it makes the thorns point at you, ready. When you get caught in the thorns, you have to wait a minute and work yourself free because they won't let go. Salty sweat makes the resulting scratches and cuts sting.

Our forward movement became very slow, and then stopped. There it was, a light-colored trail running just outside the tree line on the edge of open ground. There was just a little more light outside the tree line than inside. Brown turned to me and whispered, "First up." I turned and passed the message, and First Platoon moved silently past. Zipper stopped by me and we moved silently to the tree line, about five meters from the road. We were trained to lie down on our stomachs, facing the kill zone. That's easy in training. The ground would be dry and you can see what you're going to lie on. I decided to sit in the mud and water, with my back against a spindly tree. I couldn't hear the Claymores being set out. They would be set up on the trail side of a tree to protect us from the rearward blast. You have to be sure you choose a large tree so the blast doesn't knock the tree over on you. The explosion from the Claymore's C-4 explosives propels some 700 pea-sized steel balls in a sixty degree arc for about 150 feet. It's a dandy equalizer.

The rain let up but the water dripped on us from tree limbs overhead. Somewhere out there in the night artillery was firing, but our position is deathly silent. Rice moved close to Brown to use the radio and report we were in position and arrange for a DEFCON with our mortars. These prearranged points could be called for and quickly set on the mortar sights, giving us fast supporting fire (HE or high explosive), or illumination from flares. "Support, Alpha. Over." Rice spoke softly into the handset with his hands cupped around the mouthpiece.

"Four Alpha, Bravo Support, Go." I was close enough to barely hear the radio traffic, and understood the words mostly because I knew what they would be.

"Four Alpha in position. Request one Willie Peter (WP or white phosphorus), high. Will adjust. Over."

"Roger four. Wait." The Fire Direction Center (FDC) already knew the direction and distance to our location so the wait was not long. In my mind, I could hear the mortar squad working, and wishing I was there, instead of here. "...Deflection zero two fiyuv niner. Charge, eight. Time, 23. Elevation, zero eight niner three."

"Ready."
"Hang one."
"Hanging."
"Fire."
POOP.

We were near the maximum range for the mortars, so we couldn't hear the round leave the tube. The air burst of white phosphorus was difficult to see in the dark since there was no flash, only white smoke.

We spotted it fifteen to twenty meters up and only about fifty meters North. "Bravo Support. Four Alpha. Left fifty. No round. Out." The DEFCON was now set about twenty meters to our front.

So, there we were, about 2200 hours, ten P.M. Three understrength squads, covered with mosquito bites, sitting in mud and water in the dark, for maybe eight hours. We can't move much, can't make noise or light, can't smoke. We can't sleep or let ourselves doze off. We're supposed to wait, watch, listen, and hope some VC comes tripping down the trail. This is the way the VC fought and is one of a very few of their tactics that we would adopt. The big difference was that they usually had advance information about our movements from the local Vietnamese.

At first, you see and hear impossible things because you expect something to happen; movement, no sound. You think you see shadowy figures moving, or standing and listening, as though they know you're there. Your eyes play tricks on you in the darkness. Your imagination tries to dull your good senses and instincts. Only, it isn't fun or interesting; it's deadly serious. Minutes drag by while you listen intently. The only nearby sound you hear is water dripping from trees. Your nerves are on edge.

An hour passes; nothing. You let yourself relax a little; your heart slows a little and slides down from your throat. You become aware of the mosquitoes taking turns on bare skin. Deathly quiet. If you didn't know there were other GI's nearby, you'd swear you're sitting alone, in the middle of nowhere, in the dark.

Check safety. The radio crackles slightly for the first SITREP and you nearly jump into firing position. "Four Alpha, Bravo Support. If SITREP negative, break squelch twice." Brown has the volume turned very low, but I heard the squelch break twice as he presses the send button twice.

My eyes start their useless search in the total darkness because there's nothing else to do. Wait, listen, watch. Minutes drag by. I look at the luminous hands on my watch and see that it's 11:19. September 14, 1967. In-country 6 days and 359 to go. No, 360 because next year is a

Leap Year. Lucky me, I get an extra day in country. One day can make a difference.

I check my watch; 11:29. I rub my face to relieve the itch from mosquito bites. My face is covered with welts. Is this a proper way for a free citizen to spend a year? Is this going to bring freedom to these people? Living like an animal in the elements day and night? Sitting in the rain; soaked, tired, hungry, muddy? Just doing our duty.

The long day begins to catch up with you. The dripping from the trees becomes rhythmic, hypnotizing. Hours of no sound except the drip, dripdrip, dripping. At first it's irritating. Then it's numbly accepted as the only stimulus to your senses, almost a friend keeping you company. Your body relaxes a little more and your thoughts wander aimlessly. You realize you're getting too comfortable, complacent. You hold your cool, wet sleeve to your face to keep fully awake.

The radio crackles lightly for the SITREP. Must be midnight, and still nothing. You begin to feel like nothing will happen, like only fools and desperate people would be out at this time of night in this weather, under these conditions. Hueys passed overhead, their distinctive sound now familiar to me after only 6 days. Other Americans are not far away, but they don't know we're down here.

Wait, watch listen. Wipe your face with your cool, wet sleeve. Thoughts of home. The rain starts again, heavier, and adds what it can to your misery.

Force your mind to be alert, to focus. Wipe your face again. You realize the time between wipes is getting shorter. You've got to stay awake all night, one hundred percent alert. "Stay alert, stay alive. Rifle at the ready."

Artillery mutters briefly out there. The radio crackles for the next SITREP.

I'm sure glad I went to college. I'm going to use that education after I get out because I'm sure not going to use it here.

Your mind begins to numb, but your eyes and ears are open. You could easily sleep sitting up, real easy. Just let go, just a few seconds, drift. No. No. Wake up. Wipe your face. Good thing you aren't lying down. You could just lay your head down, just for a minute, or even a few seconds.

My stomach growls. Mom's hot breakfast would be really good. Base camp warriors are probably beginning to return to their barracks after a movie or a few beers at the club.

My legs are starting to cramp from not moving and from being wet, sitting in the water and mud. Patience, discipline. Five more hours and it'll be over. You're almost halfway. You wish for contact so you can wake up and move. Slowly and quietly check your gear, making sure everything is ready and where you can find it in a hurry. Your gear has to be ready at all times. You have to know where everything is. Safety on. Hand grenades on my belt, right and left. Two bandoliers of magazines crisscross my chest. The magazines are in the pockets upside down to keep water and mud out, and to make it fast and easy to pull them out and insert them into the rifle.

Another glance at my watch; one forty. Time is slowing down, even more. Wipe your face, check gear. Anything to pass the time and stay awake. Still waiting for sound or movement, still moving your eyes, futilely because it's very dark. This is a good situation to use the Starlight scope, which magnifies any small amount of light, even from stars, and you can "see in the dark." It's one of the highly touted technological tools in use, but not available to Grunts. I never understood that because it's the Grunts that need that ability.

The radio's crackle for the two o'clock SITREP breaks the monotony. Then, death like silence.

You fight to keep awake, stay alert, and stir your thoughts. You feel like you're sitting on a rock. Your back begins to be very uncomfortable; your legs feel numb to the point of being useless. You wonder what you'll do if you have to move fast; will your legs work for you or against you?

SITREP, three A.M. Surely nothing will happen anymore, except, war is twenty-four hours a day. It doesn't break for darkness, weather, chow, or death. The VC must be trying to avoid the weather by not moving tonight. Artillery in the distance, then silence.

Your senses numb, your alertness slips, your sphere of awareness shrinks in size until it reaches only a few feet from you; about as far as you can see. Four A.M. Now you get more relaxed, more absorbed in thoughts and memories.

You become vaguely aware of a sound off in the distance that begins as a low rumble and gradually intensifies. It builds slowly, louder and louder. It sounds as if the earth is collapsing, falling into itself, and the brink is approaching you. The ground shakes under you, until it runs all the way through your body. The rumble continues for fifteen or twenty minutes, then ceases abruptly. Saturation bombing; the Ho Chi Minh Trail receives its daily quota. The North Vietnamese and the VC move down the trail at night so B-52 bombers drop at night as well as during the day. The planes fly so high you never hear them. When the bombs hit, the planes are long gone. Maybe the VC knew of a bombing scheduled for this general area and that's why we've had no movement.

How do they bomb so accurately in the dark? I wonder if someone will forget to tell someone else when we're out on patrol and wipe us out.

Four thirty A.M. Your body is completely numb and your mind isn't far behind. Keep watching, keep waiting, don't let your guard down. Mosquitoes are thick and sometimes are sucked into your nose when you breathe, but you have to get them out without making any noise, if you can.

Maybe that's not a trail out there. Maybe it's just a clear area and we're at the wrong place. Maybe I counted wrong, or Rice read the compass wrong by a few degrees.

Sleep is getting harder to fight off, you're exhausted. Still no movement out front, just dead silence. It would be so easy to lean back against a tree and doze off in seconds. Your head gets heavy and your helmet seems to weigh twenty pounds.

Crackle. Five A.M. You can make it now, just a little more. The sky begins to lighten, even though it's still cloudy. You look around at your buddies, hunkered down inside the tree line. What a sad looking group; wet, wrinkled, unshaven, caked with mud and stink. Sunken red eyes, always the eyes. Do mine look like that yet? I haven't seen a mirror lately. Faces and hands are covered with mashed mosquitoes, welts, scratches, and smears of blood.

To the northwest is a cloud of dust barely visible in the early dawn. A monument to the saturation bombing.

Zero five forty five. Sgt. Rice passes the word to bring in the Claymores and trip flares, grab a smoke. but maintain security. Legs are stretched, flexed and massaged. Backs are turned for urination – civility even here, when possible.

Dry cigarettes are taken out of fresh packs and plastic bags. Lighters click, canteens gurgle. The movies have it all wrong; after being up all night, water tastes like a warm spoon, cigarettes taste like smoke from a brush fire. You wish you hadn't lit up, but, smoker or not, the smoke helps keep the mosquitoes away.

A night of that 90% sheer boredom. It's no wonder smoking is so prevalent in combat units. When there is absolutely nothing to do, and you need to keep occupied, smoking is about the only choice. They are free in C-ration packs, so it's almost a natural.

Day seven. A new day and what do we have to look forward to? More? Worse? Six A.M. Brown radios Support that we are on the way in. Rice and Brown move forward to Fourth Platoon and we move out. We travel a different route because the VC may have set up mines, booby traps, even an ambush, if they detected us and knowing we would return to our camp. Obviously, you need to be just as alert returning from a mission as you were going out; there is no tactical difference.

The column automatically stretches out to five-meter intervals for minimal casualty susceptibility. Since it's daylight, snipers are a threat also. Look down for booby traps, mines, and punji stakes. Look up for snipers. Look left and right for an ambush. Look everywhere, including where you're stepping. The ironic part is that where you're stepping is probably the only thing you can see. Snipers, ambushes, booby traps - they'll be hidden and camouflaged with expertise. If you see them, it'll be too late.

On each side of our column there's a flank guard about thirty meters out. They help protect the main body by detecting or forcing any waiting ambush or sniper to fire before their optimum time; in effect, sacrificing the few to save the many. The flank should stay just in sight of the main column, the distance being determined by the density of the vegetation you're moving through. The only difference between flank and point (the first position in the column), is that the point has the main body right behind him. Point sometimes must hack a trail in thick jungle. Very tiring and sometimes there are several point men trading off to let one rest. I'd still rather walk point than flank.

The return trip was as uneventful as the night. We avoided trails and moved through heavy undergrowth. Same routine: Stay alert, eyes moving, squish, slosh, weapon at the ready, swat at mosquitoes, step-kick-step-kick off the mud building on your boots. Check safety. The mud build-up on our boots seems heavier than before because tired bodies tire easily. Breathing is labored, heavy sweat runs down our cheeks and drips from chins. You have to push yourself to keep moving, causing attention to focus on your next step, dulling your sense of alertness to danger. Heat and humidity smother you like a blanket. Somehow, the human body always finds a little more strength, then a little more, and a little more.

We moved across paddies like flies exposed on an empty table – easy targets. Then more brush. Moving into heavy brush from an open area is very dicey because you can move blindly into any of the dangers.

We reached the open area, and camp was in sight, about a kilometer away.

Have we brought this place another day closer to a democratic heritage? Half a day? I'm half a day closer to home. Now, it's only 359 more. All that was only half a day – this will be a very long year.

We pass through the perimeter, reach the mortars, and drop our gear, ready for a rest. Sit down, lie down or fall down. Time for sleep, and eat later.

Lieutenant Young came over and said, "After you guys eat your C's, we're going to Tay Ninh to get mortar ammo, and fire the guns today and tonight. Tomorrow we move back to Dau Tieng."

Infantry by day, mortars by night. Guess we can sleep when we get home, or in the airports waiting for the plane that takes us home.

9

There's no breakfast quite like a cold can of pork and beans with congealed blobs of grease floating on top; fare fit only for the Queen of Battle – the Infantry. Might as well get used to it. At least the night was only uncomfortable and miserable. It could have been worse.

After one night, with no baptism with fire, I felt a little more like one of the guys. I looked and smelled the part, anyway.

Breakfast was followed by a mirrorless cold-water shave with a blade ruined by a squad of men. We cleaned off some of the mud, grabbed our gear and climbed into the bed of a waiting two-and-a-half ton truck, better known as a deuce and a half. We never went anywhere without our rifle and helmet. The entire country was an insecure area. You needed to protect yourselves at all times. Quite a few of the troops in forward areas (away from large permanent base camps) wore their flak jacket twenty four hours a day, but because it was so hot, not everyone was willing to put up with it.

The ride over the rain eroded roads was painfully bouncy. It reminded me of popcorn in a skillet. The truck had to move reasonably fast or it would become an easy target for the enemy, so the smallest bump threw us up in the air and we landed with a bone-jarring, tooth-clicking thud.

The scenery was nice. Mile after mile, all we could see was rice paddies, crisscrossed with dikes. It looked like an all green checkerboard, dotted here and there by an island-like stand of trees, some of which had a deserted hooch in the shade of palm trees. Most of the farmers had moved to a large city for safety, but still worked the rice by day. The rice farmers were at work, wading in the mud and water behind a water buffalo pulling some kind of plow. The iconic picture of the World's Rice Bowl, Southeast Asia. Quaint. Timeless.

The trees were green, we wore green, our truck was green, the rice shoots sticking up out of the water were green, even the water in the paddies looked green.

During the drive, we passed through hamlets and villages. There was always a group of kids by the edge of the road, waiting. When they heard the truck's engine, they ran out to the road and waited. Then, "GI give chop-chop," they all yelled. Wesley tossed them some packets of chewing gum, cookies, and a can of Ham and Lima beans, our hated meal in the cases of C's. He said, "Watch this." The kids scrambled after the items but the one who got the can of Ham and Limas threw it back at our now distant truck. He laughed, "They don't like them either." I made a mental note to carry something to throw to kids if I ever rode on a truck again. In the background were Vietnamese, sort of lurking. Some looked at us with hostile faces, others were indifferent. In the shadows of trees, it was difficult to see them clearly, which makes you tense up, and ask yourself, "What's that female carrying? Is that a weapon, or don ganh, shoulder sticks to carry things? What about the kids right here by the truck? Any of them hiding something behind their backs?" The stink is here in the villages, just like everywhere else.

We passed through part of the city of Tay Ninh. The narrow streets were choked with pedestrians, bicycles and Vespa motor scooters, but very few cars. Our truck filled the road so that the Vietnamese had to stand aside as we passed. They all looked the same; you couldn't tell a farmer from a merchant from a VC. Most of the people seemed friendly, but we had to be careful, because it would have been real easy for someone to shoot or throw a grenade into the truck. I don't know what I expected to see, but I was surprised to see so much open activity and freedom of movement. War or not, life must go on, especially if someone else does the fighting for you.

We stopped briefly at an intersection and I looked over the milling crowd. On one corner was a youngish male, begging for money. He looked like he could have been a war veteran, crippled for life. Fate could have made him a hero, but he was in the wrong place at the wrong time. Now, he's an outcast, no longer needed by anyone. Two flesh-peddlers came up to the truck, each trying to elbow the other out of the way. "Hey, GI, I have plenty virgin for you." Said one… "No, him numbah ten. My numbah one, young," yelled the other as we drove off, weaving through the crowd.

The ammo dump was in the Army compound on the edge of the city. We were directed to a stacks of boxes which had evidently been standing in water at one time because there was a watermark about one third of the way up. Since we were directed to the ammo, we assumed it would be good.

Just as we were about to finish, a dangling metal band sliced my wrist right on the vein. The heat and exertion caused our blood to pound through our veins, and caused my blood to squirt out about six inches from my arm, making the cut seem a lot worse than it was. I grabbed my wrist with the other hand to slow the fountain and waited while the other guys finished loading the ammo. Then they took me to the Twenty Fifth Field Hospital (a Quonset hut) to get some stitches. The Doctor cut off my fatigue jacket so I wouldn't have to release the pressure I was applying. After treatment, the Doctor told me to be sure and keep the cut clean because infection sets in very fast under our conditions here. I told him I was in the Infantry, in the field, and he stopped giving advice on cleanliness and hygiene, and said to come back in about ten days so he could remove the stitches. I explained that I would probably never be back this way and I didn't know where I'd be in two or three days, much less ten. He looked at me like I was refusing to cooperate.

All through the treatment, the Doctor kept asking me if I was OK, and if there was anything that I needed to tell him. I think he was afraid I had cut my wrist intentionally, and I was a candidate for suicide.

When it was all over, I threw what was left of my shirt on my back and walked out the door. As we were walking toward the truck, a Military Policeman (MP) stopped us. We were standing in front of a hospital, in a combat zone, bandages all over my arm, my shirt obviously cut off, and this half-witted MP wants to run me in for being out of uniform. We walked away laughing, leaving him mumbling something about letting it go if I promised to get into proper uniform.

The ride back to the mountain was wet. Heavy rain soaked us and turned the road into a swamp. The truck slid all over the road and almost hit trees several times. A good soaking rain was the only means available to wash off some of the mud, but it insured we would continue to be wet and sour smelling. Vietnam receives about 100 inches of rain annually, so we can expect to be constantly soaked, especially during the monsoonal season when the rainfall is even higher.

We unloaded the truck, and then Sgt. Bauer said to break for chow before setting up the guns. We were tired from being awake all night on ambush, and carrying ammo crates, so we decided to sleep instead of eat. We rolled up in our ponchos and lay on the wooden ammo crates so we wouldn't be on the ground in the mud. About an hour later, someone woke us. It was still raining, but it didn't matter because we had been sleeping in a sweat inside our ponchos. Sleeping in a poncho in heavy rain is a wonderful experience. The heavy raindrops beat on you like a drum but if you are exhausted, you'll sleep.

We still weren't in the mood to eat cold C-rations, but we were reminded to take our malaria tablet. We were supposed to take a tablet every week. The other guys threw their tablets away but I decided I didn't need to risk malaria so I took mine. I asked why nobody else took one and Dean told me it was because the pill was extremely bitter and gives you the trots, bad. Besides, why prevent something which would get you a ticket out of the boonies? They were right on all three counts, and it was the last time I took a malaria tablet.

Back to work. Before we could fire the mortar, we had to work on the mortar pits. The protective sandbag walls were sagging and the stacked bags were sliding off because of the rain. The ground inside the pits was really soupy where the base plate had been pounded in and dug out, many times, from firing the mortar. So we spent the rest of the daylight hours trying to shape things up. Rain eased so mosquitoes returned. The sun broke through the clouds and turned the air into a sauna, incredibly hot and humid. Breathing was difficult and physical movement required great effort for our tired bodies.

Sweat was streaming from faces, into eyes and down backs. Shirts came off but it didn't help much. I realized now why we were issued four canteens and a large supply of salt tablets. Until you are acclimated, you run a very high risk of dehydration and heat exhaustion. I learned to always have a canteen nearby, in addition to my rifle. I wondered if my kidneys would wither before I could adjust to the heat and humidity.

In a few hours, we repaired the sand bag walls and replaced the soupy mud with drier mud. During those hours, I got a much better idea of how things were. War stories were mostly avoided. The chatter was mostly about home, back in the World, with only an occasional mention of events here. I was surprised at how close this group was, almost like brothers. They knew each other's favorite C-ration meals. They knew when each other last heard from home and if the news was good or bad. It was as if they had been chipped off the block of young people back home, transplanted in another country, and continued with life. But, these guys never met before they came here. This close relationship was in part a defense mechanism, partly a diversion, but perhaps mostly, a mutual morale assist; if I help you keep your morale up then you help me with mine. All you have going for you is your buddies. You're living in the elements, day and night; you're overqualified for your trained occupation; you resent having to live like this; you're short on sleep, and long on worry; you're tired and becoming bitter; you eat out of cans, cold food you don't even like; you get shot at; you may die painfully today; your country doesn't seem to be appreciative, or even aware of, what you're going through. Without help from your friends, your morale would evaporate.

We fired the mortars for a while and it was like seeing a long lost friend. It had been almost two months since I fired a mortar in training and I found myself mentally reviewing some of the things to remember; keep your head below and away from the muzzle to prevent damage to your eyes and ears from the flash and concussion; don't have your toes under the edge of the base plate when you fire the first few rounds because you'll lose them; realign the sights after each of the first few rounds slam the base plate into the ground and tilts the gun throwing off your aim. An earlier lesson was reinforced; training is always under ideal conditions and weather, but combat isn't. The mortars we used in training were in pretty good condition. These guns were missing parts, losing the constant fight against corrosion, and had many dents and nicks. I took the rainproof plastic cover off the barrel, set the sights, and fired the first round. This settled the base plate and also threw out a spray of mud and water that covered all of us. Another layer to keep the bugs off.

We fired until we used the old lot of ammo already here and saved the new lot from Tay Ninh for night firing. It was supposedly Harassment and Interdiction (H and I) firing which was a target chosen because the VC had been active in the area and may be there again.

Then the time came for work. Firing those rounds drove the base plate into the mud and we had to get it out and repair the ground for night firing. Digging it out was like digging up a tree stump – the ground just didn't want to give it up. In training, the ground was always dry and hard so the base plate was driven down at most a couple of inches. We never thought about what would happen in mud, and were never told.

I was beginning to realize we were fighting two enemies – the active enemy, which I had not yet met, and a passive enemy, the elements, which I had known for only a day or two. A thought passed through my mind. What if the VC could team up with the elements and increase their effectiveness? Maybe they already have, and that's why some of the tactics they used were successful. This is their natural habitat.

Hours later we had the pits repaired and the mortars were ready for the night. My fatigues had been soaking wet since I arrived here. If it wasn't pouring rain, the heat and humidity caused constant, heavy sweat. Always wet, I kind of thought this would not be a good thing for our skin and problems would show up and begin developing. The rain did wash off some of the mud and stink for a while, but poor hygiene would surely take its toll.

The sun was just setting as we broke out the C's. What cuisine shall we enjoy tonight? New guys get last choice, which was almost always Ham and Limas. Nobody liked them, including me.

The date stamped on the C-ration case was Nineteen Fifty something, over ten years old. Only the best for America's fighting men.

The mosquitoes are absolutely relentless as they moved in for the night.

Sgt. Bauer came over and briefed us for the night firing which was to set one DEFCON, coordinated with the nightly ambush, and then to fire H and I, every hour on the hour, on coordinates we would be given later.

The rain is relentless too, and the heavy clouds blocked all light from the full moon. Redford told us to get some sleep before the ambush called in, maybe in an hour. When a gun crew is to be available for fire support, that means there will be a crew awake and ready, immediately, at all times. When a unit needs your support, they need it now because they are in imminent danger. They do not have time for someone to wake up and stumble around, and maybe set the sights just slightly off, which is bad news for the unit, whether it misses everything or it hits them. This also means someone will be on the radio at all times. Here, buying them time may mean buying their life.

Sleep was not long in coming even though everything hurt from head to toe; feet, muscles, guts, skin, even our hair seemed to hurt. We slept on the sandbags with no cover or shelter. Using ponchos replaced one problem with two others, so why bother? Redford woke us and said the ambush should be calling soon. They must be miserable out there as we were last night; rain, mud, mosquitoes. Few of the guys kneeled behind sandbags and tried to light a cigarette in the darkness; the rain made it hopeless.

A tracked vehicle called a Duster, with two forty-millimeter cannons had come into our camp while we were sleeping and positioned itself to have a clear shot at the rock with the curious cave-like crack in it. Somebody told me it came every night and fired six to eight rounds every thirty minutes, then left at dawn. I assumed the idea was to protect the camp in case there were VC in the cave, but the effect seemed to be to disturb anyone who managed to have time to sleep. Just one more sound of war to get used to.

Dean got the radio call from the ambush patrol and got the mortar sight settings and charge from the Fire Direction Control (FDC). I set the charge and the time fuse for an air burst. The round was fired and a sheet of water and mud covered us as the base plate sunk below ground level. Wesley knelt in a mud puddle and reset the tube because now it was off the proper settings – now it could hit the patrol. I quickly reset the sights – have to do this quickly and accurately because another round may be called for, HE or Willie Peter. The patrol requested an adjustment and another round. Set charge and fuse, fire, adjust tube again. The patrol wanted an adjustment but no round. Check the setting on the sight in case the patrol called for support. Their DEFCON was set.

We readjusted to one of the H and I points and fired HE from the new lot of ammo from Tay Ninh. The CO's position was directly in front of the gun. When the first round was fired, it didn't sound right leaving the tube – the sound was too weak. We waited and never heard an explosion. Shortly, Lt. Young walked over and said he heard the round thud into the ground right in front of the CO's position. These rounds have a self-arming mechanism which activates after it has traveled for a certain period of time, usually 1.25 to 1.5 seconds. Fortunately, the round didn't travel long enough to arm or we would have killed our own CO.

We aimed the mortar in another direction and fired a few rounds. They were OK.

The duster started its night firing. I figured he woke anyone sleeping. I thought I was going to get some sleep but it didn't look very promising. The next mortar crew was due in an hour and my crew due back in two hours, giving us an hour off – one on, one off. With the guns firing, that hour off would probably be more like thirty minutes of sleep, maybe.

About ten thirty, the second crew took over. We lay down on the wooden ammo crates again and dozed off. At eleven o'clock the duster woke me. At eleven thirty it was our turn to fire the mortars again. At twelve thirty we slept a few minutes until the duster fired. Then we slept from one to one thirty, our shift. We got about three hours of sleep, total of a few short naps. Only the second uncomfortable night. I hoped it was two of only a few, but it was just a hint of things to come.

So the night went; rain, mosquitoes, guns, wet and muddy, very little sleep.

Near morning we had a second short round. It fell just outside the perimeter and exploded. The CO said to stop firing that ammo from Tay Ninh. The next day, he had some of the ammo sent in to Ordnance to be checked and found out that we shouldn't have been firing it because it had gotten wet at the dump; it had been standing in water.

Dawn and no enemy contact. Word was passed to pack up the mortars. Choppers would pick us up and we would return to Dau Tieng for showers, beer, hot food, clean fatigues, and sleep. Tomorrow we would move out to the field on a Battalion size operation – the real thing.

We dug the base plate out again and oiled the mortar as best as we could. Then we got our gear ready to move out and ate cold C's for breakfast while we waited for our flight. The perimeter stayed intact for security. When the choppers came in, those men could leave their positions.

I was sitting next to Sgt. Bauer and said, "Hey, Sarge. How were we supposed to sleep with all the firing going on?"

While he dug peanut butter out of a tin with a cracker, he said, "John, couple more days and you won't wake up. Your mind will be able to tell you if it's incoming or outgoing, and tell your body, 'Don't wake up. It's us.' Then you'll get some sleep."

We heard the Hueys coming while they were still a long way off – their distinct pulsing, thrumming drone of the engine, and the whop-pop-pop of the blades.

10

The first time I saw Dau Tieng, it seemed pretty crude and primitive. After only two days in the mud, it looked like Paradise. We dropped our gear and stampeded to the shower, which was outdoors, no walls, and used a suspended jet wing fuel tank with nine valves. I shared a valve with eight or nine other guys. They had been in the jungle for over three weeks before I joined them at the mountain, so I showered quickly and left them to soak off some of their crust and stink. They earned and deserved a good shower. Sloshing back to the hooch, I realized that nowhere else in the world could you be muddy up to your knees and still feel like you are clean.

The holiday didn't last long. The CO passed the word to be ready to move out at 1600, or 4 P.M. The change in plans disappointed everybody. Not staying in camp overnight meant no hot food, no sleep, and an extra night in the boonies. At least we got a shower, clean fatigues and wrote a letter home. It was just another reminder that "You better give your heart to God because the rest belongs to Uncle Sam." You now have no rights, no time, and no say in the matter.

I was fortunate to spend a couple of days at the mountain before going into combat for the first time. I was better able to prepare my gear for maximum effectiveness and minimum weight, and myself for the living conditions. So I thought.

We were issued C-rations for two days – it would be two days before a resupply helicopter would bring more food, water and ammo. So, in addition to helmet, rifle, and C's, I took all four canteens, twenty four loaded magazines in two bandoliers, gas mask, extra hand grenades, extra salt tablets, first aid pouch, rifle cleaning kit, extra socks, extra boot laces, twenty sandbags, one Claymore mine, one smoke grenade, one LAW (light anti-tank weapon, like a bazooka but much smaller and lighter; also used against bunkers and personnel), poncho and poncho liner, backpack, bayonet, flak jacket, entrenching tool, extra insect repellent, camera, and my only link with home, a picture of my family.

Since I was the new guy, I got to carry the squad's shaving gear, machete and a file to sharpen it with.

Quite a few of the guys hung a towel around their neck to mop the sweat from their eyes; they knew from experience what was coming.

I was also elected to carry three slap-flares, hand-held star cluster flares ignited by slapping the bottom of the tube while aiming them upward. Three flares, three colors; red meant we were being overrun, adios; white meant all clear; green meant fall back to the LZ (Landing Zone), or, come in and regroup here.

The C-ration cans fit perfectly in the extra pair of socks, two meals per sock. The long tube of cans in the socks were tied to a belt loop above each leg and kept from banging against my legs by hanging them down into the big cargo side pockets found on jungle pants.

The smallest piece of gear, by no means the least important, was the P-38 can opener. It usually took about 38 punctures to open a can of C's. At any rate, you didn't eat without this little tool which was about the size of a quarter.

When I was a lot younger, I enjoyed looking at pictures of Infantrymen during combat and noticed all the gear they were lugging around. I often wondered why they were carrying it, why not stash it somewhere, lighten your load, and come back for it later. It never dawned on me that each man had to be self-sufficient. He had to carry all his day's needs with him because there isn't anyone who is going to bring it to him at day's end. The other reason is that there isn't a "somewhere" to stash the gear. There is no closet, building, barracks, or spot to which you will return for sure. You constantly move around all day and have no idea where you will set up for the night.

The RTO (Radio Telephone Operator) usually carried as much as we did, plus the 25-pound radio, plus the heavy extra battery. The machine gunner and his ammo bearers carried their basic load plus extra belts of ammo for the gun. The Weapons Platoon often carried the mortars with those fifty-pound base plates, and ammo. Carrying all this gear through rice paddies, streams, and muddy jungles was like carrying an anchor in a swimming pool; you sink to the bottom with each step. I had well over seventy pounds of gear, but it was by no means the heaviest load I would carry into combat.

After assembling all the gear, we had to make sure it worked properly and that we carried it in such a way that we could get to it quickly. All the gear in the world is worthless if you can't find it, so you have to know where it is at all times. If you are pinned down behind a log, or in the dark, you need to be able to find everything without spending precious time searching.

We assembled in the Company area, put our gear on the ground and waited for orders to walk to the helipad. Most of the guys lay on the ground, head on their pack, and taking advantage of the free time to catch up on lost sleep. A few wrote letters or just doing anything to keep from thinking about going back to the field.

Ski came over to make sure I was doing OK. He and Dean went out of their way to help me get adjusted; they were like a couple of big brothers. Dean said, "Use insect repellent only when you have to. It's hard to get that stuff. When you're out, you'll have to rub mud on yourself. Anything for relief.

"You've got a lot of gear to lug around. Couple of days out and you'll find out what's important to you." Since it was my first time out, I didn't know what to take, so I took just about everything we were issued. A couple of old timers walked by, fuzzy-faced kids barely old enough to shave. One said, "Forget the C's. Take more ammo and water." The other said, "Don't take much of anything 'cause you can't move fast, and any extra weight tires you out. Ski added, "You never know how the operation will turn out. If we hit heavy contact, you'll wish you had more ammo. If it turns out to be routine patrolling, you'll wish you had more food and less heavy ammo. Have to be ready for anything."

I looked around at the rest of the Company. Everybody's selection of gear was different, adjusted to their personal needs and preferences; not like training where we all had exactly the same gear and had to wear it the same way. I also noticed quite a few Lucky Pieces in the bands holding helmet camouflage covers on, and on dog tags; a Crucifix, a rabbit's foot, an Ace of Spades, a feather, even a rifle cartridge. I'm sure they represented quite a collection of stories.

Rain eased up a little and the sun broke through the heavy clouds, but we were already soaked. By dark, we would be muddy and smelly already. We might as well have waited to shower.

Lt. Young walked over from the Orderly Room and said, "All right, Weapons, here's the plan. We'll chopper to the other side of the Iron Triangle, sweep through the Ho Bo Woods, then the Boi Loi Woods, and wind up here at Dau Tieng. It's a big area so we'll be out about three weeks. We expect the LZ to be hot (we'll have incoming fire). Artillery will prep the LZ (artillery will be fired into the area to kill or drive out the VC before we insert troops). We do expect hostile action; the bad guys are definitely in there again. Resupply choppers will bring the mortars out on their first run in two days.

"This is a Battalion size operation. Alpha, Charlie, and Delta Companies will sweep on our left. We'll have Song Saigon (Saigon River) on our right part of the way. Saddle up and move to the LZ in ten or fifteen minutes."

I turned to Ski as I started putting my gear on, "Ho Bo Woods? Sounds like a hideout for derelicts."

Ski chuckled and answered, "Sounds like it but it will not be a picnic. We had Operation Cedar Falls there earlier this year and the whole Triangle was a VC hideout area, big time. The village of Ben Suc was a headquarters, so it was destroyed. Thousands of acres of jungle were leveled. Must have been a hundred miles of tunnels, down maybe five to ten levels. Underground world; 100 bed hospital, ammo dump, barracks. You name it – unbelievable. Had to pump the tunnels full of acetylene gas and ignite it. Only way to reach every corner," he grunted as he put his gear on. "Must have taken years to dig. Miles of tunnels but no dirt around. Hid it somehow. No wonder they can have a good size army this far south; they moved North Vietnam down here and put it under our feet, within spitting distance but out of sight. VC were popping out of holes uncovered by the bulldozers leveling trees. Some gave up; some got cut in half by the 'dozers blade. Almost a half a year ago. They've had plenty time to rebuild.

"That and a couple other operations made the VC change their strategy. They moved their large base camps back across the border to Cambodia and kept small guerilla units and camps over here."

"Couple other operations?" I asked.

"Yeah," he continued. "LZ Gold, Battle of Soui Tre. We were there. A thousand mortar rounds came in first, then human wave attacks. They overran some of our perimeter, hand-to-hand. Sixteen choppers shot down. Sixteen! Big air strikes. Point blank artillery. They were crawling over tanks. Bad shit. Bad. Killed over 600 of them little suckers and somehow lost only a few dozen GI's. Shot 'em into little pieces."

Little did I know those days weren't over. Not yet.

Here it is, the big one. The last six months, even the last few days, were just practice, fun and games. Combat assault on choppers into a hot LZ, a few weeks in the jungle, "We expect hostile action." This is the point at which civilization and rationality become memories, and where movies and photographs can't capture whatever it is that's left.

Walking to the LZ, I looked around at these guys and saw what I've seen in movies and pictures. Infantrymen walking, bent forward under a heavy load (humping). Rifle in hand, not talking. Not thinking of tomorrow but concentrating on the next step, the most basic element of combat. All the marching in rows and columns has been left behind in the States as if to make up for circumstances. March in straight rows, salute and play war games; don't march in straight rows, don't salute in a combat zone and don't play games in war. Make up your minds, which do you want us to do? Which one is the real soldier? Which builds Democracies? We arrived at the airstrip and readied ourselves for an Eagle flight on the slicks (helicopters with slick sides, no rockets or miniguns hanging on the sides like gunships).

We formed a staggered line of groups of seven, about eighty feet apart, took off our gear, and waited again. I was thinking I always seem to be the one waiting, wherever I go. It sure would be great if someone else had to do the waiting on me.

Clouds moved in and their shade made the temperature drop from about 100 degrees to a cooler 90 degrees; another monsoon rain was coming. Maybe it'll rain so hard they'll postpone the operation until tomorrow; one less day in country, one less night in the field.

Several of us had just dozed off when the drone of Hueys nagged us awake. We slowly put our gear back on and watched the choppers form a dotted line as they circled to approach. In my group were Ski, Dean, Wesley, Redford, Lt. Young, and Brown. The radio was tuned to monitor transmissions between our CO and the flight leader, Little Bear Six. The choppers flared and eased into position on the ground, each near a seven-man group. Dirt, rocks and debris swirled around us like a dust-devil. How can there be so much dust if it rains so often? It made me try to hold my breath and close my eyes. The noise from the engines was so loud we had to communicate with hand signals. The first three men to board sat on a small canvas seat. I sat on the floor in the open doorway, legs dangling outside above the skids. There were no doors on the slicks which not only saved on weight but also allowed faster entrance or exit under hostile conditions. We were ready to lift off in seconds.

We took off to the south, climbed slowly and soon turned to the southeast. The view from the air, maybe two thousand feet up, was nice. The land looked less hostile. The air blowing in the door was cool. We'd never be allowed to ride like this in the States, sitting in the open door, feet dangling outside, as if we were on an amusement park ride. We were doing a lot of things here that we would never be allowed to do in the States. In fact, I didn't really feel I was in the same Army I trained in, but just using similar gear. It's definitely more lax here; emphasis was not on how we did something, but just getting it done. You could wear your uniform and gear however you wanted, within reason, with no petty harassment.

Talk was impossible because of the engine noise. We circled and began our descent to the LZ. Lt. Young kneeled between the two pilots, and then shouted in turn in our ears, "Lock and load. Hot LZ." We put magazines in our rifles, chambered a round and put on the safeties. All eyes were on the tree line looking for movement, tracers, or smoke. Before we took off, Redford said artillery prep of the LZ was a waste. Not only did it tip off the VC that something big was going to happen, and where, it didn't do much good anyway. I guess he was right. There were fresh craters everywhere and blasted trees leaning against other trees, but there were green tracers reaching for our chopper. That is a very helpless feeling, being shot at and having no place to hide. I pictured us falling out of the sky like a rock.

Our tracers were red, most of theirs were green. The convenient difference was by chance as far as I knew.

Our door gunner fired back, raking the tree line with his M-60 machine gun. Huey gunships fired into the trees with miniguns and rockets, hovering around the clumps of trees with their nose angled slightly downward. It reminded me of big fish darting for little fish around rocks in a lake at home. Tracers kept coming up at us. They seemed to float, to just hang in the air, and then zip past. The closer we got to the ground, the thicker the tracers became. I'm sure our chopper took several hits, but we were still flying. I felt like the condemned man in front of a firing squad, without a blindfold; no place to run. Just wait and watch. We didn't shoot back because we couldn't see them under the trees. Wait until we get on the ground, Charlie. Just wait.

At about fifty feet up, we stood on the pipe-like landing skids outside the chopper and held onto the door frame, rifle in the other hand. The heavy packs and rush of air made balance tricky. The LZ was short grass and mud. When the choppers hovered at about three feet above the ground, we jumped down and sloshed outward to form a circular security line around the chopper so the pilots could get those big targets out fast. It took a lot of guts to fly one of those things right into the VC's line of fire. Since we were between the VC and the choppers, we were also targets. WHAM. WHAM. Small mortars. We hit the mud, SPLAT. Our front half was now covered with mud, our rear half was still clean. Our heavy load of gear pushed us deep into the mud. We looked like turtles with heads slightly raised, looking for the VC in the tree line; looking for smoke, movement, anything. Tracers grazed across the LZ; green, answered by red. Several rounds whistled inches over my head. If I had held my right hand up, I would now be called Lefty. I emptied a magazine into the tree line, then another. Explosions, rifle fire, machine gun fire, helicopters diving, grenades. There was no place to get cover. "What do I do now, Drill Sergeant, Sir?" Completely exposed and pinned down, we waited while the gunship pilots earned their pay. Rockets whooshed and mini guns burrrrped. My pucker was definitely tight. I had to try to hide behind a blade of grass.

After the choppers left, it seemed very quiet, and the feeling that came over me on this first assault was abandonment and isolation. Dumped in the middle of some swampy field, completely exposed, on my belly, wondering what was in the trees ahead. No choppers were down and no wounded so far. The LZ definitely qualified as hot, but now that we were on the ground the incoming was light. So, the gunships circled and waited for the next Eagle Flight to come in for a landing. The quiet didn't last long. Small arms were POP, POP, POPPING. Ski had crawled over to my side, trying to keep his shotgun barrel from getting full of mud. "AK, John. He's not shooting at us. Time to hit the bush." (AK-47, a rifle, the VC's primary weapon) Somehow, we got unstuck from the mud and kept low as we squished and sloshed as fast as we could toward the trees about a hundred yards away. That was the longest hundred yards I have ever covered. The mud was like bubble gum, and we seemed to be running in slow motion. When we got there and were kneeling behind some brush, I made up my mind to reduce my load of gear in the very near future. This pile on my back made it too difficult to maneuver. I had to give up some of my heavy luxuries if I was going to be "the quick" and not "the dead." For starters, it would be flak jacket, bayonet and gas mask.

POP. POP. That distinctive AK firing sound again, like a large cork gun. It was deceptive because the thirty caliber round could easily take half your head off. Faint memories came to mind; a young boy playing was with a wooden rifle. This didn't even seem like the same thing. POP. POP. The rounds sizzled by overhead, slapping leaves like a stick raked across a picket fence. Bullets carry their message, loud and clear. No sir, this just isn't the same as the war game.

A voice yelled out and several M-16's opened up. Somebody finally had a fix on the VC's position. There was a long, heavy exchange of rifle fire, and the harsh chatter of the M-60. Bullets whined, ricocheted and thunked into trees. Leaves and twigs fell all around us. A grenade launcher thumped, followed by the explosion. Then another. Shouts. Curses. Yells. Somehow, this didn't remind me of the movies.

I had to remind myself that, even though it sounded like a combat assault training course at Fort Polk, this was the real thing. Half those bullets were coming in my direction; they're trying to kill me. Those bastards want my life. It's a difficult thing to relate to, and to assimilate. No one has tried to kill me before now. My eyes were everywhere. My mind was trying, but couldn't, to remember what they said to do in training. "To hell with that," I said to myself. "THAT was them. THIS is me." Ski said, "Might be just a few men or they may be baiting us into an ambush. CO's got to decide." He did, and word was passed to move out and follow to the left. We took off, searching for the enemy. Word was also passed that we were following blood trails. The gunships may have been responsible. The chopper pilots would be like guardian angels during the next year, saving many a GI.

Redford told Wes and me to take right flank. We edged away from the column about twenty five meters. The trees were very tall, some easily two hundred feet, with extremely dense underbrush. It's dark in a jungle, eerie dark. The dense canopy blocks most of the sunlight. We had to parallel with the main column through twists and turns, but maintain visual contact while staying out as far as possible. If we lost contact for too long, we could easily get lost. We had to hack our own path and maintain our own security; that's why there were two of us. Front flank man cuts the path and maintains security at ground level; rear keeps visual contact with the column and keeps an eye in the trees for snipers. Wes said he would take lead to start, and we would swap when he was exhausted. Sounded good to me. I gave him the machete and we started through the brush that obviously had not been penetrated in quite some time, if ever. It was a nightmare of tangled branches, vines, thorns, and bugs. We often had to sling our rifles so we could use both hands to pass through. There was no breeze in growth like this making breathing labored. We were soaked with sweat in minutes. The high humidity hung on us like a wet blanket. The damp ground smelled sour and the odor of rotting undergrowth was stifling. I kept my head moving, eyes wide; look left to the column, up in the trees, right to the dense jungle, down on the ground and back, to make sure the VC didn't attack from the rear; then again, left, up, right, back,... In training, methods are of primary importance; in combat, the enemy is of primary importance and methods are just consequences.

The bush is just one big thorn; thorns are on everything. So far, the only things that grow here are rice and thorns. I was almost surprised that rice didn't have thorns, and that the national flag didn't have a picture of a thorn on it. Bugs of every imaginable kind were attacking us; they all bite or sting. Rain or shine, day or night, the bugs attack. Better put a bug on the thorn on the flag. This country that is so picturesque from the air is very hostile.

It's spooky out on flank. You feel even more abandoned, and very exposed. It's easy to lose your bearings in thick jungle, can't figure out which direction to go, no landmarks, no points of reference, every direction is the same scene – just like being in a thick fog.

As we moved along, we experienced the mud build up on our boots, building with each step until it got so heavy it fell off. Then it started all over again. It's difficult and tiring to walk with a two- or three- inch glob of mud on your feet, but during the rainy season we'll get plenty of practice.

An even more frustrating thing started its year-long life, too. Our rifles had a flash suppressor at the end of the barrel to help hide the tell-tale flash when fired. Whoever designed it left it open in front, like the tines on a fork. When you move through vines and brush, they get hung in the open slots like tangled hair in a comb. Every few feet, you have a tug of war to get your rifle free from the tangle. It's a constant battle just to keep moving. When you finally jerk free, your rifle looks like it's growing leaves out the end of the barrel.

We snaked along for about an hour around occasional craters from the artillery barrage and a few small open areas. Bugs buzzed around our heads, salty sweat stung our eyes. No sign of the VC. The column stopped. Wes and I dutifully stood facing away from the column, leaning back with our packs against a tree to take some of the weight of the heavy gear. If we sat, we wouldn't be able to see five feet, and the column could slip quietly away, unseen by us. Besides, with this load of gear on our backs it was difficult and painful to stand up from a sitting position. We took a good drink, popped salt tablets and lit up. Smoking is not supposed to be allowed during troop movement but if they hadn't heard or seen us by now, it wouldn't hurt a thing. Wes said he'd better sharpen the machete. Dense jungle dulls a machete fast and a dull machete makes you work harder. I told him I would take front for a while because he looked beat already.

No more sniper fire. Could be good news, or bad. There were far too many tracers in the LZ for just a few snipers. Somebody ahead, somewhere.

The sun would set soon. Have to set up a night position.

A sip of water. Insect repellent was rubbed on; easy, has to last two days. Resupply helicopter couldn't get to us in this mess anyway.

Mosquitoes and other bugs hovered all around us. From the column, Redford gave a soft whistle to let us know we're moving again. I took front with rifle in one hand and the machete in the other. It wasn't too bad at first, but the heat quickly sapped my energy. Then my pack made my back hurt and the flak jacket hindered movement. Sweat dripped in a steady stream from my chin and made the machete handle slippery which caused me to almost lose my grip with every swing. The beatup machete handle caused blisters and eventually cuts in my hand. I tried to concentrate on front security; I should look and then swing the big knife but the undergrowth was so thick I had to swing and then look. Thorns raked my hand and arm but at least the rain had stopped.

No blood trails out here.

About half an hour before sunset, the column stopped and we were signaled to come in. It felt much better being in a "crowd" than being isolated on flank.

Lt. Young said to dig in here for the night and he would spot the positions properly to be a preferred position in our perimeter. We had to dig fighting holes and surround them with sandbags because it was too late to cut tree limbs for overhead cover. (We would normally cut large tree limbs and small trees to form a strong, flat roof, and cover that with sandbags in case of rocket or mortar attack).

We didn't join up with Delta Company so we formed our own circular perimeter with three-man fighting positions at about every fifteen feet. Close enough to see the next position in the dense growth. Each platoon had to send a two-man LP out about one hundred meters, with a radio, for early warning of enemy movement. The LP would come in at dawn, or if and when we were attacked. They wouldn't get much sleep, if any, trading off every hour. Our day wasn't over even though the sun had set. In fact, the second half was just beginning.

Talk about night life, this was ours, every day. Ski started digging our hole and I filled sandbags, holding them open for each shovel full from the hole. Dean opened C-ration crackers to eat while he cleared brush to give us a little elbow room and a clear field of fire. After a while, we traded jobs.

Between the mosquitoes and thorns, our faces looked pretty gruesome. Ants and leeches added to our misery. The only sounds I could hear were those of the Company digging in and occasional artillery barrages somewhere off in the distance. The LP's were in position but we still had to have one man on guard while the other two worked. I ate a can of something. It was so dark now I couldn't see the lid and read what it was. I was so hungry I didn't care. While I ate, I set out two Claymores and two trip flares.

Trip flares give you a certain amount of security. They operate on the same principle as a booby trap. A trip wire, attached to the triggering device on the flare, is strung across your field of fire about shin high. Advancing enemy, walking or crawling, hit the wire and set off the flare, not only warning you of their presence, but also illuminating the area. At less than a pound, it's definitely a necessity.

You're supposed to clean your M-16, ammo and magazines every day. You can't. Besides having too much to do, it's usually too dark when you have the time. If you drop one of the small pieces, you probably wouldn't find it. So, we skipped rifle cleaning. We could clean our ammo in the dark, if we could muster the willpower to put off sleep. That usually didn't get done either.

We changed off again. It takes a lot of digging to make a hole big enough for three men, especially with the small entrenching tool we were issued.

We all had a chance to put on several layers of mud before we finished about nine thirty. This wasn't considered a busy evening. Ski and Dean filled me in on a typical day's end. Usually we would also have to cut tree limbs to make overhead cover for our bunker. Also, carry supplies, food, water, mortars and crates of mortar ammo from a LZ, set up the mortars, fire H and I and ambush support during the night, and guard duty. I asked when we'd sleep, and Dean said, "Go AWOL, 'cause you sure won't get any here."

The Artillery FO (Forward Observer) was setting up the DEFCON's for the night. He started away from the perimeter and adjusted closer and closer, at several points around the perimeter. Every time a round came screaming in, it sounded like it was going to hit right on top of us, and I found myself continually ducking. Large chunks of shrapnel whizzed and whirred over our heads through leaves and limbs. I sure was glad he knew what he was doing; at least, I thought he must know since he was an Officer (We were to never question the judgement of an Officer).

Each position of three men had one on guard for an hour while the other two slept; one hour on, one off. Guard duty was usually about 8 P.M. to about 5 A.M. The new man gets stuck with the last hour which means he was awake for the day at 4 A.M. That makes for a long day. Since it was almost 10 P.M., I stayed up for my first shift. This arrangement could give you as much as six hours sleep, broken up several times by an hour of guard, if you were lucky, and the night was quiet. Starting this late, I'd get four hours.

The day hadn't been too dangerous, but it was very active. That, combined with very little sleep in the past few days, made everyone anxious to skip important duties and just sleep. You have to sleep near each other for several reasons; you need to be near the bunker in case you're attacked; you need to be able to find the next man for guard easily so you don't want to stumble around in the dark and give your position away or get shot (night in the jungle is so dark that you can't see your hand in front of your face and lights are out of the question). It's also very easy to lose your bearings in total darkness and get completely lost. If you must move around, you don't want to step on anyone, or urinate on him; you may need to communicate quickly and quietly. So, it's best to sleep side by side, heads toward the perimeter, and rifle in hand. At least one of you has to have a watch with a luminous dial to keep track of your hour. No one ever mentioned this in training, and we weren't issued a watch. Fortunately, I had my own, and I was the only one in the squad who did.

I sure hope we get a new guy soon. I was getting worn out from all the "new guy gets the crap."

Here I was again, exhausted but awake, looking out into the night, waiting, listening, not making any noise, not using any light, trying to stay awake. In a prone position, your head keeps nodding, so you have to sit up. It doesn't help much, but if you do fall asleep, the fall will awaken you. If you're lucky, you have guard duty at night. Otherwise, you'll be doing something far less desirable like getting shot at, going on ambush, sitting on LP, or firing the mortars. In fact, just about the only way you can look at combat is to tell yourself it could be worse, because it definitely can.

It isn't easy getting enthused about keeping awake. Inevitably, your thoughts turn to home. That feels good for a while, until you realize home is a year away, so you change your thoughts to the here and now.

Here in the brush, there seem to be many more bugs than I've encountered so far; mosquitoes, wasps, ants, centipedes, spiders, leeches and about a thousand other creatures. Besides keeping you awake, they have one thing in common; they attack you by stinging or biting. Always here, I wondered what they bite or sting when humans aren't here.

Soon, I had to get up and take a leak, the first since early in the day. The profuse sweating drains you of moisture so your body habits change. Great for your system. Irregular meals, when you can, small amounts, throw off your regularity, and cause your stomach to shrink. Your insides can no longer tell night from day; only your eyes can.

This is just great stuff. How did you spend your youth? Well, because I was healthy, I was drafted, sent overseas, ruined my health, and came back a medical mess.

Too tired to do anything about the bugs crawling all over me, I continued to sit and wait. At first, I thought it just takes time until you get used to it. But, now it has become obvious that you are just too tired to make the effort, you just don't care. Your entire body hurts; feet, back, muscles, arms, and face.

Same routine as on ambush; wait, watch, listen, for any piece of sensory information. Wipe your face to stay awake. Your eyes are open but your mind keeps trying to turn off. You fight your body to stay awake. Check your watch, and then start all over again. And again. Bite your tongue; pinch your thigh; anything to stay awake. Eleven o'clock slowly dragged around. I woke Dean and gave him the watch.

I couldn't believe it; my turn to sleep, which won't take long. There won't be any tossing and turning or insomnia. What a luxury, and I don't want to waste a second. As I lay in the mud, I was vaguely aware of some sticks and rocks under me, but I didn't care because I didn't have the energy or the time to dig them out. What was the use? I was asleep before my head hit the ground.

It seemed like only a few seconds later when Ski woke me at 1 A.M. for guard. My first instinct was to check the time and make sure he didn't make a mistake. Two hours of sleep doesn't do much except leave your mind befuddled. Now it seemed even more difficult to stay awake. It got very dark, very quiet, and even though you could reach out and touch a friend, very lonely. You count the minutes as they drag by, another minute of your life gone forever, spent looking at darkness. It was strange that we never heard any animal sounds, day or night; no crickets, no frogs, no owls, no creatures rooting in the dirt and decaying leaves for something to eat. They must have all been eaten, killed or chased away.

Somewhere in the darkness came the sound of artillery.

The stay-awake routine starts all over again; wait, watch, listen, check the time, wipe your face, think of home, bite your tongue, pinch yourself, anything else you can think of. Again. Again.

I remembered Ski's story about the tunnels and having half a year to rebuild. Maybe there were VC under me right now, listening, waiting for the right time to pop up out of their tunnels and spider holes.

My fatigues were drying a little by now because the rain had stopped and I was not sweating. They're made of rip-stop poplin especially for this climate because they are lighter weight material and faster drying than regular fatigues. But, the thorns and thick brush would shred the rip-stop material. It was a losing battle anyway because a soaking rain began.

I knew that I would never see rain again, ever, without thinking about miserable nights in the jungle, just sitting in the rain, getting wetter. I also began to have serious doubts about just what we were doing and how we were going about it. This drudgery was accomplishing nothing; going through motions which result in boredom and inactivity. Nothing was being accomplished, no progress was being made. What is our strategy? What is our plan? Do we have a plan?

I think I was seeing the results when politicians micromanage a war and not leave it up to the military.

About 2 A.M., Sgt. Bauer felt his way to our position and said the LP to our left front had movement and every position was now to be 100 percent alert, everybody awake. If the LP was allowed to return to the perimeter, Sgt. Bauer said he'd let us know so we wouldn't mistakenly shoot them on their way in. I woke Ski and Dean and all three of us sat there looking into the darkness, waiting, listening. The time crawled while we waited, but all we had was rain hitting leaves.

2:45 A.M. The rain poured and our fighting hole literally became a swimming pool, full to the brim. Great; if we are attacked, do we stay out of the hole and get shot, or do we jump in and drown?

3:30. The rain stopped. POP. A green tracer sizzled by just above our heads. We couldn't fire back because we might hit the LP. It was too dark to see, so it had to be too dark for the VC to see us. They were trying to sucker us, or the LP, into firing and giving away our exact position. So we waited some more. The guys on LP would be having no trouble staying awake; alone out there, isolated. We strained our ears for any sound, our eyes for any movement. I had my rifle in my hand, Claymore detonator on my leg, grenades by my side. I was ready, just waiting, and hoping for something.

No word from Sgt. Bauer. No more incoming. So we waited in silence, wondering if we would get a chance to return fire, or get some more sleep.

Four o'clock. Half past. Nothing. I wondered if the base camp warriors were having a good night. Dry clothes, hot breakfast. If I'm the one in ten that is in the boonies, I hope I find my nine base camp friends someday.

Five A.M. and it's time to wake up, as if we haven't been awake for several hours already. Time to start a new day, a new beginning. I stood and tested my joints; stiff as a board; muscles ached, skin hurt, everything hurt. So, we started the day like every other day in the wet season; wet, muddy, stink. The day was gray, soggy, dank, and a wispy vapor hanging motionlessly just above the jungle floor.

The stand-off wasn't over, though. The LP couldn't come in until it was light enough to see them as they were coming in to the perimeter. While we waited for the day's instructions, we ate breakfast. Ski schooled me in the fine art of heating C-rations and coffee while in the boonies. "Don't eat that stuff cold, John. Here's some C-4." He handed me a small ball of the plastic explosive about the size of a marble. This stuff is very powerful and is used, among other places, in Claymore mines. I took it carefully, suspecting what I was supposed to do with it, but not daring until he explained it to me. He said, "Touch a match to it, and hold your open can of C's to it. Burns hot. Stir the food so the bottom doesn't burn. Don't step on the C-4 while it's burning. You'd probably go home with one and a half legs." I believed him, but I watched him closely before I tried it. HOT FOOD. Hot cans, too. "Leave the lid connected for a hobo handle." What a luxury. Hot beans for breakfast. It felt good.

Shortly, the CO walked by with Lt. Young and said, "The LP's are coming in. After a mad minute, destroy your swimming pool save your sandbags for tonight, reload clean ammo, and saddle up. We've got some VC to catch."

Dean explained mad minute to me. "For about a minute, everyone fires their weapons; rifles, shotguns, pistols. Everything. Supposedly you not only reload with clean ammo, but you clear the area around the perimeter of any VC in hiding. There may be psychological reasons, too."

We grabbed a fast, mirrorless shave with a blade that felt like it had a saw-toothed edge. There had always been something private and personal about shaving, until now. Using the same razor as someone else is one thing. Using the same helmetful of water, with soap and whiskers floating on top, almost seemed like your last corner of humanity has been given up. The CO required us to shave to help promote personal hygiene and prevent skin problems, which could become serious, so we shaved the best we could.

We dumped all cans and trash into our bunker turned pool, followed by the dirt in the sandbags.

After filling the hole, we pulled in the Claymores and trip flares just in time to hear Lt. Young yell, "Mad minute, fire." The perimeter erupted in an awesome display of firepower. Sure enough, my rifle jammed on the second magazine, failure to extract the spent cartridge. I assembled my cleaning rod, shoved it down the barrel and forced the casing out. The mad minute was over before I was ready to fire again. At first I was embarrassed because it implied that I didn't clean my weapon and ammo. Then I was worried because I knew it wasn't that dirty, but it still jammed. Something isn't right here. If that happened in a fire fight, it could be fatal. I wished for the M-14 I used in training; old faithful never gave me any problems. Fortunately, we received no return fire.After all that work and breakfast, several of us heard the call of nature. I put on my helmet, grabbed my rifle and entrenching tool, and the incredibly small packet of toilet tissue from the C-ration package. As I headed out of the perimeter to a nearby bush, I yelled "Man out front"so nobody would hear movement and shoot me. Having just negotiated mud, thorns, and buttons, I heard "Saddle up." I decided there is no time to be human in a combat situation. I had heard the other guys tell about the year-long bout with the trots. It's caused by a steady diet of treated water and C-ratios, malaria tablets, dirty living conditions and a stomach constantly knotted from this lifestyle. The dirty living conditions usually led to stomach worms. This was truly an "All Expenses Paid" year to forget.

We reloaded magazines and strapped on our gear. I have definitely got to lighten my load. I watched Dean, who was sitting on the ground, tuck his towel under his pack shoulder straps to ease the pain. Then he grabbed the tree he deliberately sat next to and pulled himself, with his heavy load of gear, to a standing position. That's the way I need to do it.

If my Drill Sergeant from training saw my rifle, covered in mud, I'd be doing pushups for the rest of my life. The outside was dirty but the inside was clean. That's OK here but not in training. On the other hand, he has been here so he probably understands.

Next to my rifle were new friends. Ants had found droppings from our meals. They were big, mean looking ants and I had an uneasy feeling I'd be seeing a lot more of them.

We moved out, and I started my eighth day in country. Eight very busy days that seemed more like several weeks.

As we moved out, we went part way around the perimeter and it was amazing how the thick growth had been turned into a campsite in such a short period of time. The brush had been cut and trampled at each position for bunkers, sleeping and for a field of fire.

I didn't have to walk flank. Moving along with the column took a lot less work and concentration, which gave me time to think and wonder some more. What, exactly, is my goal, my mission? Why are free people, many of us college students and graduates, living like this, caked with mud and stink? Why aren't the people we're "helping" out in the boonies with us? Why aren't they out here instead of us, and we in base camp? Why are we fighting in the South when the enemy is in the North? We're more of an occupation force than an army on the move, but I can't communicate with the natives, nor do I know anything about their culture and customs. I'm totally ignorant about the people, their history and their country. Why aren't we back home, going to school, or the beach, or a football game?

The sky started to clear, promising us a sauna down in the bush. Meantime, we started some of the daily drudge; mosquitoes, thorns tearing at our skin and fatigues, sweat, mud building on our boots until it was so heavy it falls off or we "kick" it off, rifle flash suppressor hanging on vines, looking for snipers and booby traps. This seemed to be our job instead of the military tactics we had been taught.

In about two hours, we stopped to coordinate movement with Delta Company. This is when I learned where the ragged hole in the helmet camouflage cover came from. Instead of sitting in the mud when resting, it was more convenient to take off your helmet, turn it upside down, and sit on it. The rounded top was a swivel chair, and after a few weeks on the trail the ragged hole appeared and grew larger and larger. When we stopped, we had to keep spaced apart; if you bunch up, a sniper couldn't miss. Hot water washed down salt tablets. Eyes kept moving, trying to penetrate the jungle and find the VC. Our backs were sore and our feet ached already, and we're just getting the day started. We moved out silently, slowly, only as fast as the point man wanted to risk, and as fast as he could hack a trail.

The ground became very swampy. We were wading in mud and putrid slime-covered water, up to our waist at times, in an area of lighter vegetation. Each step had uncertain footing. Many a hand was extended to help a buddy. We had mud splashed up to our eyes, filthy ammo and weapons, and a large number of new friends hanging on us; leeches, swollen with blood to the size of a finger. Mosquitoes were alert and airborne, waiting in swarms like black clouds.

I already knew I would never enjoy water sports again in my life after this year. I would look at being wet as an unwanted thing, and even try to avoid getting wet, other than a shower. I also knew I would not enjoy watching it rain, remembering the countless hours of being in it, and the many days that followed of being soaked and miserable.

On the far side of this muck, the vegetation changed to thicker jungle. As the point man approached the far side, POP POP POP. A sniper started shooting. POP. POP. Several other snipers joined in. "Medic." Somebody was hit. Part of the unit was caught in the open in this muck. The VC planned it that way. M-16's erupted in vengeance, spraying trees and brush. GI's were trying to move low and fast on hands and feet in the muck, trying to get to cover. Some just went head first into the slimy, putrid water, knowing they probably were too far from cover to make it. Small geysers of water shot up around us from incoming meant for us. More rounds hissed by overhead. A machine gun opened up in long bursts, searching. Grenade launchers thumped, shotguns blasted. Orders were shouted between the shots; "... base of fire...", BAM "...move to the far side...", BOOM "...cover the right flank...", WHAM. Leaves and limbs fell like rain from the sparse growth around us. The heavy fire bought men time to get to cover.

I wasn't into the most open area yet so I stood behind a tree and shot up into the trees on the far side. In the fourth magazine, my rifle jammed again. This time I wasn't worried, I was scared. This no good son-of-a-bitching pea shooter was going to get me killed. I wanted the heavier caliber M-14, Old Faithful.

Zipper kept moving forward slowly as he shoulder fired his M-60. His assistant gunner had already hooked several belts of ammo to the gun. Zipper sprayed the area where the shots came from, heavily. The sniper fire stopped and we moved forward to better cover as fast as we could through the sticky mud.

The CO said to make a circular perimeter around the wounded man. If he's hit bad, he's in big trouble. There's no way to MEDEVAC wounded from this area without some clearing done by hand with machetes.

POP POP POP.

The CO told First Platoon to go get those snipers before they caused more problems. They were to take any volunteers from the other platoons. Ski and Dean turned to me and said, "Come on, John, let's get that bastard.

Good experience for you. We can get'em." I didn't feel comfortable in the jungle after only one day so I said no, maybe next time. This was still my guiding principal; Follow all commands but do not volunteer for anything. They took off to join First Platoon, and the group fanned out into a line to sweep through the area where the firing came from.

Sgt. Bauer moved around the perimeter and said he was picking a detail to start hacking a clearing out of the jungle so a helicopter could pick up the wounded man. "He's probably OK, but he can't travel and it's too far to the nearest LZ."

By this time, the patrol with Dean and Ski had hit something. POP POP POP. The VC's Russian-made AK's opened up. Fire was returned by the M-16's, Ski's shotgun, and a machine gun. Some tracers hit the trees just over our heads.

POP POP. More VC firing, again answered by 16's. The firefight was brief, sputtering to a finish. Somebody from the patrol came running in calling for a Medic. "Doc, two men down hard." The Medic took off at a full run.

I went to the area we had to clear for the MEDEVAC LZ. There were ten of us, five with machetes. The CO came over soon and said, "There's no way you men can clear this by yourself so I called for some Engineers to come out and blast these trees. You five cut, the other five carry away so it doesn't get clogged up around here. The Engineers will be here in three or four hours. All three WIA's are now KIA's."

We looked at each other and I asked, "Anybody know who they are?" An unfamiliar face answered, "The first one was a new guy. He was walking flank. Don't know who the other two are." Walking flank. I was glad I wasn't walking flank today. Would have been me.

We started in the center of what would become the LZ, and cleared outward. Hacking and hauling, chopping, and dragging. There were vines, brush, small trees, medium trees, and tall trees. The jungle was so thick that after an hour's work, we had cleared an area less than the size of a small house, except for the trees. At this rate, we'd definitely not finish for days. Hornets and ants were bad. Mosquitoes were everywhere; heat and humidity were stifling, sweat dripped in a stream. The machete handles became very slick and we lost our grip frequently. Blisters rose, burst, and turned into bloody messes, stung by salty sweat. Our hands and arms were scratched by thorns and branches. Our fatigues had a lot of tears. The fatigues were made so that every button had a covering, a flap, to prevent them from snagging on vines and branches. It worked well but the rest of the fatigues were fast becoming olive drab slaw.

We took a short break at the end of the first hour. I went to get my towel and salt tablets where I left my gear on the perimeter. When I got near, there were five guys just leaving, and the Medic was kneeling beside the two motionless bodies of the KIA's from the patrol. I didn't need to see their faces to recognize Dean's blonde hair and Ski's lanky body. One had been hit in the neck, the other in the head; both from behind. If I had volunteered for that patrol, I would have been walking between them, little brother style, and I'd be a body on the ground. Until now, the idea of getting killed in Vietnam seemed remote; something that happens to somebody else, not me. Reality finally pressed home; combat is impartial. The other half of losing a friend is the realization that death is just as close to you as it was to them, or anyone.

Such a loss becomes reason enough to not want to develop any more strong friendships, at least not until you are certain your sphere of self-preservation has no holes in it. My sphere had a hole in it for a short time. My self-preservation slipped at the sight of my two good friends just lying there. In only a few days of shared hardships, we had become close. They were good young men who had taken it upon themselves to help me get my feet wet, to help me return home alive. We had shared each other's workload, shared private thoughts, and even shared our food and water. They had no business in a situation like this. The only thing I could do for them now was help hack out the LZ so their bodies could be returned home for a decent burial.

My thoughts were interrupted by the Medic, "Buddies?"

"Yeah."

"They never had a chance. The line passed over VC in spider holes, the VC popped up and shot them in the back. Zipper seen 'em at the same time and stitched 'em good. One's dead, another should be; got seven rounds in him. CO says there's more out there. They've been trying to sucker us into ambushes since we landed."

First law of combat: do not fight the enemy on his terms.

I stood over my friends and allowed myself to drift in thought. There before me was the useless termination of life. Hopes, dreams, and laughter brought to nothing; the first steps as a child, the years at school, the loving care in childhood illnesses, the first date, graduation, the call to duty, the casket returning home. Why? For what? I looked up through the trees and glimpsed a blue sky, the first in days. It was a colorful sight compared to the heavy, gray days we'd been having. A nice day to die. I wondered how it would be possible to tell everyone back home, "Don't forget these guys, they died for you. They endured a lot of trouble and pain, just to die. You can't pay in money for what they've done, but you can show interest in what they did for love of country, and for you."

I decided I already knew the second law of combat: self-preservation, because no one can do it for you.

I said "Thanks" and "Goodbye" to my friends as I covered them with their ponchos. That's when and where the young boy, who once played war with a wooden rifle, was no more. Innocence must give way to the harsh reality of the cold world. I repaired the hole in my sphere permanently, and returned to work. We chopped and hauled in one-hour shifts, trading off. Most of the guys have a towel around their neck, and a canteen and salt tablets nearby. The heat and humidity required you to wipe your face and eyes every few minutes, and a sip of water.

Two Engineers arrived in the afternoon. Their chopper hovered above the trees and they rappelled down a rope. Their gear was dropped from the chopper and crashed to the ground. Choppers at our disposal didn't have winches to raise or lower a load. That's why we had to cut an LZ to extract the bodies, and the Engineers to rappel. They went right to work, strapping chunks of C-4 explosive to the bases of trees and yelled, "Fire in the hole." I don't have any idea where that expression came from, but it didn't take us long to learn we had about 15 to 20 seconds to get to cover and watch another tree fall. Late in the afternoon, our CO told us to dig in for the night, and finish in the morning. The Engineers kept blasting; they would share a bunker with the Headquarters section in the center of the perimeter.

It hadn't rained all evening and the sky was still clear, almost promising a bright night lit with a full moon.

The CO called for resupply a day early because of the unexpected activity cutting the LZ. When the chopper arrived, it hovered just above the trees and water cans were pushed out of the door. It was just too high and most of the cans burst. Another worry added itself to our list; the fear of running out of water, food, and ammo.

After working all day in the heat, and losing friends, we didn't feel like eating or digging in. It didn't matter how we felt though, we had to dig in for safety. We dug the hole, filled sandbags, and cut limbs and logs for overhead cover. Might as well get used to the routine; it'll be a daily duty for the next year. After a day like this one, we had a body ache, from head to toe. Seemed like every muscle ached. Our hands were frozen in a half-open claw. Fortunately, the VC hadn't come back. Rumor had it that they were waiting for the MEDEVAC. If that were true, we should be able to get a few hours of sleep tonight. The guys on OP came in and were replaced by the LP for the night. The OP had no movement all day.

Time to get things ready for the night. Our fatigue jackets were almost dry, but they were dirty and torn. We had to wear them because we needed as much protection from mosquitoes as we could get. Our jackets were covered with a white, powdery stain from profuse sweating, and taking all those salt pills. When they dried, it left a layer of salt. We set out trip flares, Claymores, cleaned rifles and ammo, and set the detonators and grenades where we could easily find them in the dark. We split the hours for guard duty, one up and two down, ate a can of something, drank a lot of water, and collapsed on the ground.

I was desperately anticipating sleep but, BOOM, the FO was setting DEFCON's for the night.

My first taste of the jungle was bitter. What little security I had to lean on, my new friends, was taken away. We tried to make the best of this rotten situation, but it was no fun anymore, no shared adventure. You can't win, just survive. In fact, I realized that if you survive, you've won. I felt my morale slip another notch or two.

My two new partners, Wes and Blue, asked me if I wanted to trade my jamming rifle for Ski's shotgun. No, it wouldn't seem right somehow, as if it was his personal possession. Wesley was a lot smaller than anyone else in the Platoon, Blue a lot larger. They were known as Littl'un and Big'un. Both had been in-country for a while and knew the ropes. They were easy to work with, and that helped me temporarily forget about the day's events. Ski and Dan were their friends too, but they had learned how to develop that protective callous to protect themselves.

It started to rain again, heavily. Sleeping in the rain already became a way of life.

We were very happy that the night was uneventful, no attacks or probes by the VC. We finally got a good night's sleep; six hours, two at a time. In between times, on guard, I realized something about this war was not right. Sort of like we weren't really fighting the right way. We were just here, going through some motions, not accomplishing anything. We seemed to be constantly on the defensive, even though we were acting like we were on the offensive. I felt all this was useless, wasted lives, effort and money. Useless is a bad feeling for us trying so hard.

Another night passed with the usual routine; you sleep a while, a hand shakes you awake, the watch is put into your hand, and you struggle to a sitting position to help you stay awake. It's deathly quiet. You don't move, make noise or light; you do wait, watch, listen. Artillery sounds in the distance, aircraft fly by. These sounds go on, day and night. It'll be our turn soon.

Morning. You open your eyes, then close them, hoping it's all a bad dream. But, it isn't. Sgt. Bauer is on the job; "Work detail to the LZ in ten minutes. Get moving. Don't tear down your bunker." The previous day's work on the LZ had taken its toll on us. I was so stiff that I thought I may have hurt myself permanently. I was beginning to realize how mental numbing can protect you from physical, as well as emotional, pain.

The Infantry, God love 'em. What did that poster at Ft. Polk say? "Infantry: covers a wide range of responsibilities. Requires good physical and mental coordination. Strength and stamina helpful. Thorough on the job training. No related civilian job. Confidence and leadership acquired may be applied to any civilian occupation." That's the most white-washed description of Combat Infantryman I've ever heard. It should have said something like, "Covers a range of activities like killing, and living like an animal. Physical and mental stamina absolutely required to survive, but are no guarantees. Related civilian occupations: hit man, hobo, nomad. Bitterness and frustration acquired must be lost before applying for any civilian occupation."

Several of us shaved, using the same helmet-ful of cold water and that razor with the saw-tooth blade. Breakfast was a cold can of beef slices, peanut butter, and crackers. I made a can of hot instant coffee with the last of my C-4 and took off through the brush to the LZ. On the way, Blue joined me and said, "Know that VC they got? The one with seven rounds in him? That sucker is still alive." I made a detour to look eyeball to eyeball at the man who probably killed my best friends. I walked over to where the bodies were laid, wrapped in ponchos. Nearby, propped against a tree, was the VC. They were all to be put on the MEDEVAC chopper. The VC's eyes moved slowly to meet mine. They had the glassy stare of someone who was going to die soon. What little clothing he had on was raggedy and blood-stained. A few bandages had been applied to his wounds. The rest of his body was covered with smears of blood. He was a scrawny guy. I'm not a big person, but I made two of him. Besides looking underfed, I realized he didn't have a uniform or boots. His foot gear was Ho Chi Minh sandals; a piece of rubber tire tread for the sole, with rigged straps. No gear, no helmet, no hindrances. They were nobody's fool; they traveled light and fast, dressed to keep cool and didn't spend a lot of time and energy fussing with a pile of gear. I made a mental note of this lack of gear and how you can still be effective as a soldier; there's a valuable lesson here. Travel light means travel faster and longer.

It occurred to me that in combat you try to kill the enemy, and if he doesn't die you try to save him. I wasn't surprised that an American Medic bandaged his wounds. I don't think we'd have it any other way. But, it seemed so strange to be here, living like this, to kill the VC, and then send him to our medical facility to try and save his life. It didn't seem to be logical. Do we want to kill him or not? I guess we don't really want to. He was shooting at us, so to save us, we shot him. If we fail, we'll try to save him. Did we shoot him to save him? I looked at the poncho-wrapped bodies of my friends, then at the VC. I wasn't sure what I felt. Do I want him to die? Do I want to kill him? That could be me someday, propped against a tree in a VC camp. I turned to my friends and said, "*Sin loi* (I'm sorry)."

The Engineers were already working when I got back to the LZ. They yelled, "Fire in the hole", explosions shook the ground, trees fell, and a chain saw buzzed until the next yell.

Mid-morning it started to rain; the daily quota. The CO passed the word that the LZ would be finished by noon, and the mission would continue with a patrol around the area. We were low on rations and water, some guys were out. The chopper coming to pick up the bodies was supposed to bring C-rations, water, ammo, and a limited supply of fatigues to replace those torn most. The CO didn't want us to look like a rag-tag army, and fatigues did offer some protection from bugs and brush. The CO did think of his men and tried to keep them as comfortable as he could make possible. Besides, it was the least Uncle Sam could do for our "All Expense Paid" wardrobe.

After hours of sweating heavily, dragging logs and sliding in the mud, the LZ was usable. The chopper snuggled down between the tall trees in the small LZ. While we unloaded the cargo and loaded the now five bodies, the pilots walked around trying to figure out how to get the chopper up out of the LZ. I never realized until now that a helicopter doesn't take off straight up, especially with a load. It lifts off the ground slightly, tilts forward, then climbs as it flies forward, like an airplane. In an incredible display of skill and guts, the pilot lifted off and flew the very short distance to the wall of trees ahead, climbing slightly. He stopped, hovered, and not having nearly enough room to turn around, backed up to the other end of the LZ. Repeating this maneuver several times, he lifted free of the towering ring of the still standing trees without hitting them. I didn't know helicopters could back up, but I saw it. I'd watch many more skillful and gutsy chopper pilots during the next year.

The VC didn't hit us when the chopper came in, so they must have left the area. It would have been a good time, though. I'm sure every eye in the Company was watching the chopper, none on security.

I put on my replacement fatigues. They were actually well used, but were washed, by South Vietnamese labor, in the Saigon River. Since the river is used for everything from bathing to a sewer, they smelled almost as bad as we did, but for different reasons. The material felt strange, stiff, and harsh. A day or two in the sun would break them in.

By the time I filled my canteens, the only C-ration meal left was Ham and Limas. They were always last to go. Dean had told me how to make them taste pretty good by adding lots of salt and heating them.

Shortly, word was passed for First and Weapons Platoons to saddle up. First would leave the LZ going north, circle left, and return on the west side. We would leave southward and return from the east. Sgt. Bauer told us Delta had found a small camp and, while investigating, had casualties; two were killed by booby traps and a third stepped on punji sticks.

We took off with me on right flank. That's the most miserable feeling I had experienced so far. You have to keep the column in sight, break your own path and watch for danger to your front, while you become the column's exposed buffer to ambush. You're very busy out there, but it doesn't ease the pressure.

The jungle seemed thicker somehow, as if it had grown twice as dense overnight. The semi-darkness of the dense jungle is ominous as you perform your hostile drudge. Thorns hang on your fatigues and skin. Vines and tangle hang on your gear and in the flash suppressor on the rifle. Rifle in one hand and machete in the other, you back up, untangle, and move forward. Mud builds on your boots. Sweat runs down in streams but is lost in the rain. You struggle to keep one eye on the column, one on your work and one looking for danger. You tire more easily than yesterday, yesterday more easily than the day before. You continue finding a little more strength to struggle on, punishing tired, strained muscles, fighting the wet, hostile, green hell. You pick up a leech, then another, but you don't have time to stop and get them off. The heavy rains have swollen the jungle streams; it's rained every day, sometimes all day and sometimes all night, too. Sometimes the water is deep; sometimes the muddy bottom is deep, too. You don't know if you can pull yourself free from the muck because it seems to be trying to hold you down, and force you to use the last of your strength to pull free.

As I looked down one of the streams, I could see one of the Platoons crossing it, and had a good laugh. I hadn't realized it before, but I, and everyone else, reached for my canteen so often that when I returned it to its cover on my belt, I never snapped the retaining cover flaps closed, which keeps the canteen from falling out. This way, I could reach for water and not have to fuss with the flaps snap, sliding the canteen quickly in and out of its holder. When a canteen is empty, or even half empty, the water tight lid makes it buoyant. As the Platoon struggled across the swift, chin deep stream, empty canteens were popping up to the surface and being swept downstream by the swift current. So, there was a line of heads bobbing across the stream and a line of canteens bobbing down the stream. I enjoyed that little laugh because I needed to change my focus and lighten the stress.

Still no VC, but we knew they were here somewhere. You feel like you're ready to find them. At least, you could get off your feet, and take your hostility out on them. They are why we are here, struggling through this crap. Have they been looking for us, or have they been watching us looking for them?

Through the rain, dense foliage and lack of light, I saw a small clearing ahead. It was difficult to tell what size it was or if it had seen activity. The column stopped while two men were sent to check it out. When they returned, Lt. Young radioed the CO. In a few minutes, Wesley came out to my flank position and filled me in. "Small camp ahead. The CO told the Lt., the VC must be gone, else they'd probably have sniped at us by now." We were supposed to form a line, and sweep through for a search. Watch for booby traps, and keep spaced in case of snipers.

Even though we weren't expecting to see any VC, I was a little apprehensive about just walking into the camp. It seemed like we should have watched a little while, scouted the surrounding area, or something. We formed a line and swept through the camp. There was no resistance, so we began searching the area and destroying anything of benefit to the enemy. The camp was fairly new, and small. The few crude bamboo structures were roofs to provide shelter from the rain as well as camouflage to hide from air observation. Wesley and I chose one and destroyed it with the machete. Someone called out that they had found a grave, or freshly filled in hole, and Lt. Young told him to dig it up.

Wesley and I finished and went to the perimeter to help form security. For what little comfort it added, Wesley took off his helmet, turned it upside down and sat on the open side, as if to work on the already large ragged hole in the cover. It takes many breaks on jungle trails to wear a hole through the cover. It was sort of like the sunken eyes and bitter attitude; the longer you've been in country, the more prominent they become. Taking your helmet off in a situation like this is an unsafe practice. But, since I didn't want to sit in the mud any more often than I had to, I sat on mine, too. Scanning the jungle, wet from dripping rain, I watched Wes try to light a soggy cigarette with damp matches. "Wesley," I asked, "Why dig up the grave? If the guy's dead, he's dead."

"Well, since we're not fighting for villages or mountains, you've got to measure victory somehow. So, after every firefight, we've got to turn in a body count. Could be one body in that mud, or five. It could also be where Charlie keeps extra weapons or food. Could be booby trapped, too. You never know what you'll find."

I was so tired my head started nodding while I looked at the trees. I stood up to keep awake but, it didn't help much.

It's an eerie feeling to enter an enemy campsite, tear it up, and dig up a grave. Sort of like vandalizing someone's home while they're gone.

My mind was jerked awake by, "All right, we're hattin' up. Let's go, let's go. We'll be late for the movie. Resume your positions and move out." Back to the hostile grind in the wet, green hell. Slosh, squish, hack, and chop. We pushed on though our tired and sore bodies told us they didn't want to. We struggled back to our perimeter through the mud, rain, sweat, and thorns. Negative contact.

Using the extra boot laces Dean told me to carry, Wes and I set up a jungle hooch made from our ponchos. We crawled inside and got out of the rain, the best thing that happened to us in what seemed like years. We listened to the thrumming of the rain on our shelter while we ate a cold can of something that smelled vaguely like food.

While I checked the Claymores and trip flares, Wes went out front to take care of the trots, mumbling, "Maybe Charlie will crawl through it if he pays us a visit."

Sgt. Bauer came by checking the perimeter for the night. He always had a few minutes for his men. "Hey, John, any mail from home yet?" he asked.

"No, still too soon," I answered.

He looked at our hooch. "You guys gonna' sleep out of the rain, but in the mud?" He chuckled. "You're getting soft."

"Yeah. Hey, did we find anything in that camp today?"

"Nothing to get excited about. The grave had a piece of a body. The kid who dug it up threw up all over, not used to blood and guts yet. He will be. The camp was clean except for a few footprints and Chieu Hoi leaflets. Some government agency goes to a lot of trouble and expense to print messages in Vietnamese telling the VC to surrender and we'll treat them well. Then we drop'em from planes by the millions, and the VC use them for toilet paper. ARVN's do too." (Army of the Republic of Vietnam)

A centipede about ten inches long undulated his way into the hooch. Sgt. Bauer said, "Let me show you how to take care of your little friend." He squirted insect repellent on the centipede and dropped a lit match on him. The burning creature shriveled in a noxious cloud of smoke with a few crackles and pops. Sgt. Bauer continued, "Jungle's a tough place to live." As he got up to leave, he said, "Don't let the bedbugs bite." Great way to start the night.

Wes and I agreed to two-on-two-off for guard, me first. No DEFCON's to set tonight since they were set last night.

The night's routine began; the daily grind followed by the nightly routine. I sat in the dark once more, watching and waiting, with no noise, no light, no nothing, except for sore muscles, bugs, and the drumming of rain on the roof. No bats squeaking, no owls hooting. Just me and this rifle. The rifle was beginning to feel like it was a part of my arm, like some giant growth. Every time I looked down, there it was. I felt insecure without it, even guilty. Someday, I'll be able to walk around without a weapon, and I'll be able to stay out of the mud and rain, instead of living in it. Someday.

During my second watch, about 2:30, an artillery barrage hit not very far away. It must be Alpha's turn to have some fun, and be awake all night. Wes didn't even stir.

Somewhere in the distance a flight of helicopters droned by. Flying missions of support or mercy, all day and all night.

5 A.M. Sgt. Bauer came by and said, "Let's go, up and at 'em, we're headed to the Promised Land. Gimme an Amen."

Since there was no enemy action during the night, we got 5 hours of sleep. What a luxury.

It's difficult to be a "Lean, mean, fightin' machine" on five hours of sleep, especially when five is an extraordinarily long sleep. How much of this can you take? I was already getting to the point of enjoying about all I could stand.

Still raining, but time for the daily grind and new adventures. I think our bodies, and minds, had developed a permanent ache, residents of the days and nights of nonstop strain.

After a cold can of C's and cold coffee, trash went into the bunker turned swimming pool, followed by mud. We packed the Claymores, trip flares and ponchos, sharpened the machete, checked the rifle and ammo, rolled down sleeves, applied insect repellent, swallowed some salt tablets, hung our gear on, then pack and ammo. What a ritual; by now you can do this in your sleep. I did decide it's best to put your gear on while kneeling or standing, because if you're sitting it's very difficult to get up with all the cumbersome, heavy gear, unless there is a vine or branch nearby to pull yourself up.

Redford came over while buckling his gear on and said, "John, you're on flank again. Let's move."

From Draftee to Trainee to Grunt. I always thought any progression in life was to go up, but it seemed to me we were going down. In fact, this had to be the bottom. In fact, like our DI said in training, "You're lower than whale shit." Wonder if he was trying to prepare us for the truth.

Out to flank; you know the drill because it never changes.

Two hours pass, three, and finally the jungle thins out a little. We stopped for a break, shoulders sagging from the rain-soaked packs. The straps are cutting into our shoulders like knives from the heavy pack and all the other gear. I recalled one of the big cadence calls from training, "We're on our way to Vietnam, we're gonna' kill the Viet Cong." Somehow, I didn't feel we were fulfilling our mission.

Sharpen machete, check safety, light a cigarette to burn off a leech, salt tablets. What a strange daily routine.

Wes came out from the column to relieve me. I owe him a big one. I got in the column close to the CO. He was on the radios, a hand set on each ear; one for Battalion, one for Company. "Say again, Flame Six. (Flame was the radio call for Battalion, Bravo for our Company. Bravo One was First Platoon, Two the second, up to Six which is the CO. The tall trees must be breaking you up. Over." While he listened, he looked down at me. He was at least a head taller. A no-nonsense soldier, he went by the book as long as it fit. All the guys I have talked to say they would follow him through hell; a very high compliment. Watching a man of his caliber somehow gave our war effort integrity again. I was told he was a school teacher but changed his career to military service for some reason. I thought to myself, "If he's here with us, in this wet, green hell, going through the same thing I'm going through, then I'm not too good to be here."

"Roger, Flame Six. Wait." Then he spoke on the Company radio. "Bravo Elements. Six. Change to secondary LZ. Delta needs assist. Resupply as scheduled. Any requests? Over."

"Six, Four." I could hear Lt. Young. "Make sure Muleskinner brings a tube."

"Roger, Four."

Back to the Battalion net, "Flame Six, Bravo Six. Send one 81 mike-mike (81 mm mortar) with the hot chow. Over." He gave the handsets to his RTO's and smiled at me again. Rain and sweat dripped from his chin, just like everyone else's, and fatigues just as grungy. In a lowered voice, he said, "Can't ask you to fire your mortars all night on cold chow, John. Hot supper's on me." In a loud voice, he said, "Saddle up, we're growing roots here. Get the point element a new compass heading. Let's go, shake it, Delta's waiting." God lov'em, where does America get good leaders like this.

I signaled Wes to move out, because we might leave him sitting there. Movement was easier in the thinner brush, but the grind was still the same, with the mud, thorns, vines, bugs, sweat, rain, watching, listening, and moving in silence. A square of toilet tissue was on the ground where point marked a booby trap. Whoever was on point had good eyes because the trap was old and blended with the trees and brush real well. It was a swinging mace type; a tree limb cut off and hinged in a crotch, swung up and tied so the trip mechanism would release it like a giant pendulum. The end that swings down to hit you looked like a porcupine with sharp bamboo stakes sticking out all around it. My skin crawled when I pictured what it would do to you. The last elements of our column would destroy it after everyone else had safely passed.

Minutes later, another tissue marked a punji pit. I looked down into the pit, maybe ten feet deep, and saw the sharpened bamboo stakes sticking upward. They probably had been dipped in something septic like water buffalo dung or urine. Nasty way to get hurt. The fall would ensure that you would be impaled on the stakes.

The column stopped a little longer than the usual get-untangled pause. Several minutes passed and the CO demanded, "What's going on?" Just then, there was a lot of commotion in the brush ahead. I looked just in time to see somebody start slapping the point man's back. He was completely naked and dancing around like he'd lost his mind. Ants. Weaver ants make a nest by weaving together leaves on branch ends. The point must have been under the nest when his machete hit their limb. The vibration knocked them loose and they fell on him.

What did the survival manual say? "Weaver ants, large red; are used as seasoning for raw fish. Eggs may be fried and eaten." That was just before "Cockroach; may be eaten raw, but usually fried. Eggs edible." (The manual doesn't say where to get a frying pan in the jungle.) But, in the jungle, you can eat it if it doesn't eat you first.

How can a group of guys, strangers to each other, go through this kind of hell and not be bonded like brothers. How could anyone survive all this, if not for the efforts of everyone?

Back to the grind, with a pack and gear that seemed heavier than when I took it off for our break. Hour after hour, the steamy, sour-smelling jungle reluctantly lets you move along slowly. It almost seems to be alive and trying to close in on you to hold you back.

No VC, no signs of VC, nothing.

A large, natural clearing appeared just ahead. It was under water but it would be our LZ and defensive position for the night. We were expecting water, ammo, a mortar, and hot food. I think we wouldn't care what or where the LZ was as long as we got some decent food.

Sometimes, the chopper would come back in the morning to pick up the mortar and bring it back out to us at the next perimeter near a suitable LZ. Otherwise we would carry it through this green hell of a jungle or rice paddy. Sometimes more than one gun was brought out to us making it even more work if we had to carry them.

The CO picked up the Battalion net to receive transmissions from the resupply chopper.

"Flame Bravo Six, Muleskinner. ETA two zero minutes."

"Two zero. Copy."

"I have a northeast-southwest vector, I'll ID your smoke. Over."

"Roger, Muleskinner. Standing by. Out."

Smoke grenades with colors are used for two things. The primary reason is to identify the correct LZ for the pilot. The second is security. Sometimes the VC monitor our radio transmissions and try to divert the chopper to a different LZ, where they are, and shoot it down, if they happen to have a smoke grenade of the same color. This can still happen, for example two yellow smokes, so we have to wait until the "last second" to pop the smoke so the VC don't have the chance to duplicate.

Sgt. Bauer said, "We need security. John, over by that lone tree. Blue, Redford, Wes, spread from there to the left. Move out."

I waded through the knee-deep putrid water toward the small tree. It was on a tiny island; higher ground, about ten feet across and two feet above the water. As I waded, I opened a C-Ration tin of cookies, and kept my eye on the LZ's tree line for Charlie. I was planning to sit with my back against the tree and rest my aching body.

About five or six feet from the island's water line, almost under a limb, I froze. At first I thought my eyes were playing tricks on me. The island was completely covered with ants; I could not see the ground under them because they were so thick. Seeking refuge from the water, they headed for the high ground. The island was seething with layers of ants crawling over each other. From there, they went up the tree, out to the tips of the limbs, and were crowding each other off the ends of the branches. You couldn't see the dirt or the tree; just the constant movement and shifting of ants, red, black, large, and larger. I backed up a couple of steps and realized I was holding a cookie to my mouth. I tossed the cookie onto the island, and the reaction made my skin crawl. I didn't know ants made noises, but I heard it easily from ten feet away. The cookie disappeared pretty fast amid a sound that I can only describe as an angry, hissing buzz.

I heard a Chinook helicopter in the distance, so I backed away a little further and turned to watch the arrival of our hot food. The Chinook had a sling hanging under it, a large net full of supplies. The CO yelled out, "Pop smoke."

A yellow smoke grenade was thrown out for Muleskinners ID; he saw it and turned toward us as he descended in his approach. Just as the chopper came over the edge of the LZ, about two hundred feet up, the sling broke and all the supplies splashed into the water, heavier items, like our mortar, sank deep into the mud. A hundred faces watched our hot meal fall, but only a few made comments. It seemed to be accepted as just another daily disappointment; "So, what else is new?"

A detail of men waded out to the mess to salvage what they could. The containers of food and water had popped open and gotten contaminated by the putrid water. Dry fatigues were soaked, and the single mortar was buried deep in the mud. Mortar ammo probably wet and useless. We carried the mortar to where we would make a firing position about two hundred yards away. No one ever volunteered to help Weapons Platoon lug all the equipment because it was no picnic, especially after beating the bush all day. Each of us would make more than twenty trips carrying the mortars and heavy crates of ammo; splashing through the putrid water, squishing and sliding through the mud, tripping over brush and the uneven ground, in the dark, in rain. Great for building strong backs and legs, but not so good for building strong mental outlook.

So, another routine of the daily grind was added. Ski had told me about them. "When we set up a night position, no matter how beat you are, you'll make a million trips from the LZ; dig your bunker, fill sandbags, cut trees and limbs for overhead cover; oil, set up and fire the mortars; guard duty, usually one on, two off. In the morning you undo it all; dig up the base plate from deep in the mud; carry everything back to the LZ; destroy your bunker. Then, it's just another day of the same."

While the rest of the Company set up their positions for the night, my squad cleaned the gun and set up on a slightly higher spot for night firing.

The sun hadn't quite set yet and the clouds had broken enough to create a sauna. After four days of being constantly wet, I decided I better take off my boots and see if I still had toes, or rotting nubs. Our boots were specially made for this type of use, from canvas and rubber, since leather would rot very fast. They had two holes just above the insole to drain water and nylon mesh inserts designed to act as a pump when you put your foot down with your weight on it. My boots were holding up well, but the nylon inserts were already disintegrating, absolutely worthless. When your feet are in muddy water constantly the inserts and your socks act as strainers, pumping and straining the water, retaining the sediment. Your boot is soon filled with the muddy sediment, and this grinds at the nylon insert and soon tears it up. It doesn't do much for your feet, either. I threw the useless inserts away. I took off my putrid socks. Bad mistake. My feet looked like dead jellyfish and started burning uncomfortably when the sun hit them. My soles were so deeply wrinkled that I had to force the wrinkles open to literally dig out the mud sediment. Hopeless. This after only a few days in the bush. I decided clean, dry socks would be useless in this kind of situation and never carried any again. I never again took my boots off during an operation until we returned to base camp, no matter how many days.

The Artillery FO began his routine of setting DEFCON's for the night. WHAM. Shrapnel whirred through the tree limbs. It seemed to get a little closer each night.

Night came and with it the feeling of being isolated from the rest of the world by a curtain of darkness; alone, in the middle of nowhere. Not helpless or forgotten, but cut off from everything familiar and secure.

Hungry, tired and filthy, my crew laid on the muddy ground to sleep until our turn to fire the gun. A couple of large red ants crawled on my arm and I watched them to see what they would do. They were almost an inch long, and unlike any ants I had ever seen because they had a large pincer in the front. They closed their razor-sharp pincers, slicing the skin and drawing blood, and to inject their venom, raised their rear ends into the air until they were vertical. They didn't have the usual stinger, but it was painful.

Just before I fell asleep, the gun crew fired their first round and settled the base plate. I was vaguely aware of being splattered with mud. I didn't care or move; I figured, "What the hell, it's not like I'm clean."

Sgt. Bauer was right about not waking up when our guns fired. My subconscious knew it was our gun, and my body was too tired to react anyway, so I slept through the two hours.

Somebody shook me awake and I was standing before my mind started working; I woke up and was already standing, which is my normal routine for guard. After a few quick instructions, we familiarized ourselves with the gun's lay. The base plate had already been pounded six or seven inches into the mud, promising to be a back-breaking struggle to dig it out. Great way to get your day started.

The mortars were set up according to SOP, inside the perimeter, for our safety because if we set up outside of the perimeter we'd be exposed and unprotected; suicide if the VC were nearby. There are times when there is no choice and the gun must be set up outside the perimeter. Since we were inside, we could concentrate all our effort and time on the gun, and the mortar pit.

During the firing, I had my first serious bout with the Tropical trots; it finally caught up with me. The constant diet of canned food, heat, constantly filthy conditions, treated water, salt tablets, malaria tablets, and guts knotted from anxiety takes its toll on the strongest of constitutions. Once it starts, it lasts the rest of the year. When it strikes, it's always at an inopportune time. I stopped moving and nearly doubled over from the cramps. Then I made a hasty retreat. As I returned going through some positions on the perimeter, somebody whispered, "Eat more peanut butter and cheese. It'll do it every time." Someone else whispered. "Bull shit.

Doesn't matter what you eat, it comes out the same. Only way to stop it is to get out of the bush."

Struggling with all the usual daily challenges of being here, I now had to add stomach cramps to the long and growing list. But, we struggled on with our duty. It was the only way available to us to pass the time; the year, the day, the hour just before you could lie down and sleep. Our time with the gun was finally over, and we, miserably, laid on the water and mud for a little sleep. There's nothing to do but to do it.

Another night without, but we got five hours of sleep, broken into several parts, and tried to mentally prepare to drag ourselves through another day of the same damn thing.

Digging up the base plate took most of the energy we gained in sleeping. The base plate had sunk more than a foot and almost decided it was going to stay there.

We packed the gun and unused ammo and began the multiple trips to the LZ, back and forth, squish, and slosh. We cleaned our weapons and ammo, and ate something from a can. Muleskinner came and took the reloaded sling away, and we were set to begin the grind.

"Saddle up. VC are waiting."

On go the packs and gear, straps cutting into our shoulders; got to lighten this load! No flank today; it was like a vacation to be in the column.

A hot shower would be good, or even cold. I'd settle with just washing my hands. No telling what was on them when I ate.

We never did link up with Delta so I guess their contact broke off, maybe because they found out that we were coming. Grunts were usually not given the big picture so we just had to guess using what little we knew.

The wet, green hell wears you down another notch, real fast. All of the usual challenges are still there, always there; squish, slosh, mud build up step-kick-step-kick, jerk at the tangle, pull off the thorns, stink, bugs, sweat. You duck, twist, turn. Meter upon meter slides slowly and silently by. Occasional Chieu Hoi leaflets, moldy from some long ago air drop, stares back at you from the brush.

Cramps gnaw at your guts, shoulder straps cut into your shoulders like hot knives, check safety, keep moving your eyes; up in the trees, out to flank, ...

The big guys seemed to have the hardest time moving through the jungles. Besides having more body weight to maneuver, they also had more surface area to get through the thick wall of vines and brush, and to get snagged on the thorns, and scraped. Brawn isn't necessary to survive in combat. In fact, carrying and supporting a massive body is an extra burden. To survive, you need endurance; physical and mental. Smaller men slipped through the jungle growth easier, but struggled more with their load of gear because it was so high in proportion to their body weight.

I again wondered if my face was beginning to look like those of the troops I saw going home when I got off the plane; sunken eyes, distant stare. The numb, burned out, hollow shell of a body. No, John, not yet. You've still got 349 days to go.

We stopped to rest and eat, maintaining column position during movement. Every other GI faced outward left, the other right; security is maintained. "No bunching up. This is a tactical situation here, not a picnic. Keep spaced apart - five meters."

Most everyone can force down only one can of food, about six ounces. Not much, but stomachs have shrunk due to heat, thirst, irregular meal times, limited time to eat, diarrhea, just not eating because of the monotony of C-rations, and the preference of using the time to try to nap. Shrunken stomachs can hold only small amounts periodically, not large amounts three times a day. Besides, food makes you thirsty. More cigarettes are smoked than food eaten.

Noise discipline; you wait in silence. The heat and exhaustion takes its toll and my head starts nodding.

I promised myself that I'd never again, as long as I lived, go camping or hunting if it required living out in the elements. I'll never again go out in the rain, for anything. Most of all, I'd never, ever, let a day go by without taking at least one luxurious hot shower, with a big absorbent towel to get dry.

The afternoon passed the same way, with no signs of recent activity. "Charlie, where are you Charlie? You're not playing fair. We came halfway around the world to play and you won't come out. Come out, come out, you son of a bitch, come out."

I again started having that vague feeling that we were not fighting this war the right way. "We have no front line here, men, and no rear area that is secure." What the hell kind of war has no front line? That's what we were trained for, to go to the front and shoot, to fight. Why don't we make a front line, like the DMZ, and wipe out what's on the other side? You need to be able to locate and identify your enemy. Here in the South, they're all mixed in; you can't tell who's who, friend or foe. In the North, there's no problem. Let's put a serious hurt on the enemy; none of this bombing halt business because people are getting hurt. They're hurting us, so let's hurt them. We're just fighting symptoms here in the South. We need to go to the North and get something done, get serious.

Before now, my feelings about the war reflected the nature of the war itself; ambivalent, unresolved. Then my feelings turned to hostility toward the war. Now, that hostility was more and more directed toward the methods and strategy of our war, or, the absence of them. Let's take the politicians out of the waging process, or just go home.

The same back breaking, stinking shit every day. Every day. No relief, no change.

We reached the night's defensive position and LZ, which was not flooded this time.

The CO set the Company up just inside a tree line, but the mortar pit would have to be outside, in the LZ, because of the tree limbs being in the way if set up inside the perimeter. So, we would be alone out there, in the dark, no security on three sides. This is OK if you're sitting quietly on ambush, or LP, but we were going to be busy, making noise. If Charlie was watching us set up in the evening light, there's no doubt he'd be back after dark. Maybe we were supposed to be bait. Who knows, but I don't think he'd pass up this chance if he was around.

Muleskinner came in to red smoke, and set the resupply sling down very gently. The side gunner gave us a thumbs up; hot food tonight. As they lifted off, the wash from the powerful twin rotors blew us over, as we turned our backs to the stinging blast of dirt. It was a Chinook helicopter, and very well named after the Chinook winds. The rotor wash was a dry, very hot blast from the twin turbine engine's exhausts. The Chinook was a real workhorse. It could carry over thirty fully equipped troops inside, or twenty thousand pounds externally. Chinooks brought food, water, ammo and mail to the field. Hueys, a smaller chopper, carried us in and out of the field most of the time; alive, dead or wounded. Helicopters were an indispensable support tool for the Infantry.

First things first; the CO let us eat the hot food. Half of the Company got their food, leaving the other man in the two-man positions on the perimeter for security; never drop your guard. Then the other half got theirs, though it was no longer hot. The CO always ate last at his own insistence; he was always making sure his men were taken care of first. A Medic checked everyone in the chow line for anything that needed attention; infected leech bites, deep cuts. Infection sets in very easily in these filthy, warm, wet conditions. He was especially interested in Jungle rot, a fungus growing on constantly wet and dirty skin, whether you had cuts and scratches or not. Every one of us had Jungle rot, some worse than others. He smeared some kind of white cream on the spots and we hoped for the best. Going through the chow line, everyone had white smears of medication, making us look more like clowns than GI's.

We inhaled our food so we would have a little time before sunset to carry the heavy supplies in from the LZ; mortar, ammo, C-rations, and water. You never hear about this in training, or anywhere, but it's how we spent a lot of time. Weapons Platoon was always a part of this detail because no one would carry the mortar for us; back and forth, trip after trip, grunt after groan. Just basic daily requirements for a company of men makes a big pile. Always on our feet; moving, busy. Walk all day, work some more at night. Push, and push some more. Tired bodies keep moving out of reflex and discipline.

All around the perimeter, the nightly routine is underway; holes are dug, sandbags filled, limbs are cut for overhead cover, mines, flares,... DEFCONs are set. Will Charlie hit us tonight?

We set up the mortar on a fairly dry spot in the LZ, filled sandbags to encircle the gun in case we are hit so we have a little security; about three feet high and twelve feet in diameter. Ammo was uncrated and placed strategically so we could operate efficiently, even in the dark. Ready to play soldier, in the dark.

We were definitely uneasy about being outside of the perimeter, in the dark. I could think of many places I'd rather be; in fact, I couldn't think of one place I wouldn't rather be.

We went back into the perimeter to sleep for about an hour before firing. On the way, we checked the food containers to see if there was anything left. Dumb idea; wiped clean, nothing left but the smell. We settled for water, salt tablets, and mosquito repellent.

It started raining while we were sleeping. When a hand shook me awake, my first thought was that somebody was peeing on me in the dark.

We moved quietly out of the perimeter, as if no one would ever know we were out there. As we walked by a bunker, someone whispered, "Have a good time."

Check sights, set charge. Hanging. POOP. Shot out. The muzzle flash seemed bright enough to see all the way back to Houston. We half expected to see some green tracers coming at us, now that we gave away our presence, and location. We fired a few rounds on the first setting and changed to another. After an hour of fun in the dark, we went back into the perimeter and slept for an hour. Our second firing was uneventful also. Our third firing started out smoothly. We had the routine down so well we could do it in our sleep. As dark as it was, we might as well have had our eyes closed. On the fourth round, there was no POOP of the round leaving the tube. There was only the slow release of gas, like a giant whoopee cushion. I had no idea what had just happened, so I just stood there trying to figure it out. Wes and Redford turned and ran into the sandbag wall, tripping heels over head into the mud. In a couple of minutes, they came back and Redford said, "OK guys, we're in some pretty shit now. We've got a hung round and we've got to get it out." The mortar tube is open on one end only, so we couldn't open the bottom end and push it out, like we have to do with our rifle barrels. When a round is hung in the tube, it could be for any of several reasons, all of which involve big problems. I tried to remember what we were told to do in training and I knew we were about to earn our "All Expenses Paid" for the entire year.

"Gentlemen, the first choice is to call Ordnance and let them handle it. If you are on your own, you'll find out what you are made of."

Redford kicked the bottom end of the tube several times to see if the round would discharge. Nothing. Again. Nothing. He felt the barrel and said it was cool, meaning there was no danger of a cook-off (the propelling charge being ignited by heat), and no components would be too hot to handle. The round seemed to be stable and was probably not armed to go off, but must be treated as if it is for your own safety. Now for the fun. Redford said, OK, who's going to catch the round coming out of the tube, John?" Nobody said anything, but they both looked at me and Redford said, "OK, new guy, shit rolls downhill, and you're at the bottom." I moved to the muzzle, Wes took the other end, and Redford said, "I'll give the instructions, and don't do anything on your own; wait for my instructions." Following instructions, Wes removed the tube from the base plate and tilted it to horizontal with the muzzle end still resting on the bipod legs. If the round fired at this point, it could be bad news for all of us because of the recoil being against our hands, and the danger that the round could become armed by some defect. I put both hands over the open end of the tube, forming a circle slightly smaller than the bore, leaving the center open so the detonator in the nose of the round wouldn't hit my hands and possibly explode. Wes tilted the barrel more so the round would slide down the tube and I could catch it. Nothing. Wes tilted more. Nothing. Redford jiggled the tube. Nothing. Redford said, "This ain't supposed to happen." The round was really stuck; bad situation. Nervous sweat was running down our faces. We took the tube out of the bipod yoke and moved to a wooden ammo crate. Again placing my hands, forming a ring, over the open end, Wes tilted the tube almost straight down and, with Redford helping, we banged the edge of the muzzle on an edge of the ammo crate. Sweat was stinging my eyes but I had a tiger by the tail. If I removed a hand to wipe the sweat, and the round came out and hit the ground, we could be evaporated by the possible explosion. Just when we were ready to give up, I felt the round scraping slowly down the tube and bump into my hands. Weak kneed, hearts thumping, holding our breath, we laid the tube, and the round, gently on the ground and sat in silence for a few minutes. Wes said he needed a cigarette, and Redford said, "You need to quit smoking those things, they can kill you." We looked at each other and laughed a nervous laugh of relief. We did laugh about that many times in later weeks; an inside joke of our group bonded by shared danger.

We couldn't fire the mortar anymore, except for defensive action, because the tube might be faulty and cause another problem. So we returned to the perimeter to sleep the few hours until dawn. Sleep didn't want to come, though, because of adrenalin and keyed up nerves.

After two hours of sleep, we woke up to a light rain. Time to start the new day, but with the same old activities. Dig up the base plate. Carry the mortar, ammo, water, canteens, and food containers to the LZ; trip after trip, lugging the heavy gear. Destroy the camp, cold water shave, eat a cold can of something,..... It was almost a day's work just getting ready for the day's work. Caked with mud and stink, wet and tired, stomachs knotted, we put on our heavy gear. With pack straps cutting into our shoulders, we moved out. We felt like we wouldn't make it through another day.

"John, right flank." Are we having fun yet? Enjoying our "All Expenses Paid"?

The machete feels ten pounds heavier, the jungle ten times denser. When will it ever end? Will it ever end? The column spaced itself automatically to five meters between elements, a reflex action by now. The mud, thorns, bugs, tangled brush, mosquitoes, gear getting tangled, hacking a path; it's all still there, step after step, hour after hour. The monotonous daily grind in the wet, stinking hell.

The jungle reluctantly lets you pass, holding you back with all its might, until you pull free, only to catch you again with the next thorny member.

Every one of us would have liked to quit, stop. "Ok, I've had enough. I've enjoyed all I can stand. I'm going home." We couldn't, even if we tried, because we couldn't get out of the country without orders. But I, and all the guys in this unit, wouldn't try because I know we were loyal enough to the U.S. to fulfill our assigned duty. We were committed, so we served our time the best we could.

Mid-morning. The sky cleared enough to let the sun come out and create a greenhouse effect under the thick canopy of the jungle. Breathing is difficult, and every movement required monumental effort. Sweat-soaked fatigues were glued to our skin.

I often wondered, if the VC were hiding and operating in cities and towns, would door-to-door, building-to-building warfare be any easier? It would certainly be better environmental conditions, and somehow, I couldn't help but think it would have been much better duty.

Near noon, the CO calls for a halt for food and rest. Security, silence, watchfulness. Helicopters and artillery sound in the distance, but nearby, are only the sounds of P-38's opening cans of C's. Some guys lost their P-38 so they are being tossed from one buddy to another.

In every direction was dense jungle. Someone could be a few feet away, watching, and you wouldn't be able to see him. From flank, I see someone stand to urinate, no rifle, no helmet, no flak jacket. POP. POP. POP. Bullets ricochet nearby, looking for the man standing. Sniper. The standing GI dives into the mud and water under the brush for cover, eyes wide, tensed to crawl back to his weapon. Cans scatter as we drop our meals and shoulder our weapons. Eyes are moving through the brush, and up in the trees. Waiting, listening, watching. Nothing.

The CO sent a light fire team in the direction the shot came from. When they came back, they reported finding a narrow, well used trail about one hundred meters ahead. This could mean one of several things; a VC is stalling us so others could get away; the enemy is trying to sucker us into an ambush or booby trap; both, or even some other tactic.

The CO forms a killer eyes patrol; two riflemen for security, a machine gun for firepower, and a volunteer. After finding a place on the trail that seems to be the most clear of danger, the volunteer, in a prone position, will toss about fifteen or twenty feet of line, with a weight on the end, down the trail. Pulling the line back to him, he can snag any trip wires and set off a booby trap. Advancing fifteen or twenty feet at a time, they cover the trail slowly and carefully.

The patrol set out, the Company behind them, until they hit the trail. We waited there while the patrol set out. You imagine them going through their routine, but we waited, watched, and listened.

Bored from watching the leaves that enclosed us, I watched the bugs crawling on me; mosquitoes on my arm, flies on my fatigues, and ants on my boots. Every kind of bug imaginable was trying to make a living off us.

Probably a waste of time, I thought, another dead end. Then, BOOM, BOOM. We expected a call for a Medic, but thankfully it didn't come. The patrol tripped a booby trap, but they are still working. An hour passes and the patrol hit no more booby traps or an ambush. The patrol returns and reports to the CO there is some kind of camp ahead.

We moved out, following the now cleared trail, with me on flank and half expecting to find the enemy by some kind of contact. We moved slowly, stalking, looking for signs of danger. The VC know we're here but have either left the area, or are waiting for us. The camp should be close; weapons are ready with safeties off, muscles are tense, hearts thumping, adrenalin building. Every movement sounds loud as thunder, but you have to keep moving. You've got to see them before they see you or you can hang it up. We keep moving slowly, carefully, quietly.

Sweat is dripping into our eyes. Eyes are moving, searching. There, ahead. I saw brief movement through the brush but I couldn't identify it. Stop. Keep looking. Maybe it was a shadow playing tricks. Don't move because movement attracts the eye, and you don't want that. There, a VC rose slightly from a crouch to shoot at the column to my left. He has an RPG and intends to take out a bunch of us at one time. I'm surprised that I was able to go undetected but I did. I raised my rifle slowly to shoot him. He saw my movement and turned his head toward me. He knows it's over for him. I shot at the same time as another M-16, and a grenade launcher. The VC crumpled. I don't know who hit him, and it didn't matter. Was that for Dean and Ski? No, not really. Even living like an animal, and losing my friends, training, reflex and cold emotion still controlled my response; he was just another target with a human silhouette, like the targets in training. No vengeance, this time.

I realized I had shot nearly half a magazine; six, maybe eight rounds. Do I need to put in a fresh, full magazine? Will there be more VC? You've lost control of your immediate security by concentrating on the VC for too long. Quick, scan the area; catch up with what's going on around you. There could be another around here. I didn't see any, but neither did Dean and Ski. The column started moving, so I moved ahead cautiously, still alone on flank, edgy.

When I got to where the VC had been standing, the body was gone. Lt. Young came over and said, "There's a blood trail and marks where he was dragged away. See anything?"

I shook my head, realizing there are more somewhere close by. Lt. Young said, "Ok, let me get a patrol and we'll follow their trail." Another damn patrol. That's how my friends bought it.

In less than a minute, we took off. I was glad Zipper was going. He was good, almost lucky, but he had a lot of jungle savvy.

The trail didn't go far. The rescuers must have given it up as a lost cause. We found the body but the RPG was gone. Lt. Young radioed the CO, and it was decided that Weapons Platoon was to stay right here and bury the body. While the other three platoons would sweep around the area, separately, in different directions, to see what they could stir up. Four of us were detailed to bury the body while the rest formed a security perimeter. This VC was scrawny, like all the others. He looked like a kid, maybe fifteen. He stunk worse than we did. He must have been living in one of those tunnels; damp, muddy, stale air. He was hit in the head, neck, and chest; a bloody mess. We buried him as fast as we could, then we sat and waited.

Second Platoon radioed the CO that they had found a tunnel opening. The Company converged at that location. I watched from my position on the perimeter as a volunteer tunnel rat took a pistol and a flashlight and wriggled feet first through the small opening, down the vertical shaft. The trap door for the tunnel opening was a work of art. The door had been left off so the VC could ambush us and crawl to safety in a hurry. It was so well camouflaged that we would never have found it if the door had been in place over the opening. We could have stepped right on it. The lift-out door was about fourteen or fifteen inches square; very small. It was made like a wooden tray with dirt on top, and short, grass like vegetation growing in the dirt. The tunnel opening had a camouflaged wooden frame. The frame held the door, but also prevented the edge from caving in during entering and exiting. It fit together like two pieces from a jig-saw puzzle, which further hid the opening. The ground around the opening was vegetation, not mud, so footprints wouldn't expose the tunnel's existence. Finally, the entrance was under the edge of a bush, a spot you're not likely to walk on or even see. The tunnel was made the way someone would make it if their life depended on it, because that was the case.

The vegetation was considerably thinner here. We could see as far as a hundred meters in some directions. We were near the edge of the Ho Bo Woods. The sky was clear, and it felt like we had returned to Earth from some faraway hell. Time to breathe a sigh of relief.

The tunnel rat came back up in about thirty minutes, covered with mud. He reported that the tunnel wasn't very long and led to a fair size room that contained rice, munitions, and medical supplies for maybe a squad sized element.

Since it was now late in the afternoon, the CO passed the word to dig in while volunteers got the enemy cache out and destroy the tunnel. Volunteers again; I'll "volunteer" if I get a direct order, not before. Besides, I'd never fit in this small tunnel opening. I did go into a tunnel once, and did not enjoy it; not my thing. Takes a special kind of person to be a tunnel rat.

Tired, hungry, thirsty, sore, knotted stomachs, and sour smelling, we set about the night's usual preparations. LP's are set out while the digging in began. Everybody's busy, always moving, always working, never a dull moment.

Green clad figures turn into shadowy shapes as the sun sets; some with soggy, rotting flak jackets, some shirtless until the mosquitoes come out. A few eat or smoke at last light. There is very little talk in low voices; not much to talk about, except going home. Painful to think about how much longer each has in country, but the thoughts are happy because it will be a joyful day when your Freedom Bird takes off.

I still want to meet those nine base camp warriors who support me since I represent the one out of ten. What can all those guys be doing? I always thought a war had most troops in the field, on the line.

The Artillery FO started setting the DEFCON's; seems even closer tonight. Shrapnel whizzed by and sure enough, someone yelled, "I'm hit. The son of a bitch hit me. Medic!" There's some commotion down the line, but soon it was quiet again. I don't know what happened to the wounded man.

Guard duty begins. Tonight, Chief, Wesley and I share a position. We sleep the sleep of complete exhaustion, not moving a muscle, out when our head hits the mud. And in the same position when we wake up, with rifle still in hand, as when we hit the ground. Wes shook me awake for the third hour shift.

Knowing there are probably VC nearby, and that we killed one of their buddies, tends to make you kind of edgy. I had visions of a lunatic running at me with a knife clenched in his teeth, arms outstretched, seeking revenge. I sat in the silence, trying to stay awake and be alert to sounds. Suddenly, Chief let out a snore that sounded like a buzz saw and I tensed up so fast I must have been sitting six inches above the ground. I clapped my hand over his mouth and rolled him onto his side. I'm sure you could have heard it all the way to Saigon. I had heard he had snore issues because of bad sinuses, but I was not prepared for that. I had no trouble staying awake after that. I waited while about thirty minutes slowly dragged by, with a free hand close to Chief in case I had to muffle another one of those nasal explosions. Finally, my shift over, I woke Chief up and stretched out in the mud. I hoped he wouldn't fall asleep and miss that VC sneaking up with a knife who wanted to slit our throats. I used my wet, muddy pack as a pillow so if it rained my head would be above the accumulating water and I wouldn't have to wake up and search for a high spot. Two hours later, somebody shook me awake. I wished we had eight-hour shifts; what we did have felt like twenty-four hour shifts.

The full moon had risen and it was so bright I could actually have read by its light. The drastic change from the deep black nights of the jungle and thick clouds is very unsettling. I looked around and could see several bunkers and men, completely visible, like daytime. I felt uncomfortable, exposed. I tried to decide which was worse; now, I could see Charlie, but he could see me just as easily. Complete darkness; you can't be seen, but you can't see anything either. Bright moonlight; you can see well, but you can be seen very well, too. Charlie knew exactly where we were, but we didn't know where he was. I held my rifle a little tighter, and checked my grenades and Claymore detonators.

Wait, watch. My stomach cramped, and then groaned. Wonderful, the trots were acting up. For relief, I moved a few feet backwards instead of going outward because I didn't want a posthumous Purple Heart just because I had to go relieve myself. As I sat on guard later, I didn't want to move my head, just my eyes, as if it would give away my position. I knew that was dumb, the moon lit me up like a spotlight.

Then I heard something right in front of me, maybe ten or fifteen feet to my front. Some kind of throat noise, then a slight rustling in the leaves. I strained my eyes. Something made that noise but I couldn't see anything. Then again, noise but no movement. I swung my rifle toward the noise because it was too close to use the Claymore. If anything moved, it was damned sure going to wish it hadn't. Every one of my senses was turned up. My stomach crawled into my throat and my heart was trying to burst my eardrums. "Coo coo coo caw caw. _uck you. _uck you." The voice was like that of a young kid, and the words were as clear as a bell. The source was so close, I could have reached out and touched it, but nothing was there. I thought maybe I was losing it. Maybe it was a VC down in a spider hole; a VC with a sense of humor. I reached to my side and shook Wes awake without moving my eyes. "_uck you. _uck you." Wesley sat up and then threw a chunk of rotting wood toward the noise and said, "Damned _uck you lizard." At first, I thought he was kidding, or maybe still asleep. Lizard?

I didn't know if I chuckled from disbelief or at the aptly named gecko lizard. Who would believe this? Sounded just like a human voice. It didn't ease the tension in my spine.

The rest of the night passed quietly, so Charlie missed a good opportunity to hit in the bright moonlight. Maybe they don't like light after living in those dark tunnels. Anyway, it was a good lesson on the unpredictability of the enemy; when you expect him, he doesn't hit; when you don't expect him he hits.

Morning, and another night of only a few hours sleep. Same routine to get ready for the day. It's strange to live day and night, for weeks, in the same clothes, never taking them off, never changing them. When we woke up for guard, or in the morning, we didn't have to get dressed because we were already dressed, boots and all. Our fatigues were a second skin.

The sky was still clear, promising another sweaty day. First and Fourth Platoons were sent out to patrol the area, while Second and Third stayed behind to destroy the tunnel and take the man wounded last night by the DEFCON to a nearby clearing for DUSTOFF.

We set out and after only two weeks in country I felt like an old hand. Same thing day after day, and I drew flank again, too. We moved through the brush for a couple of hours, with the usual thorns, bugs, and mud. The temperature climbed faster than the sun. Nothing, no contact. We stopped and were told that elements of Delta would pass nearby. Sure enough, in a few minutes, a flank came hacking through the brush. "Over here," I called out.

He came over and flopped down. "Got a cigarette?" he asked. I passed him my pack and looked at him. He looked like he hadn't slept for weeks. He was covered with mud and scratches, and smelled like the rotting jungle undergrowth. I asked, "Been here long?"

"Second day." He answered. "Jungle's a bitch. Got to think of a way to get out. We ran into booby traps yesterday. Lost three guys. Damn near got me on my first day out. I'm supposed to be a cook. I joined because they told me I would go to Germany and be a cook. I went ok, for one lousy, damn month and I got orders for Nam. Infantry. I don't even know how to work this thing." He held up his M-16. I told them I'd do anything, just don't send me to the field. I volunteered to burn the shit in the latrine, and they told me they had a waiting list for that. (Since there was no sewer system here, the excrement in camp's latrines was burned by the "hockey jockey.") I said I'd wash tanks or stuff legs in body bags. I don't even know what half this gear is for." He got up and said, "Better go before they put me in front of a firing squad. Thanks." He crashed off through the brush.

I hoped he never had to go on ambush because he'd probably get everyone killed.

After the patrol, Sgt. Bauer said we would move to the Boi Loi Woods by trucks. They'd have a water trailer and C's.

Beginning to drag from lack of sleep, reflexes slowing, losing our edge, we moved out to meet the trucks. We were just moving along with the flow, not knowing where we were going, or how far, or even care. Maybe we'll arrive before the trucks and take a nap while we're waiting.

Not much of a war for me, so far, but this is how we lived between firefights.

The brush was light, but everything else was the same; bugs, mud,... The hot sun and high humidity drained us of moisture. Heavy gear made us sag, taking each step with a grunt and a groan. We almost hoped for a sniper, even an ambush, so we could stop, hit the muddy deck, and get a load off. Our fatigues were pasted to our skin with sweat and mud.

Keep your eyes moving, if you can. Step. Wet. Step. Hurt. Step. Bugs. Step. Bitterness. Step. Step. Step. BOOM.

We hit the mud, and it felt good to get off our feet.

"Medic." Somebody stepped on a small mine and probably will lose his foot. He'll be OK otherwise. Now, he's going home; he's got his ticket out, and alive. We'll stay, looking for our ticket.

We set up a security perimeter for the Medic. Another DUSTOFF was called and we moved to a clearing to meet it. Two grunts carried their buddy to the open ground, talking to him all the way telling him how lucky he was. "You're going home, back to the World. Save some beer for us."

The chopper wasted no time and arrived at the LZ at the same time as we did, all in just minutes. They lifted off and Charlie scored another casualty without even being nearby. Or, was he? Was he in the far tree line watching? Laughing?

Reaching for extra strength, we moved on. Trucks appeared ahead; no nap. At least we got ammo, water and C's. The trucks would make four trips, one for each Company. The leave-behinds were to start moving toward the new area, making the trip a little shorter each time. Alpha trucked first, and we started walking. The line stretched out to five meter intervals, and we moved quietly along the road. There was no tree line near the road, so probably no snipers, but it was a good place for miles. We moved through an open area that was obviously leveled during Operation Cedar Falls that Dean had told me about. Six months ago. Thousands of acres of jungle were cleared; nothing of any size was growing as far as we could see. What did that accomplish? We're still here, going through the same motions. Except Ski and Dean. They didn't make it either.

Clouds gradually built up as the day wore on. The heat made us hope the rains would return so we could cool off. We stopped for C's but most of us spent the time nursing a canteen while reclining against our packs. Little food was eaten because it would just make us thirstier, and adds to the trots. Looking down the road, I saw a grunt here and there walk a few feet out from the roadside and take care of their diarrhea in plain sight. Any modesty must be pushed aside because there is no place else to go.

My helmet camouflage cover was developing a respectable worn spot on top, my boots had deep scuff marks between the mud clumps and my gear was looking bad. I hadn't seen my face for a week but somehow I didn't want to because all around me I saw how it must look.

Time to move ... grunt ... just get up ... groan ... on your feet. No tree limbs or vines here to pull yourself up with.

Bravo was still walking at five in the afternoon when the trucks came for us. Heavy black clouds started dripping. The painful, bouncy ride in the truck was a welcome relief from the drudge on foot. The moving air during the ride was the first breeze we had felt for a week.

When we reached our destination, it was dark and the rain was pounding harder than I've ever seen; but, it was cool.

This was my chance to lighten my load of gear. When we got off the truck, I left behind my flak jacket, poncho liner, bayonet, gas mask, some cans of C's, the extra grenades, and the LAW. Quite a few other grunts had the same idea because gear littered the truck bed. I felt guilty for only as long as it took to put on the remaining, noticeably lighter, load.

We sloshed through the rain to light brush at the edge of the jungle and began the nightly routine. Wes and I started digging our fighting hole but it was raining so hard that the hole stayed full of water, right up to the brim, and we couldn't even tell how deep it was; could be two inches or two feet. We tried bailing the water out with our helmets but the hole still stayed full to the top. We had to yell to each other above the noise of the pouring rain. Now, that's a rainstorm.

We dredged a few more shovels of mud from the bottom, then gave up, and put up a low wall of mud filled sandbags. If we were hit, that would work better than squatting in water up to our necks.

I had guard first. Wes and Blue tried to find a spot in the mud to sleep, where their heads would stay above water. The rain washed off a lot of stink and dirt. But, before the night was over, our damp clothes would make us cold and stiff.

I woke Wes for guard and laid down in the rain and mud. If I hadn't needed sleep so badly, I would rather have been on guard, sitting in the mud instead of sleeping in it. Mercifully, the night passed without action, but with only the usual five or six hours of interrupted sleep.

The next day was like the others had been; the same old challenges with rain, bugs, sweat,... We fought the tangle of the jungle, and all the other things, while trying to be silent and vigilant. Sometimes the vines were so thick and intertwined that we had to sling our rifles and use both hands to crawl through. I felt sorry for the big guys today, trying to squeeze their bulk through this mess.

Our position the next night was by an old bomb crater filled with stagnant rain water. We took a quick, cooling dip before digging in, clothes and all. The water was probably full of flukes and God knows what else, but it felt good. The crater had been blasted by a 500 pound bomb. That's a strange thing to learn, to be able to identify the size of the bomb by the size of the crater; 250, 500, and 750 pounders. Wonder if I can use that after the war is over?

No one looks forward to darkness. It brings on apprehension; you can't see, you don't know what's out there, and the enemy is very unpredictable. And, you don't get enough sleep.

Days aren't much better because they bring their own kind of hell, sucking life from your body, and the spirit from your soul. But, you still have this duty ...

The days start running together, time gets fuzzy, lost. Is it Sunday? Wednesday? Holidays had no meaning. Most of us, if not all of us, never knew for sure which day was his birthday, or the Fourth of July, and sometimes even what month it was. We were so tired we forgot where we were and what we were supposed to be doing. We were so tired that we just didn't care about anything.

I ran out of mosquito repellent, bug juice, and rubbed mud on my skin for protection. It's not a good idea to do so since the mud was probably loaded with bacteria, but we were constantly in it anyway so it probably wouldn't make much difference. I learned to sleep completely covered by a poncho, for protection from mosquitoes, with only a mud smeared ear sticking out to listen for Charlie.

When we got C-rations, I traded the food for toilet tissue when I could. When I couldn't, I learned which leaves didn't have sharp edges.

There was no time, or material, to write a letter home. There was usually no way to send it anyway.

I realized that the most important things in life are the simple, basic things, the things you take for granted. Back home, your whole day is one fulfilled simple, basic need after another; showers with hot water, toilets, air conditioning, clean clothes, electricity, soap, your choice of food, leisure time, safety. Here, we had nothing. Absolutely nothing.

I didn't know how much longer before we got to camp, so I removed the stitches from the cut in my arm. Had it been ten days? Ten weeks? The days dragged by; routine, monotonous, and wasted.

The jungle got thicker and very little sunlight got through the canopy. I never would have guessed such a place existed. In every direction was never ending green; up, down, forward, and back. We were constantly touched by green, wet vegetation. It was almost claustrophobic. Vines were so thick it was like being in a giant can of worms. We had to use both hands to wriggle our way through. The air was heavy, stagnant, and steamy. The only sound I could hear was labored breathing. Sweat streamed so heavily I think it stretched our pores wide open for life. Jungle rot started growing on my arm; small red spots appeared. My boots had as much mud inside them as outside. Cuts and scrapes on my hands burned from the salty sweat. If I clenched my hands in a fist, pus and blood squeezed out. I had lost a lot of weight already and my gear hung loosely on me.

Another day passed, then another. The Battalion CO radioed our Company CO and demanded to know why we weren't moving faster. He was above us in his chopper every day, and in a shower and clean clothes every night; after a hot meal. This is for you, Leader Six.

Finally, we found signs of activity; light trails, bunkers with small food caches, and graves. I decided I better clean my rifle and ammo. The magazines had a lot of mud in them. They also showed signs of going to pieces. There's no telling how long they've been banging around in the bush before they were issued to me, how many grunts had carried them before me. They were flimsy anyway, not really made for this kind of abuse, and now were likely to cause failure to feed the rounds into the chamber. If we ever get back to Dau Tieng, I decided to ask Jim to get an M-14 for me. Old Faithful, it'll be a lot heavier, both rifle and ammo, and the flash suppressor is closed so it will not become hung up in the brush and vines. It won't fail me like the pea shooter M-16.

Another night. It was so dark under the jungle canopy in the daytime that it was almost spooky. At night we might as well have been on guard with our eyes closed. We set out double trip flares and Claymores.

The next day I drew flank. The underbrush was eight to ten feet tall and so thick you could see only a few feet or less. Above that, below the topmost canopy, it was open except for tree trunks and vines, and you could see for up to two hundred feet between the trunks, if the sun was high. But, you couldn't see through the top canopy. This created a layer effect; dense underbrush, open area with tree trunks, and canopy. I lost the column twice in the very dense growth. The first time, I watched for moving vines high up, above the thick brush. Sure enough, I saw one move and headed in that direction, hoping it was us and not them. The second time I lost the column, I thought it would be just as easy by watching the vines. I panicked because nothing was moving. I decided the column must have stopped. I moved in the direction I thought they might be, and there was no column. I went further and, still no column. I came to a light trail but it showed no signs of heavy booted traffic. I backed away because I didn't want any part of a trail, a path of least resistance. Now I doubted my bearings, not knowing which way to go. There were no landmarks, and I didn't have a compass. Nothing like this was covered in training. Should I yell and give our presence away? Charlie probably knew we're here anyway. I sat down and mentally retraced my steps. I decided the column had stopped a long time ago, and I was in front of it. So, I decided I better wait for the column to move to me; I didn't want to move and get shot when the point detected movement. Twenty minutes passed and I saw the vines sway gently; here they come. I'd wait until they were forty or fifty feet away and then whistle to hook up. Before I got the chance, BOOM. The point must have been checking out the trail and hit a booby trap. I closed in on the smoke and entered the area cleared by the explosion. I expected blood, but not what I saw. It looked like a whole squad of men had been blown up. There were pieces everywhere; smoldering tatters of skin and fatigues, chunks of bone, wet stuff dripping from leaves, flesh stuck to tree trunks, one boot with a foot still in it; and no rifle or helmet in sight. On the other side of the clearing lay the remaining part of the slack man, and another grunt. Their faces and chests looked like hamburger. Standing over them were the CO and his RTO's. I wanted to help the Medic, but there was nothing I could do. Let him earn his pay. I turned around and joined the security perimeter being set around the grisly scene.

The RTO on the Battalion net was behind me and I listened to the traffic while comparing luck and fate. That could have been me, except I don't do trails. I wonder why the Point did. Which of us had luck, and which had fallen to fate?

"Leader Six, Bravo."

"Bravo, Leader. Go."

"Leader, we have to detour to nearest Lima Zulu. We've got one Kilo (Killed) and two Whiskeys (Wounded). Over."

"Roger Bravo. Are you in contact? Do you have a body count? Over."

"Negative, Leader. Negative contact. Booby trap."

Somebody nearby mumbled, "Come on down. Yeah, we got bodies. Three Grunts bleeding American blood in this God-forsaken shit hole. Come on down. I'll give you some contact."

So it went, day after day. I knew this lack of action wouldn't last forever, but I was beginning to hope anyway. Charlie didn't have any large units in the area, so we floundered around in the bush looking for the little guerilla units. No warfare, but the guerillas nickeled and dimed American blood, like ticks on a dog, drawing blood until anemia sets in. But, that was their plan from the beginning. Don't confront large American units with all their fire power and support. Hit and run. Bleed them and drag it out until they get tired of it and go away.

Days were spent in the body numbing routine, elements wearing you down. We wondered who would hit a booby trap next. Nights brought a mind-numbing routine, and insecurity; will tonight be the big one? We watched and waited, wanting to sleep.

Finally, word was passed that the next day we would walk through the Rubber trees and return to Dau Tieng. Camp; home. Be it ever so humble. That crude place would sure look good after this. Everyone talked about sleeping for a month. This was exciting. There's nothing there in Dau Tieng, but we wouldn't be out in the bush. That's enough by itself.

The next morning, the routine didn't seem to be as bad; it even stopped raining. As I put my gear on, I noticed the hole in my camouflage cover. Though small, it was sort of like a badge of initiation. Big deal to think about such a thing.

We took off and hit the rubber plantation in about an hour. Once again, we felt like we exited from some never land and re-entered the world.

The trees were spaced far apart compared to the jungle, and the ground cover was kept low by the rubber workers. It felt strange to have so much elbow room, and a breeze.

Word was passed to keep spaced way apart because this was ideal sniper country, wide open. We had to walk close to the trees because booby trap trip mechanisms were usually set up in the middle of the rows; the path of least resistance, the easy way, most open. If we found a booby trap, care was to be taken in following the wires because the wires themselves were often booby trapped. As we walked by the trees, I saw how rubber workers harvested the latex sap from the trees. A gash is cut in each tree, by hand, and only bark deep, like a stripe in a barber pole. The tree bleeds the sap, which follows the gash down to a small drip bowl hung on the tree, about waist high. The worker moves up and down the rows filling a bucket from the bowls, and the bucket is emptied into a tank trailer. It's hard, monotonous work.

Rubber plantations are divided into thousand-meter squares by dirt service roads. This breaks the area up into a grid; very handy for a mortar crew. If a VC worker saw us, he could tell a guerilla unit Americans are two roads over and one down, for example. Then with simple math, distance for a mortar could be calculated quickly and accurately. If they didn't know simple math, they could still estimate close enough for an area burst weapon, like a mortar, and adjust. Then quickly fade away.

We were introduced to another friend; large orange and black spiders, about the size of your hand. They spun their webs from tree to tree, which were twelve to fifteen feet apart along the row, and about twenty five feet between the rows. A twelve- to fifteen-foot spider web is a big web and has to be very strong. When we walked into the web, its strength made it feel like a giant net. I think they were from the tarantula family. I don't know if they were poisonous but we always gave them a wide berth.

We came to a hamlet where rubber workers lived. In Vietnam, these hamlets were everywhere and didn't have official names. They were just small settlements of convenience. So, five or six were grouped together and given a name to form a village. This hamlet, or Ap, was number 6 of the village Bis, so was designated on maps as Ap 6 Bis. One through five, and any over six, would be nearby. We were to search here for any signs of VC activity. First and Second Platoons cordoned, or circled, the village, Third and Weapons were to search the hooches.

As we went into the village, the kids came running out to greet us, yelling, "Hey, GI, you give chop-chop." "Give me gum, cigarettes." Most of the youngsters wore only ragged shorts and nothing else, a few had shirts, and some had no clothes at all. They all had smiles on their faces, and delight in their eyes. They had been through this before and knew GI's were soft-hearted suckers for kids. They split up into ones and twos and clung to our arms and fatigues. Out came our hearts, candy, gum, and anything else we had that would give them joy.

We continued with our business and began searching. Wesley and I paired up to go hooch to hooch. I didn't know what to expect but I figured the village was friendly today since we didn't receive any sniper fire coming in. Just outside the front doorway to her house, which like all the others had no door of any kind, a mamasan was squatting on the porch feeding her family of four kids from a pitifully small bowl of rice. I could eat five times that much for a meal. Meager as it was, she offered me some. I don't know if it was out of hospitality or fear. I smiled, said no by word and hand motions, and walked into her home. Through my mind went thoughts of Hepatitis, children going to bed hungry, and pity. I went back and gave mamasan several cans of C-rations. She smiled ear to ear, showing teeth stained black from chewing Betel nut. She spoke in Vietnamese. Vietnamese is a strange language to English speaking people because it's a tonal language. It has five tones which give some words five meanings, one for each tone. In the same sentence, a speaker can sound very happy and also very angry. I told her she was welcome and continued with my duty of tearing her house apart.

Most of the hooches were bamboo walls with a thatch roof. A few were made of something like adobe, and a few even had wooden floors. None had doors or windows, just the openings, and lizards ran all over the place. Beds were wooden frames with slats, and a woven palm leaf pad only a quarter inch thick to sleep on. There was usually only one room with curtains hanging here and there to form smaller rooms. The kitchen was always separate from the hooch and amounted to little more than a thatch roof over a fire pit. There was no electricity, no refrigeration, no pantry, little food, no running water, and no comforts. Nothing. I thought to myself, "What these people wouldn't give for a house in America. They probably wouldn't know what to do. This has got to be a miserable life, but if it's all you have ever known, you can't miss a better life." In one of the kitchen areas, I asked Wes, "What is that smell, like something dead?"

"*Nuoc mom*. Armpit sauce. Fermented something. They put that stuff on their food. Maybe it keeps the bugs away, or something."

We searched under, over, and behind everything for weapons, tunnel entrances, or anything indicating VC related activity. Nothing.

I spotted a small conical hut hidden in the brush and thought it looked handy, but out of sight. I stuck my head in the small doorway, half expecting to see something suspicious. Instead, I found a large pile of Chieu Hoi leaflets and a horrible odor; it was an outhouse. I tried to decide if the smell was from the *Nuoc mom*, or from eating too many C-rations thrown to them.

Our search of the village turned up nothing. I'm sure the mamasans didn't appreciate having to put their household back together. I'm also sure it wasn't the first time GI's had to make a shambles of their homes, or the last. As if to prove me right, a withered, old mamasan was chasing a GI around her yard with a stick. She was yelling at him, he was trying to apologize, a couple of scrawny chickens were running and squawking, and the kids were laughing and cheering him on. Later, he collected some C's and gave them to her. She was still unhappy until he gave her some menthol cigarettes. Then, everyone was happy.

It is really uncomfortable searching someone's home, as though you were breaking and entering right in front of them, watching you.

There usually were no young men in the villages, unless they were in the militia. All young men had to be in the military service, leaving only old men, women, and children. This didn't preclude the possibility of their being VC, or of VC activity. In fact, the VC would probably move back in as soon as we left.

We sat around in the shade for an hour or so and played with the kids. Out came more gum, cigarettes, and canteens. Then the kids showed us how to play their games, most using rocks and sticks. One of the boys hit me up for a drink from my canteen. He had raw sores and bumps all over his face and I thought about how I could avoid sharing my canteen with him and being exposed to whatever he had. The other kids, Wes, and Blue watched me to see how I would get out of this. It was kind of a strained moment. I remembered my canteen cup, which I never used, and poured water in it for him. Everybody was happy. I let him keep the cup and he was proud of it.

While we played and visited, the youngsters stroked the hair on our arms and chests. It fascinated them because their race isn't very hairy and their curiosity took hold.

I showed them the picture of my family and each one studied it closely, for quite some time, reluctant to pass it along. One boy looked at me earnestly and asked in Pidgin English, "Babysan belong you?" He pointed to my younger sister and brother in the picture. "No. No have babysan. Sister, brother," as I pointed to each in turn. He was quiet for a moment and said, "You can numbah one boysan. Nguyen (pronounced nwin) go America you." He pointed to himself, smiling. These little guys knew something wasn't right with their lives, something was missing. No father at home to be a pal, shooting, dying, and hunger. I saddened him when I gave him the only possible answer. "*Sin loi* (sorry), Nguyen. No can do."

These were good kids and it was difficult to leave them to whatever fate awaited them, including the likelihood that they would be indoctrinated by the VC. I hoped the time we spent with them contributed to resistance to the VC.

As we left, they ran along, for a long way, saying goodbye.

We finally got back to Dau Tieng, and there was Jim, waiting with a big smile, and a cold beer. "We followed you on the radio all the way, John. Go wash that God-awful smell off and I'll find you another cold one."

"How long were we out?" I asked.

"Twenty five days."

I went out with a group of friends, and came back without them. I went out with pride and dignity, and came back without them also. But, happily, I settled for survival. I felt less like a soldier than a pawn. I felt less like an American citizen than a victim.

A month without a shower, but constantly wet. Almost four weeks of wading in the mud and water made me very reluctant to take my boots off. Four weeks of stink, hurt, diarrhea, bugs, jungle. On future operations, those four weeks would very often stretch out to six and seven weeks.

Forty seven more weeks to go.

All our previous backgrounds were worthless; not just wasted, but meaningless, unrelated.

But, I survived. I did survive. That counts for a lot. In fact, that's all I can say for the time spent. So now, it's time for a bar of soap, and letters from home.

Survival is what it all becomes; survival, endurance, patience. Slowly, this life smothers you. You don't control it, it controls you. You just try to survive.

11

When I arrived at Cam Ranh Bay four weeks ago, I felt uneasy about safety and security. At Cu Chi, I was more apprehensive. Dau Tieng seemed most risky and vulnerable. I'm sure the support personnel at Cu Chi would rather be at Cam Ranh. But now, coming in from the bush, Dau Tieng seemed very safe. In fact, it was so welcome that I forgot about home for a short while, as if going home was a sure thing now that I'd made it back to Dau Tieng.

After a beer and a shower, and a beer and a shower, and a beer and a shower, it felt good to be able to sit and not have to do anything. Absolutely nothing.

It felt strange to be confined by walls, such as they were, and not have to sit or sleep in the mud. It was even stranger to see myself in a mirror; I almost didn't recognize myself at first. Chairs looked strange, lights, floors, not carrying a weapon, seeing clean faces, not looking around for the enemy; everything was strange, as if I was in a different world. The simple, basic things, the things you take for granted.

At sunset, the CO personally led a Memorial service for our fallen comrades. Afterward, he announced, "You can take your boots off, men. We'll be here for a day or two." That's exactly what we did.

The next day, we kept dry and aired our skin, and feet, which were in a mess. It was amazing how luxurious such a simple thing could be. Immersion foot was very common; cracked, bleeding feet from being constantly wet and filthy.

We also applied fungal medication for jungle rot. We looked like clowns with smears and dabs or whitish medication all over us. We wrote letters home and slept. That's all we wanted to do; that's all we could do, anyway.

In the evening, it was time to clean our gear and get ready to go back to the field the next day. There was a lot of horseplay, whooping, and hollering; anything to divert your attention, to escape, so you didn't think about tomorrow, being back out in the bush. There was a lot of warm beer, but no marijuana or drugs. They were available from the villagers, so I heard, but nobody wanted them, or needed them. At this time, we took the war seriously. No one wanted to be in a helpless stupor at any time, nor have to depend on someone all spaced out while in a life or death situation, which is the types of situations our missions always were.

Some of the guys in the Company, not in Weapons Platoon, had perimeter guard that night and one of them accidentally shot himself in the foot when he tripped on a rifle in the dark. So he said. Rumor had it that the Dr. who treated him at the Aid Station said the angle of entry was all wrong for that to be the case; the wound had to be self-inflicted. In either case, he didn't have to go back to the boonies.

In the morning, we moved slowly out to the Company area with our gear and waited for the word to move out to the helipad. This time, I watched the few new guys fuss with their heavy loads of gear. Been there, done that; they too will learn quickly, just as I did.

I had finally reached a compromise in weight versus gear. If I traveled light, I knew there would be some things I'd leave at camp that I wished I had taken along. It's so difficult to move quickly with too much gear, and you tire much easier. So, I learned a lesson from the VC; carry only what you need to survive, namely; weapon, ammo, food, and water. You can adjust to the inconveniences of not having all that other gear, the luxuries. I had to chuckle when I thought of the Military posters I had seen showing Infantrymen with full field packs, gas masks, mess kits, bayonets, shelter halves, and more. We were better off living out of our pockets than lugging all the other gear. Fortunately, our CO placed emphasis on performance and let each man decide on his own selection of gear.

This operation we would be near the Cambodian border, in an area named the Parrot's Beak because of its shape, as easily seen on a map. Military Intelligence had detected many small units crossing the border and moving in the general direction of Saigon. We were supposed to patrol, make contact, and destroy. Maybe this would be the big one. Maybe Charlie would be ready and waiting for us. I knew the elements would be.

I still had my pea shooter M-16. Jim told me the few M-14's the Company had were always in demand. He gave me some new magazines and promised to check around the Battalion for an extra M-14.

While waiting for word to move out, it started raining on us. When I was new in country, I had the instinct to look for cover, to get out of the rain. Not anymore, it's useless. That was just one of the many civilized things that had to be unlearned.

I slipped my helmet on, newly decorated with my personalized graffiti; "Vast war, half vast plan." This seemed to state my feelings well about the methods, the means to the end. It seemed to me, now more than ever, that the war was not being fought properly, if we really wanted to win. We weren't going to where we knew the enemy was, there was no aggression northward. We drew lines to the north and west, the DMZ and the Cambodian border, which we didn't allow ourselves to cross. So, the enemy stayed just across the lines, safe and sound. We were just running here and there, putting out fires, because someone saw the enemy. By the time we got there, the enemy had either crawled into a hole or put on a disguise and blended in with the Vietnamese.

This kind of strategy leads only to self-defeat. We can't win this war because of unrealistic rules we have imposed on ourselves, in effect tying our hands. The enemy couldn't defeat us militarily, but we would defeat ourselves. That makes you feel real good; to go through all this living like an animal but it will all be for nothing.

While walking to the helipad, I realized I had developed the ability to sense where every member of my squad was located, in relation to me, without looking around. The first two weeks out, the boonie life was new to me and absorbed my whole attention. After getting adjusted, I started to mentally position everyone without realizing it. I could also sense who was struggling to keep up, and who was scared, without looking around me. Call it what you will, need for survival, reaction to insecurity, whatever, it did give me some peace of mind when we were in a tough position.

The LZ was cold, no enemy fire. It was covered with Elephant Grass six to eight feet high. The pilots wouldn't attempt a landing in the grass because the VC liked to hide helicopter booby traps in it; sharp, erect spikes to puncture the chopper, or, erect poles, which, when blown over by the rotor wash, activate an explosive device. We had to jump out from about ten feet up and hope we wouldn't be impaled by a spike, or break a leg. The Grunt is always the pawn, the sacrifice. I don't think the Grunt was particularly expected to make it out alive. If he did, good for him, but if he didn't, well, that was his problem.

We were on our own again, cut off from the World, wondering what was waiting for us.

Trying to get the troops organized in the tall grass was as difficult as trying to get organized in darkness. When we were briefed for the op, we weren't told about the tall grass, so there was no plan for regrouping. With no plan and no means for visible communication, we floundered around in the grass for quite a while. Pushing through the sharp-edged grass made painful cuts on hands and arms, and even faces. It also easily sliced our fatigues. Heavy sweat and mosquito repellent made the cuts sting. Mosquitoes found us very quickly.

Rain started falling, flash suppressors hung up on the grass. We were soaked in sweat from head to toe. Welcome back to the hostile grind; the drudge of the wet, green hell.

The same routine as always; tune in your senses, keep your eyes moving, mud building up on your boots, sweat, rain, mosquitoes, stink, slip in the mud, wade through chest deep putrid water, more weeks with no shower or even taking our boots off, leeches, booby traps, lonely, afraid of running out of water, walking flank. Day after day, every day. Nothing to look forward to except more of the same. Snipers. Ambush. Pain. All sucking the life out of you. No way to measure progress or even what progress is. No goal. No objective.

We patrolled and reconned and searched but turned up few signs of the enemy, though occasional booby traps reduced our numbers.

Artillery in the distance, helicopters passing over head. Everybody was busy, but no enemy. We thought this was a little strange, this long without contact of some kind. Maybe the VC are avoiding us while they are preparing for something big that involves all of them.

We looked forward to evenings so we could get off our feet. The air was cooler then, and another day was almost over. But, we didn't look forward to night, not knowing what it would bring, except not enough sleep. A human can make many adjustments and do without many things, but not sleep. Sleep is almost a dirty trick. Sooner or later you've got to sleep. Your instincts tell you to stay awake but you are so ragged-tired you can't fight your body's demand. You've got to turn off all your senses and place your life in the hands of a buddy on guard, but he's tired too. Sleep brings insecurity, night brings fear. Sleeping at night in the boonies makes you very vulnerable.

In the evenings, the resupply helicopter comes in and you start the routine; carry supplies in from the LZ, dig your bunker, fill sandbags, set up the mortar, wake up every two hours and fire the mortar. Dark, lonely, exhausted. Wet clothes cause stiff muscles and joints. Skip eating to sleep a couple of hours in the mud. Morning routine is always there, it's a grind, but necessary, day after day. Then we moved out for the day's adventures.

The second day out, I learned another thing the extra boot laces are good for. I tied the laces snugly just below the knee on both legs, to keep the leeches from crawling up my legs, under my pant legs. The pants also snagged less on the brush, and made less noise scraping against the leaves and branches.

We came to a large area that had been defoliated by American planes spraying Agent Orange, an herbicide. The idea was to deprive the VC of hiding places in the heavy vegetation. There was no mistaking what had happened here, because the area was very bleak and emaciated; no color, no green vegetation. Dirt and skeletal remains of trees and brush was all that was visible for a long way. We went across the area into thick vegetation, and as I entered it, I looked back and wondered if this really would be helpful to our efforts. It seemed we were slowly destroying the country we were trying to save.

Later in the day, Wes and I ran into a hornet nest while walking flank. We rubbed mud on the bites to ease the pain, and kept going.

During the second night, while I sat on guard, I kept seeing bright flashes of light like the sun was blinking on for a split second, then off. The light flashed about every five seconds and worked its way along a straight line from far left to far right. I thought I was losing it again. Brilliant flashes of light, but no sound. Then, it came back by, a little closer. It wasn't until the third pass, directly overhead, that I could accept what I already knew it had to be. I heard the silenced airplane engines whisper by, no louder than an electric fan. Some guy was spending his tour shooting pictures from a plane, looking for VC. I wondered if he would come back by and take a picture of me. Some job, but I guessed somebody had to do it. Then I had another thought. Why not get us out of the nasty ground pounding by combining these two methods; defoliate and take pictures. If there were signs of the enemy, bomb the life out of the area. Then, send us in to investigate. It sure would get my vote.

The next day, we followed a dirt road that led into the jungle. Toward evening, a couple of young Vietnamese females appeared on the road and tried to sell their virtues to the GI's. They followed us until we stopped to set up camp for the night, at which time the CO ran them off. "They won't be back", he said. "There's a village nearby. Probably theirs."

That night we were mortared. It was no coincidence as far as we were concerned. The females had been waiting to see where we would camp. They were VC. The night was uneventful until about 4 A.M. In the still night, there was the distant POOP of a mortar, then another, and another. The first round got everyone's attention, whether asleep or on guard. When the second shot sounded, we were diving for our foxholes. I dove into our hole at the same time as three other guys, all of us head first, feet sticking up in the air. The three rounds missed our perimeter and we scrambled for our mortar to return fire. I was so anxious to return fire before the VC moved away that I forgot to keep my head below, and away, from the muzzle. We fired eight rounds, searching and traversing the impact area, and by the time we were through, the concussion of the muzzle blasts had scrambled my brains and gave me a headache that lasted for days. It was the same kind of after effect as a severe hangover; headache, queasy stomach and a generally dazed feeling. I don't know why it didn't puncture my eardrums, but no other damage was done, so I thought. You can't go take an aspirin and lie down; you just have to live with it. I never forgot again.

By the time we packed everything, it was almost dawn. We took off into the jungle in the direction of last night's target to see what we could find, and finally arrived at the village. There were fresh craters around from our fire. A few brave villagers were pointing to the ground as they ran along, talking excitedly in Vietnamese. They stopped and pointed to the jungle. The VC had set up their mortar in the village. Our rounds had hit some of them and they took off for the trees, leaving behind blood trails and bloody bandages. Setting up the mortar in the village was a typical VC tactic. Hiding behind innocent civilians, they thought we wouldn't fire back. We didn't know they were in the village. We fired by direction of the sound and guessed at the distance. Fortunately, no innocent people were hurt. This time.

Do we search the village and possibly give the VC more time to escape? Or, do we forget the village and go after the VC? We took off into the jungle, forming a column with flanks. Rain started falling heavily and soon washed away the trail of blood drops. The elements were working against us once again. We kept searching and sloshing and hacking through the tangle. Muddy, soaked with rain and sweat we were ready for a fight. Silent anger was building inside us at the enemy who wouldn't stand and fight, only snipe, run and hide. The enemy who hid behind civilians, killed one or two people, GI's or civilians, then ran.

We came to a large clearing in the jungle. Scattered around were prehistoric-looking mounds, six to eight feet high, made of dirt packed hard as a rock; termite hills. I thought we'd get hit working our way around them, across the open area. Nothing.

The villagers may have been VC and led us in this direction while their mortar crew went safely in another direction.

The rain stopped and the sun blazed. We hit elephant grass which blocked any breeze so the air was very steamy. We stopped for radio coordination. I was rear security, the last man in the column. Whenever we stopped, rear security faced rearward to watch for a VC attack from the rear; another of their favorite tricks. Heat and exhaustion caught up with me and my head nodded. I jerked it up and then I nodded again, dozing off in a sitting position. I jerked awake sometime later and looked around. The column had moved on and I was alone. My first thought was that the VC had enough time to sneak up by now. I looked around, rifle ready, expecting to see little brown men coming at me. Nothing moved.

Time for me to hat up. Fortunately, a company of men moving through Elephant Grass will leave a trail. I caught up with them in about thirty very worried minutes. I learned the easy way that you better not get comfortable because, if you do, you'll not only get complacent, but you'll probably fall asleep. I was also reminded that you have to be ready at all times. Needless to say, I gave the man in front of me a bad time for not signaling me when the column started moving. Something he needed to learn for himself, and his buddies.

The next couple of days were fruitless so we got other orders to move to a nearby LZ and chopper to a different area. We linked up with Alpha Company and waited in the tree line of the LZ.

There would be three lifts, or flights, and I'd be in the last. The first came and left with no problems. The second came and left but must have gotten the attention of some local guerillas because they fired a few rounds. Circling Command helicopters radioed and told us the VC were moving toward the LZ and could get close enough to do some damage to the choppers, or us. The final lift came in after smoke-laying choppers had put a smoke screen along one side of the LZ. These were the gutsiest pilots yet. They laid smoke inches above the trees so it would penetrate to the ground and conceal our positions. They flew the contours of the tree line, looking like a roller coaster, nearly crashing into the taller trees, and making ninety-degree banking turns. These guys must have had a death wish, but they put their smoke on a dime.

We lifted out with no incoming rounds, probably because the VC couldn't see through the smoke. Our flight quickly left the jungle behind and we were over rice paddies, a checkerboard of greens and browns. My gut told me paddies would be no better than jungle, just different challenges and problems.

The choppers hovered just above just above the water, inside the large, loose circle formed by men from previous flights. We jumped into the water and began the sloshing and wading. To prevent certain small items from getting wet, they were placed under helmet camouflage elastic bands which hold the cover on the helmet. I looked around and saw helmets adorned with toilet paper, packs of cigarettes, pictures, and socks. Each GI had their own idea about what was valuable to them. Yes, the paddy life may be just another pain.

The RTO's had their radio aerials bent over to hide them. This was a safety precaution because VC snipers aim for RTO's first. They're easy to spot with the antenna sticking up in the air several feet, and an army without commo is lost; no coordination is possible.

This won't be a casual stroll through the open area, chatting idly with a friend, sharing the scenery.

The stagnant, putrid water stunk of algae, mud, and water buffalo excrement. The sun was intensely hot and blinding as it reflected off the water.

Rice paddies are wide open, just like a shooting gallery. If the VC hit us in the paddy, there's no place to go for cover. We wouldn't be able to get there anyway, because you can't run in knee-deep water and mud.

I had the feeling that the whole idea was that we were to be bait, to draw fire. Our eyes didn't stop moving while thinking we'd be hit from a distant tree line by rifle or mortar fire. We soon smelled like the stinking water, and were covered with crud.

A few new men thought they would take the easy path and walked on top of the dikes. The CO said to pass the word to let him know if they found any mines. They got back down in the water even though sloshing and slogging through the paddies was a struggle. Each step splashed the contaminated water up to our faces. Our feet sunk deep in the mud and schlucked when we lifted them out. It was no mystery to me how the name Grunt originated.

Mosquitoes were here, too, as well as sweat, wet, leeches, stink, bitterness, and anger. Progress was painfully slow. The Battalion CO radioed our Company CO and wanted to know why we weren't moving faster. From his viewpoint in the sky, it must have looked easy, what he could see of it.

We broke for rations while sitting in the water, leaning back against the dikes. Covered with mud and stink doesn't stop anyone from anything. You can't go clean up, so you just keep going about your business.

Before we moved out, the Battalion's CO's chopper hovered over a dike. He got out and said, "Let's go." We were supposed to follow him; he'll show us how it's done. He slogged through the paddies only as far as the next dike, where he got out of the water and walked on the dike. Looking like a shooting gallery target, he kept moving along. He got ahead of most of us, turned, slipped, almost fell, and said, "Move it, men." He was having a good time, just like the "Follow me" posters I saw at Ft. Polk.

POP. POP. POP. A sniper opened up from the tree line, and green tracers almost hit the Battalion CO. He slid down the dike and hit the muddy, putrid water face first, SPLAT.

POOP. POOP. Somebody yelled out, "Incoming. Hit the mud." An automatic weapon opened up on us and small geysers of water danced all around us.

Zipper had already set up behind a dike and he opened fire.

WHAM ... WHAM. Their small mortar was searching for us. M-16's returned fire at the tree line even though we hadn't located the enemy position yet. Men caught between the dikes turtled through the mud and water for cover.

Orders started flying, "Gimme a thumper up here. Gimme a thumper now, damn it..." The Grenadier crawled forward through the mud. "First Squad, move up behind that dike and flank them. Third, go over there." They tried to move out from behind the dike but the VC saw it and their machine gun put a stop to that.

"The bastards have us pinned down. Get some big guns or fast movers." The FO radioed for air support or artillery.

We kept firing back, waiting for somebody to cut us some slack. No one wounded yet.

The Battalion CO was covered with mud; he looked just like one of us now. There was a look of frustration on his face, helpless frustration. I felt like saying, "Welcome to our world, SIR. How does it feel?"

The wait for support wasn't long. An artillery barrage screamed in and hit the tree line. We had a new FO. The CO got rid of the one that called DEFCON's too close to our perimeter and hit somebody. The FO adjusted and our CO said, "Two more and start making your way toward the tree line between rounds." With each barrage, we made our way from dike to dike. The artillery stopped and we made our way into the tree line. No more incoming, but we got under cover of the trees anyway. It felt good, not so exposed and naked. I'll never curse a tree again.

We spread out and started searching. We found nothing except one Ho Chi Minh sandal. (Footgear for the VC, this sandal is made from old rubber tires; the sole is the tread part of the tire, and straps are fashioned from any other part of the tire. This made an easy way for the VC to keep something on their feet at no cost, and almost unlimited availability from just one tire.) When the first barrage came screaming in, the VC ran for it and one of them ran right out of his sandal. More searching turned up nothing.

Time to set up for the night, so we started that routine, and LP's and an ambush were sent out.

The days were spent like those in the jungle; searching, sweating, wading in the paddies until we got a ring around the middle from the putrid water, sun glaring, then rain, constantly wet, stink.

We began to suffer worse physical effects with widespread foot infections, jungle rot, severe diarrhea, and weight loss. The nights were spent sleeping in the mud, fighting mosquitoes, and fruitless ambush patrols. We didn't get too concerned about how the war was doing elsewhere, just around us, trying to get through another day.

We wished for ice, cold drinks, showers, bed, and escape from this stinking, wet hell.

After more than a week in the paddies, we choppered in the direction of Dau Tieng, into a part of the rubber plantation. The LZ was cold. Hopping out of the chopper and going through the wide-open area between the trees was comfortable. It might be sniper country but there's no paddy water to wade through and no green tangle to hack through. The days are long and strenuous, rainy and sweaty. The nights are almost sleepless after the usual LZ detail, digging in, and firing the mortar. The same grind and nightly routine, just a different location. It's all still there, even the large orange and black spiders. Our presence doesn't seem to change or accomplish anything.

The first night and the next day, it rained constantly. Shoulders sagged under the weight of the soaked backpacks. I wondered if we would develop a permanent stoop or other back problems; maybe we wouldn't, or couldn't, have to stand at attention when we got back to the States.

We searched for the enemy, moving eight, ten even twelve grueling kilometers each day. At night, tired like you wouldn't believe, we dug our bunkers and fired the mortars. Gotta fulfill our mission here.

We were told to go easy on chopping the Rubber trees for our overhead cover because the U. S. Government had agreed to pay Michelin three hundred dollars for every tree damaged or destroyed. Sounded like we got suckered into something, and of course, we had to go easy on our protection to save a few dollars. Thanks a lot for thinking of us, whoever you are. With all the bombs and artillery falling, there will be a lot of trees hurt. Our use for cover would be a very, very small percentage of total hurt trees. So, the Grunt again gives up something necessary; protection.

The second day, I walked point. It's kind of spooky up there, but I have to admit, it's better than walking flank. Every so often, I could see my flank guards way off to the side, maybe a hundred meters out. Look out for snipers, guys.

Even though Charlie hasn't been active around this area of Vietnam lately, you can't drop your guard. Keep your senses alert, eyes moving, and weapon at the ready.

We stopped for radio coordination and someone else took a turn at point, so I moved back to Weapons at rear security. When we moved out, I looked back and saw Blue leaning against a tree, gear still on. I whistled softly but he didn't move. I went over to see if he was sick. He wasn't, but he was sleeping while leaning against the tree. Exhaustion was catching up with everyone. Being on alert, disciplined and strenuously active twenty-four hours a day will grind you down and makes good men useless. It takes the edge off your reflexes. We don't punch in and out on a clock, eight to five with rest in between. But these American boys are Can Do people from a Can Do nation, that kept soldiering their guts out. This war effort we have been assigned seems to be a test of endurance more than anything. Not a test of fighting skills, but of physical stamina.

Most GI's tended to have a small group of close friends who, since we spent twenty four hours a day together, eventually thought and acted alike. We communicated and maneuvered without the need for words, knowing what each other was thinking. Infantrymen become more than friends because they must depend on each other more than on friends depend on each other. They must rely on each other for survival. Every action taken is for their survival as well as your own. We weren't focused on the war so much as for each other. There is no counting of actions to make sure you aren't doing more than your equal share, there is no waiting for a thank you. You just do what needs to be done and struggle on to whatever end waits. The bond is not based on emotion, but more like parts of the same body; the eye helps the ear, the hand helps the leg. Eventually, you help each other through, so you all have a chance to survive.

To keep our sanity, to think of something besides the war, we invented little games. Sometimes it would be a joke, sometimes a riddle. Sometimes we'd compare similar memories from home. The most popular was a guessing game; any subject, no rules, no time limit. It wasn't unusual to pose a riddle or question in the morning, and not get a response until late at night, the next day, or even a few days later.

The fourth day in the rubber trees, one of our Medics was MEDEVACed. His weapon, a forty-five caliber pistol, discharged in his holster and hit his leg. He claimed the weapon had been unsafe, faulty, but no replacement was available. An Officer checked the pistol right then, on the spot, and said there was nothing wrong with the weapon, it worked properly. These accidentally self-inflicted wounds were becoming fairly common. This extent to escape our daily duties was an indication how intolerable this life was.

Several days later, we choppered back to base.

The past two months had been a dry spell in the war in our area. It's unlike Charlie to be inactive for so long, unless he's planning something and needs to keep a low profile.

IV

Circumstances

12

Base camp was a welcome sight, a respite from hell, especially the shower and mail. One package from home had cookies, which meant I would not go to chow for a while. I can still, years later, taste how good those cookies were. After all the C-rations, they were a delicacy. They were also memories of home and happier days. I ate a few cookies, slept a while, woke up and ate a few cookies, slept a while ... They were gone before we went back to the boonies. I thought I may as well enjoy them now because I may not get back.

Weeks without a shower or change of clothes makes you feel less than human, or at least an abused human; weeks without taking off your boots, socks, or clothes. It felt strange to be clean, to shed our accumulation of scunge.

Jim and I talked late into the night. He filled me in on what was happening back home; demonstrations against the war, rumors of peace talks, college football scores.

Still no M-14, but I received my first promotion, to Specialist Fourth Class, or Spec-4. It didn't mean much except a few dollars more per month pay. More importantly to me, I received the Combat Infantryman's Badge, or CIB, the award that is worn above all other medals, if you were in the Infantry and served in combat.

The second morning it was back out to the drudge, the next operation. After the light contact we'd been having, we expected more of the same. This operation was in a heavily forested area. I had no idea where we were, which direction camp was, or how far. I just didn't give a damn because it didn't make any difference anyway.

All the problems and challenges were still there, waiting for us. It never went away, and it never got better.

The next morning, we got up as usual and started getting ready for the day's grind, when Lt. Young came by and said, "Pack everything and get ready to lift out now. We're OPCON to the Big Red One (1st Division). They need help like right now. They're at Loc Ninh and Charlie is throwing their heaviest stuff at 'em. Heavy. It's no wonder we've been stumbling around, all the VC are up there."

Just at first light, we were at a nearby LZ watching Hueys land in a V formation for our extraction. It was always fascinating to watch them.

We landed at Dau Tieng, were given ammo and rations, and were told to stay at the airstrip to board a C-130 aircraft. The extra ammo was for our individual weapons, for the mortar, and the recoilless rifle, giving each of us near a hundred pounds of gear to hump. While we waited, everyone again had that faraway look in their eyes while they silently fidgeted with whatever. A very uneasy feeling settled over the old-timers and didn't go unnoticed by the new guys.

The airstrip at Dau Tieng was not very long, though it ran from fence to fence across the base camp. It was also in very poor condition and on a slight incline. It looked like it had never been maintained and was full of potholes where the heavy rains had eroded it.

C-130's are large, four engine aircraft. As we watched the first plane approach, I wondered how the pilot would land that monster here, and then take off with a very heavy load. The cargo hold usually held about ninety men plus their gear. About one hundred twenty of us, plus the extra gear, were crammed in. Standing, we were literally back-to-belly, in rows from front to back. Each row of men held on to a cargo strap which was stretched from side to side in the aircraft.

The pilot was good. He didn't seem to have too much trouble landing, but stuffed with live men and live ammo, on a short, washboard airstrip not meant for such a large aircraft, he was about to earn his wings again. The plane creaked and groaned to the end of the runway, and turned around. We were ready to go in our chariot to hell. The pilot applied the brakes and started revving the engines. Inside the stuffed and stuffy cargo hold, the deafening scream and vibration of the engines made us think the plane was going to fly in pieces all over the runway. When the pilot finally released the brakes, the plane lurched forward and sent us stumbling backwards, holding onto the strap for dear life. I don't know why or how, with all those men pulling on the straps, the sides of the aircraft didn't collapse inward, but they held. We lumbered and bounced down the runway. Looking out the tiny window, which is standard for a cargo aircraft, I could see that we cleared the perimeter tree line by what must have been inches. It wouldn't surprise me to learn we hit some of the small limbs. That take off will be the subject of conversation for the pilot at the Officer's Club more than once, and he may even wake up nights dreaming he crashed. But, we made it up in the air.

We landed after about thirty minutes, and walked out onto an airstrip, near the town of Loc Ninh, that was snuggled in rubber trees seventy to eighty feet tall, growing right up to the edge of the airstrip, marching away, row after row, as far as the eye could see. This was the Societe des Caoutchoucs d'Extreme-Orient, a giant rubber tree plantation about seventy miles north of Saigon, very near the Cambodian border. Located on the edge of the Central Highlands, the climate and topography promised to be a little more hospitable than where we had been operating.

Before the C-130 could take off, a flight of Hueys came for us and we choppered northeast a short distance. The LZ was very small, with waist high grass. Only three Hueys could land at one time, the others circling until the LZ was clear. As each flight landed, we set out through the rubber trees with our hundred-pound loads of gear. Gratefully, we only went about half a mile and waited for the rest of the Battalion to come in.

I realized I hadn't eaten all day, but that wasn't unusual, because no one ate much the first day out. We were too busy, tensed up, nervous; just not hungry.

When everyone finally arrived, it was late in the day and time to dig in for the night. We set up around the edge of a squarish, open area. From a very small LZ in the perimeter, I was on the far side in a high corner where dense bamboo met the edge of the rubber trees. We picked a spot and started digging in. The ground was hard-packed dirt and rock, so progress was slow. This was very different than the mud we were usually operating in.

A flight of helicopters was flying very low around our perimeter for reconnaissance. Every time they flew over our position, I started itching all over, as though a thousand mosquitoes had just attacked me. After the third pass, I realized the chopper's rotor wash was blowing the sharp-tipped hair from the outer sheaths of the bamboo stalks, and they were sticking to my shirtless, sweaty skin. The accumulation was irritating my skin and the sweat made it burn. I rinsed off with a full canteen of water, but that helped only temporarily.

When our fighting holes were about three feet deep, word was passed to fill them in because we had to shift the perimeter for better fields of fire. We filled in, packed up and shifted this way, then that way. Nothing unusual about that, but it used a lot of time. The sun had set and we weren't dug in; we just didn't have much time. This is bad because the VC like to take advantage of our lack of cover.

When we started digging in again, Sgt. Bauer formed a five-man detail to go back to the LZ to get the mortar, if it had been left there. Somewhere in the hurried shuffle, it was lost; could still be back at Dau Tieng, on the plane, or in the LZ where we just landed. We took off with only a flashlight, no weapons, and thrashed around in the tall grass for about thirty minutes before we decided to give up. Sgt. Bauer said we'd have to go back in the morning.

We were exhausted, but we had duties to perform. We resumed digging, getting only a foot deep in the hard ground, when we heard the sound of a VC fifty one caliber machine gun. Looking up in the dark, green tracers were flying low over our perimeter. Of all the times to get hit, this had to be one of the worst. I'm convinced Charlie realized we hadn't had time to get organized, and wanted to use this to his advantage.

No Claymores or trip flares set out, holes weren't dug deep enough for cover, no DEFCON's had been set. I couldn't find my rifle or ammo in the dark. Fumbling in the dark for my weapon, I realized their machine gun was set up near the LZ we just came from. If we had stayed minutes longer, using a flashlight and carrying no weapons, we'd have been dead meat.

WHAM. WHAM. WHAM WHAM. Their mortar knew exactly where we were. I low crawled to my foot-deep fighting hole. WHAM. I said to myself, "Why didn't I get this hole dug just a little deeper?"

Suddenly the whole perimeter erupted; rifles, machine guns, thumpers, grenades. The noise was deafening. Red tracers spewed outward in every direction and bounced of rocks and trees, careening crazily. Incoming green tracers criss-crossed the red, grazing across our perimeter. RPG's hit, then more mortar rounds. The sounds of war were here this time, not somewhere off in the distance. And, they were getting louder.

I had my entrenching tool in one hand and my rifle in the other trying to decide which one to use. I mentally pictured the men in unfinished positions, some frantically digging deeper, others firing. The green tracers got heavier, meaning more VC were joining in the attack. I pictured the diggers dropping their shovels and begin firing back.

I opened fire; pick a direction, any direction. The little bastards are everywhere, all crazy from marijuana, ready to do anything, even something suicidal. I threw a few grenades in case, undetected, some of them had moved in close. Keep firing. The noise was deafening, awesome, and every kind imaginable. Men, young kids really, most of them younger than me, fighting for their lives, adrenalin spreading, blood pounding, sweat rolling. You just want to shoot them and end it, but you can't see them. All that wonderful training doesn't mean a thing, except the weapons training. Reload and fire, reload, fire, pour it out. Rise up out of your fighting hole just high enough to fire a magazine, then duck to reload.

You can sense the bullets passing by just overhead and don't want to rise up and fire, but you have no choice.

I was vaguely aware that my barrel was so hot that it was cooking the oil on it. The smell of burnt gunpowder was heavy. My senses picked out all sorts of smells, sounds, and flashes of light, but were storing them away for future reference.

Where's the artillery? Where's the damned artillery? Are they at their base club, drinking beer?

I sensed movement behind me in the HQ area, then footsteps pounding past me. In the dark, I couldn't see who it was or tell which direction they were going. RPG's spewed in, more mortar rounds hit nearby. Red and green tracers were criss-crossing everywhere; the air looked like a three-dimensional roadmap.

You can't think because too much is happening too fast to dwell on anything, just keep reacting, moving, firing. The intense sound keeps your trigger finger panicked, glued against the trigger. Your nerves squeeze your hand and you fire, reload, and fire again. You fear, more than sense, movement nearby to your left, then your right. You can't hear anyone over the gunfire if they are there. No Claymore, no trip flares. Terror makes you lash out, anger makes you curse.

My rifle jammed. "Not now, please." Now you've got to fix it. WHAM. WHAM. Dirt and rocks showered down on me. I hunkered down while I tried to unjam my weapon. Where's my cleaning rod? Must find it, but I'm not prepared for anything. Tracers passed nearby. My hands can't make things work right.

You curse, and then laugh at yourself, at your nervous, unfruitful efforts. If you get your rifle firing again, it won't change the outcome of the battle. But, it just might save your life. That's what it all comes down to, survival.

The sounds of battle are intimidating, oppressive, consuming. They weigh a million tons, demanding, overwhelming. You look up to make sure the enemy isn't close, and laugh at yourself again, at the wasted, panicky response, because it's too dark to see. Your mouth gets dry, tongue stuck to the roof of your mouth. You can't swallow.

You have no idea if anyone's been hit, if the enemy has gotten to the perimeter anywhere. You can't see anything; you can't hear anything above the sounds of the guns and explosions. It doesn't matter right now. The only thing that's important is me; I'm in the most important hole in the world.

Got it, it's unjammed. Reload and start firing again. I aimed at a nearby source of green tracers and worked on it.

A huge explosion flashed nearby; a VC rocket. They're not playing with us this time. The rocket exploded so close that shrapnel whirred overhead before I could duck. Bullets thudded into the bamboo and dirt near my hole, causing rocks and dirt to sting my face. Close. Time to get closer to Mother Earth. I wondered who was on the other end of those green tracers; NVA, females, kids, Chinese advisors? It didn't matter.

I was vaguely aware of something stinging me. At first I thought it was those bamboo hairs, but it kept getting worse. Ants. I'm lying in an ant bed. They're all over me and the bites were painful. Whoever said ants don't come out at night hadn't met these.

The sounds of war get even more intense. Bullets sprayed the bamboo above my head again. Leaves and chunks of bamboo fell on me. I began to realize the meaning of the expression, "so thick you could walk on it." That also means so thick you can't get up through it. The thought of a layer of flying bullets just above my head made me feel very uneasy. It's all very confusing, intimidating.

Along the line of positions forming our perimeter, I could see the vicious tongues of flame, spitting out their deadly streaks of light, searching for a target, impartially dealing out death. Pretty colors; hot orange, red, and yellow. Red fire, red blood. Red is the color of dying, black is the color of death. Fire. Reload. Fire.

WHAM. Thunk, thunk. A mortar round sends more deadly shrapnel whirring into the bamboo, and more bamboo pieces fall on me. That's getting a little too close.

We can't communicate from position to position, or even move around. We become isolated in our own little spaces. The fight seems to be one-on-one, you and each of them. It's a lonely, isolating feeling; each man has his own war to fight, his own life to defend. You are a team only by virtue of your placement before it all began. Don't stop shooting or you will make a weak spot in the perimeter. Hold on. Fire.

At first you try to stay aware of everything that's happening around you, to understand what's happening where. You try to anticipate and control the action involving you. But, so much is happening so fast, you can't do it. The activity is a sequence of events because they just happen that way, not because they were planned. There's no pattern, no sense, so you just give up. As the firefight continues, you don't care about anything except what's happening to you. That's all that's important.

WHAM. The fiery spray of a nearby explosion sends dirt and shrapnel over me. The shrapnel thuds into the bamboo thicket. The bright flash lights up trees, brush, and VC. Your night vision is spoiled for a short while. My gear is scattered all around me. In the darkness, I can't organize it so I can find it as I need it. No time for that anyway.

New sounds come from nearby; the sharp thudding of hand grenades and the louder sounds of Claymores. Some positions did get their mines set out, but when they are set off, that means the VC are close. More explosions, inside the perimeter, behind me.

Tracers help you adjust your aiming point. Adjust left to that source of tracers. He stopped. I stop so he can't zero in on me. Concentrate your fire on another source. There are fewer in front of me than while ago. But now, they are coming from behind me. Hold your position. Adrenalin must be running one hundred percent pure through my arteries, my pulse three hundred beats a minute. Sweat is streaming down my face. How long will this go on? Will we run out of ammo before they do?

Another new sound; artillery. They finally got it here. Relax your firing unless you have a good target. Reload some magazines; you've fired a lot of ammo. Check how much is left, if you can find it.

The artillery hit all around the perimeter, throwing shrapnel everywhere. Keep low; it's got to be close because Charlie is on our front porch. The barrage continued for a long time. Shell after shell came screaming in, close to the perimeter. The unrelenting urgency of the ground-jarring explosions makes you so tense you feel you could shatter like a pane of glass. When a round comes screaming in, every muscle in your body tenses. The earth heaves, and bounces you like a toy. Your brain tries to numb itself from the concussion of the explosion. You think the next shell will land on you, but they're being carefully controlled. Every few seconds, another shell hits.

I resumed firing out into the night. The incoming tracers had decreased noticeably. The flashes from the artillery sometimes highlight shadowy figures running. If you're fast with a gun, you can hit one of the moving targets. More artillery hit and I saw bodies flying in the air like limp rag dolls; just like in the movies. Red tracers reach out to the shadowy figures.

Green tracers sputtered here, then there.

The artillery eased up. There was a short pause in all the firing. I could hear movement here and there inside the perimeter, and a lot of hurried talking from the CO.

First Sergeant came stumbling by, checking on wounded and ammo. "Who's here? You OK?"

"OK, Top. No problems here," I answered, and he stumbled on, checking on his boys. WHAM. A mortar round exploded near where he was going, then several more.

Tracers broke loose again.

Artillery paused, but firing started up in front of me. I picked a source of green tracers and concentrated on it until it stopped, then adjusted to another. Green tracers started coming for me, and I reached for some grenades. I may need them if artillery doesn't come back.

Empty magazines are mixed in with the full ones; Gotta dig for the full ones.

What if the VC overrun the perimeter on the far side and sneak up on me from behind?

A machine gun sprayed through the bamboo overhead. I wonder how many men have been hit. Will the choppers try to come in the darkness and get the wounded, or wait until morning?

Another new sound joined us, screaming overhead. Fast movers, jet aircraft, made a pass to get their bearings. The twin exhaust flames climbed and turned; an F-4 Phantom jet, followed by his wingman. Their next run is low and hot; he dropped a Napalm bomb. Hot damn, show time. There was suddenly a giant curtain of fire, silently spreading, then the sound of the explosion. Then the rush of air sucked upward by the heat.

Two more jets swoop in for the attack, their engines screaming and the reddish-yellow burst of flames from the Napalm incendiary adds to your adrenalin rush. The pilots are good; their passes are close against the perimeter, where it's needed most. The bombs illuminate moving figures out there and red tracers stream toward them. The wall of flame is spreading, sending out heat and showers of sparks. Shadowy figures are engulfed by the flames. I opened fire on the stragglers and they crumpled. The light and the taste of blood make you confident and eager for more so you can get it over with.

The smell of burning flesh soon drifts by on the breeze. There are a lot of crispy critters out there.

A jet makes another pass. As he pulls up and turns, a stream of green tracers reaches up to him, but it's way behind, following harmlessly where the plane was a few seconds ago. The VC do not give up easily, but that was a little too ambitious. The jets made more runs, dropping Napalm and bombs. The sounds of the explosions were unbelievably loud. Huge red, yellow and orange balls of fire mushroomed all around us. The pilots were having a good time, and saving the day for us. But, the color of dying is all around us.

The jets left and it was deathly quiet, while fires burned here and there outside the perimeter. How long will the silence last?

Time to reload magazines and get your heart started again. I realized I didn't have my helmet on. I felt around and couldn't find it. How long had I been without it? Did I have it on when the attack began, or not have it on and panicked and overlooked it?

My ears rang from all the noise. The concussion from the bombs made them feel like they were full of cotton. I had to urinate badly, but I wasn't going to move, as if I would start it up again.

Green tracers started up again, and scattered mortar rounds hit. A firefight broke out on the far side of the perimeter. Then I heard a helicopter above and behind me, very close; a Huey. He wasn't flying by, but very slowly getting lower and closer. I looked back as if I could see him in the dark. No lights, but he was coming down in our perimeter. He must have been homing on a shielded strobe light. In complete darkness, with tracers and mortar rounds coming in, he landed for a few minutes and then took off. DUSTOFF, midnight MEDEVAC. Wounded Americans would probably live because that pilot had the guts to try it. It helps a little to know they will be there under any circumstances. I kept expecting him to hit some trees or get shot down, but he made it. Too bad he can't be awarded the CIB; he earned it but he's not in the Infantry. However, a Silver Star, or Bronze Star, would be deserved.

The firefight sputtered out, and it became quiet for a little while. Did they leave, or are they regrouping for another attack? Reload some magazines; no time to waste. But keep your senses alert for anything out there; sounds, light, anything.

Drink half a canteen of water and get your tongue unstuck from the top of your mouth. The night air is coolish, but the water is still warm from the daytime heat. My stomach was having trouble sliding down from my throat.

It's about 3 A.M. and I couldn't stand it anymore. I crawled a few feet and kneeled to urinate, still looking around but not able to see anything except lots of stars. The sky is incredibly clear and I could see millions of stars, far more than I've ever seen at home. It hasn't rained tonight, the first night in a while that it hasn't.

Combat is strange, frightening, confusing. Here is something you are a part of, but you have no control over. You've never been part of anything like this, so you can't relate to it. You just have to hang on, adding your part, wondering when it will end.

There is movement and low voices from the CP, but you can't tell who is making sounds, Americans or VC. That's why you must sound off when you move around at night, so you don't get shot.

I looked down the perimeter and saw green tracers starting up again. It was like a surreal world for just an instant because I could see the light before the sound; moving light but no noise. I was jerked back to reality by an AK's POP POP, and quickly crawled back to my shallow hole. The night's activities had all my senses keyed up, giving me hair trigger reflexes and eye movement. Every sound is noted and analyzed.

Here it goes again, green tracers coming in and red answering. Then thumpers and hand grenades, which said the VC are close to the perimeter. The recoilless rifle started firing beehive canister rounds, anti-personnel for close range. Incoming started hitting on my side of the perimeter so I located the sources and opened fire.

I've been shooting in the dark all night but I have no idea how many VC I've killed. I'll never know, but I don't want to know. It's kind of strange that in the civilized world, if someone is shot, there's an investigation to find out who did it. But here, it's just the opposite; if you don't shoot, you are guilty of neglect of duty.

The exchange of fire lasted for quite a while; you want to shoot them and end it but you can't see them. They heap honor on dying for their country making it desirable, almost like a death wish. To accomplish that, they get all wired up on marijuana and drugs so they can't think straight.

Rounds started hitting near my fighting hole. WHAM. WHAM. They had their mortar set up again. The firing started to get heavier. Here we go again; I pick out nearby sources of green tracers and began firing. This starts a duel; they open up on me as a source of red tracers. Mortar rounds hit near me again, showering me with rocks and dirt. There definitely are no Atheists in foxholes, at least, not in mine.

The night drags on and you lose all sense of time. Has it been going on for thirty minutes, or two hours?

A fire in the brush flares up exposing figures. I opened up and scored some more. They are still lurking around so be alert, keep looking.

I hear the drone of a C-47. That's got to be Puff, The Magic Dragon. Puff drops a giant flare, popping as it ignites, that lights up the entire area almost like daylight; light was never so welcome. OK, Charlie, show yourself. But, nobody is moving; it's deathly quiet except for the drone of Puff. The giant flare gently swings from side to side under its parachute, like a pendulum, the burning magnesium sizzling like bacon frying. Shadows move back and forth in response to the flare's movement. It's eerie. The trees seem to be alive, moving. Above the flare is a ghostly white trail of smoke. I never knew I'd be so thankful for just a little light.

Puff finds a target and starts firing. The hot-red, almost electric, stream of tracers makes a line of light that reaches all the way to the ground, followed by the sound of the gun. The gun fires so fast you can't hear the individual bullets being fired; just one long sound like the sky is being torn open by a solid line of tracers. The green tracers stop. The VC must be hiding, waiting for Puff to leave.

Still high above the ground, the flare burns out after several minutes. But, the crew in the plane has it timed and another flare ignites at the same time. After dropping the flare, Puff circles, searching for a target to decimate with those deadly guns. Charlie is either playing a waiting game, or has decided to *di di*.

Puff continued to circle, dropping flare after flare. I'll never know who the pilots were in the jets and Puff, but I'd sure like to buy them a steak dinner. Sometimes there is a short period of time between flares and everything is dark. You hope that wasn't the last flare. Don't leave now, Puff. The darkness closes in on you and your heart stops. Your stomach crawls up into your throat. Oh, shit, panic time. You feel stranded, deserted, left to die. Then, poof, another flare ignites.

About 4:30 A.M., Puff left. Now it's just you and the dark, holding on until dawn. Second to second, you expect all hell to break loose again. You're dead tired, but there's no danger of falling asleep.

Has Charlie left, or is he waiting to see if more war machines are coming for him? You just wait, and listen. There's no moon to see by.

The sounds of heavy artillery not too far away drift in on the night breeze. Must be at the airstrip where we landed. Sounds like they are having a big fight, too.

We've been here for only about ten hours, but it seems like a lifetime. You're numb, hollow, exhausted. You need sleep bad. You're burned out physically and emotionally; not temporarily, but another notch downward.

If Charlie hits again, we may be in trouble because we're low on ammo. Maybe we can throw our C-rations at them. They'll probably throw the Ham and Limas back.

It's deathly silent now, as though you're the only person in the world. You wonder what you'll see around you when the sun comes up. You don't know what to expect except there will be dead and wounded.

13

The sound of approaching Hueys woke me from my memories of the last eight months, and how it was that I wound up, so quickly, here in this mess. And, how I was transformed, like hundreds of thousands of other GI's who served in combat, from the boy next door to someone trying to shoot people. We'll never be the same after a year of this, it can't be done. Instead of good memories like sock hops, drag races, movies with friends, and backyard football, we will have memories of things no one wants to hear or talk about. We'll never be the innocent, fun loving boy next door. What do you do for excitement after living like this, doing what we did, and seeing what we saw?

We flew by helicopter to Song Be to form a security perimeter around an airstrip and an artillery position, next to an ARVN camp. The terrain was hilly and barren; no trees, no shade. Just across the airstrip from us was a 175-millimeter cannon emplacement. It fires a 150 pound projectile up to twenty miles. It was fired every hour, or so, around the clock, into Cambodia. When it did go off, it made about as much noise as artillery shells exploding.

The hot and wet season had made its full change to hot and dry, with only an occasional shower. Sunburn replaced jungle rot as the skin problem. Heat exhaustion became common in the hundred degree temperatures. The slightest breeze raised dust clouds which were inhaled, and covered everything, including our food. These filthy living conditions caused stomach and intestinal worms in many GI's.

The continuous days and nights of mental stress and physical exhaustion caused signs of emotional stress to show up; short tempers, depression, withdrawal, incoherent statements, and even self-inflicted wounds.

Battles like Loc Ninh accelerated the effects of the stress, and they showed up especially at night. Night brings a kind of paranoia; fear of mortars, fear of suicidal ground attacks. Looking out in the darkness, our imaginations would hear them coming. We dreaded having to sleep and tried to put it off. But, you can fight exhaustion for only so long.

When we did sleep, a "sixth sense" was very active. It was a mechanism developed for survival. It could distinguish between the sounds that signaled danger and the sounds that didn't. It let us sleep through the firing of the 175-millimeter cannon because that was definitely a sound made by us, but woke us at the snap of a twig or the lightest footfall, because that could be a sound made by the enemy as well as us. No doubt it saved many lives during the war. I don't know what the "sixth sense" was, but it did help many times in seemingly small ways. It seemed to be a deliberate effort by your body to keep aware of your daily life's usual activities so when something was out of the ordinary you immediately noticed it. It certainly wasn't some kind of ESP, but rather something that exists in the human brain and was utilized as a self-protection mechanism.

The first night, we were mortared. About fifty rounds walked all around our perimeter and wounded several men. Charlie was always taking shots at us and then running. Operating in large units, we made big, easy targets. The small guerilla teams had no trouble finding us in territory familiar to them, and unfamiliar to us, and they took great advantage of this fact. So, he was almost always on the offensive and we on the defensive. When we took the offensive, Charlie disappeared. It was a frustrating strategy, but very successful.

The next day, we stayed at the perimeter and finished fortifying our bunkers. Usually a sign we would be here for more than two or three nights. While we worked in the blazing sun, some kids came by to watch and talk. I guess they didn't have a school to attend, or any kind of work to do, so they came out to watch the war. Since we were mortared every night at Song Be, their job may have been gathering intelligence for the VC. Suspecting little kids, and females, was something unknown to all of us, until now.

When we finished, I sat down to rest and one of the kids sat next to me. Hair on chests and arms intrigued these little guys and this one absentmindedly stroked mine as we sat together during the break. We heard a C-130 taxi down the runway, so we turned to watch it take off. The runway was higher than us, on top of a high, flat area, like a plateau. When the pilot revved up his engines, an ARVN happened to be walking by, directly behind the plane. The Vietnamese are a small size people, and the blast of air from the propellers proved to be too much for him. The ARVN was blown head over heels, like a tumbleweed, down the hill. We had a good laugh at the ARVN's expense, the first such laugh for me in quite a few days. It felt good to do something more normal than the daily grind.

Night came and with it came another mortar attack. Later, someone called for artillery flares to check on movement outside the perimeter. We heard large rounds come whooshing out of the sky, and THUNK into the ground near us, but not explode. We couldn't figure out what was going on. More flares popped and more rounds came in. This time, one hit a GI. It hurt him pretty bad, but we found out what was happening. When artillery flares pop, the empty shell casing continues on its trajectory. Whoever was calling for the flares hadn't considered the fact someone would be at the other end of the trajectory from the artillery's firing position. It turned out an ARVN FO was responsible. This was the first of many times we worked with the ARVN's, and it predicted future events. Every time we worked with them, there was trouble.

The next day, it was our Company's turn to go on an airmobile assault. We choppered a short way and got back into the swing of the daily grind. The bugs, anxiety, pain, thorns, stink, and eyes searching for ambush and booby traps were all still there. The tropical sun was intense. Sweat poured as we fought our way through brush and tangle; soaked in minutes. The country was as hostile as ever. Welcome back to the hostile drudge.

The point man hit a booby trap. Fortunately, it didn't kill him but he was messed up pretty badly, and had to be MEDEVACed. While carrying him to a nearby road, which would be the LZ, we hit another booby trap. One man was killed, three wounded.

Thrashing around in the brush seemed like such a waste of time and men, but it was a big part of our war strategy; looking for the enemy to get on with it.

We came to a village that seemed to be abandoned, except for three villagers who didn't fare well at the hands of the VC. They had been tied to upright stakes, stomachs slit open, and left to die. The disfigured bodies of a man, woman, and child minus some parts and guts hanging out, were left for all the other villagers to see. The sight of tortured, helpless, innocent people was bad enough, but the child's body made every one of us angry. Flies, ants and other bugs had already started to feed on their flesh. Intentional atrocities, I knew America would never read about this because no newsmen were here. This was a favorite tactic of the VC, along with others like stealing, rape, and burning schools and houses. After an episode like this, the villagers wouldn't talk to GI's for fear the VC would torture or kill them. They were scared to death. When they wouldn't talk, GI's suspected them of hiding something. Consequently, the villagers were afraid of both sides, VC and GI's. Either side may decide to kill them. There was no place to hide. We went home in twelve months but they had to stay and do the best they could. This problem would affect the GI directly because the villagers would often say nothing to GI's about nearby danger such as mines, booby traps, and VC.

We buried the three bodies and searched the village for anything that was out of the ordinary. There were no personal belongings, food, clothing, daily household items, or animals. The VC had stolen everything they could carry. I guessed the villagers decided there was no reason to stay here any longer and probably joined the swell of Vietnamese moving to Saigon for safety.

The hooch Wesley and I searched must have been the village church. The outside was no different than any other hooch, except it was slightly larger and taller. Inside was one large, empty room. The sole piece of furniture was an ornate coffin-like box hanging, above head high, from the roof. We couldn't walk under it because of a waist high fence on the dirt floor, encircling the space directly under the box. We had no idea what it was, but it seemed to have a religious connection. What would our training manual have to say about a situation like this? We left quietly, in deference to the religious air, but I kept thinking that box would be a good place to hide weapons.

Except for our killed and wounded, the day was a waste; negative contact.

After we returned to the perimeter, before we were even able to rest, several of us were picked to go on a joint ambush patrol with some men from Company C. The perimeter had received fire during the day and we were to set up in the area the firing had come from. That sixth sense we had developed told us we would make contact; just something about it. We gathered at the perimeter just before sunset for a final briefing and a gear check. There was the usual quiet pre-ambush air while an Officer gave us the details. We were to set up on a trail about six hundred meters out. The ambush would be sprung with a Claymore. Contact was expected. Return would be after contact, or at sunrise, whichever came first. The expected target was the VC mortar team that fired on us every night. We were told to be set up before 2000 hours, 8 P.M.

I looked at the men forming our patrol and saw two kinds of guys; new guys, and the guys that had been in country for a while. The new guys, easily distinguishable by their new boots, helmet camouflage covers and uniforms, looked anxiously around them at the old timers, just as I once did, to see if they were doing the right thing, the right way. They still looked different from each other, still had their individuality. The old timers all looked the same; same expressionless look on their faces, same attitude, same emotions and same faded, dirty uniforms. They were all cut out by the same cookie cutter, the same rubber stamp image. We had evolved into the same war mechanism, moving along with the course of events, not controlling anything, just hanging on.

We moved out in single file, spread about five meters apart, quietly going to meet our next duty in the course of events that would eventually lead to home. Walking out to the trail, we were getting closer to the enemy. I hoped we weren't walking into an ambush ourselves.

I was a rifleman for this ambush, no particular duties or responsibilities, just firepower. I watched as assigned men went through the motions of their assigned duties; security, setting out Claymores, positioning personnel. We all knew the routine and got with the program.

We set up alongside the trail in a straight line, with three Claymores covering the kill zone. We were in low brush, with trees scattered around. The trail itself was fairly clear and open. Here we were again, in the dark, waiting, watching, listening, hungry, and fighting bugs. I hoped we wouldn't have to be awake all night. I was beat and would strongly prefer to shoot somebody and get it over with so I could go back and get a little sleep. I was definitely changing. I never thought I'd become such a person, wanting to shoot someone so I could sleep.

We didn't wait long. In about thirty minutes, we heard footsteps and occasional voices. I couldn't believe the VC would be so careless. I hoped the Vietnamese spoken was not by the nearby ARVN's. Shadowy figures moved along the trail. One, two, three, four of them. I hoped it was not a whole Company of VC and us with a trigger-happy patrol leader. I held my breath, hoping they wouldn't detect us, then turn and run. I wanted to sleep and they were our tickets.

BOOM. BOOM. BOOM. The signal Claymore was followed immediately by the other two. We sprayed the area with automatic weapons, rifles, and machine guns, but quickly stopped when there were no incoming green tracers. It was over in seconds. No sooner than the VC realized they had been ambushed, they were dead. Wham, bam, thank you, man. Fast, vicious, effective, the ambush was well timed and efficient. With security in place, we rounded up five bodies with weapons, but no mortar. They may have been going to get the mortar, stashed somewhere so they didn't have to carry it around.

We returned to camp and slept our one-on, one-off, for four or five hours.

At dawn, a helicopter dropped off mail bags and one mortar. We were going to be here a while, and fire the mortar every night. It seemed as though everyone was bound and determined to deprive us of sleep, one way or another.

The next few days were about the same; assaults and patrols with minimal contact; light mortar and sniper fire at night; killed and wounded due to booby traps; and stink, heat, thorns, bugs, sleepless nights, diarrhea, anxiety. We had returned to the pre-Loc Ninh pattern.

At night, we fired the mortar for H and I, and ambush coverage. The POOP of the mortar was drowned out by the giant BOOM of the 175, but we were here to protect them. It was very ironic.

Firing an hour, and then sleeping an hour, we managed to sleep about five hours a night and were happy to get that much.

We were in a dry spell in the fighting again, only small firefights here and there. It could be because we hurt the VC badly at Loc Ninh, or it could be part of Charlie's plan.

We received a group of new recruits the next day. Their number didn't bring our Company up to full strength, but every warm body helped. On the other hand, draft and recruiting standards had been lowered considerably because of the shrinking pool of qualified men, and it showed in our new guys. Among them were physically unfit, illiterates, and thugs. They weren't all bad guys, but they just weren't right for this kind of duty, at least not as a partner for me. I guessed someone felt these guys were a solution to the shortage problem but I felt it jeopardized both us and them. I was told later that these unfit men were the result of a new program by the Secretary of Defense. They were called 67's because the passing score for the Selective Service mental test had been lowered to 67 so more would pass and the numbers in the draft pool would increase.

It was about this time that I wondered if I could define combat, after thinking about how these guys should be labeled unfit. Or, if someone asked me to describe combat, what would I say? Shooting, death, blood, tension, depression, insecurity, exhaustion. All fit the common, classic description, but what about all those words you think of when you look at the methods used? Uncivilized, non-constructive, destructive, immoral, amoral, wasteful, insane, cruel, inhuman, barbaric, savage, brutal, vicious, ruthless, bloodthirsty, waste of life. It's the exact opposite of what you have learned while growing up. The exact opposite of what humans and nations strive to achieve. A step backward to go forward. Reverting to the other extreme to achieve progress. Killing to protect Freedom of Religion. Death to promote Freedom and Democracy. Violence to gain Peace, and to defend the right to vote. Dying to preserve life. Live and let live, or I'll kill you. It's all this and more, something that was slowly forming in my mind, but still nebulous.

All I know for sure was that my sense of right and wrong was getting confused, and that I was an insignificant number in the chaos. I understood nothing. I was just trying to survive.

After almost three weeks out, we boarded choppers to return to Dau Tieng. During the flight, I thought about how good a shower and clean clothes would feel. I looked at my grungy arms and fatigue jacket. They were stained white from the salt in sweat, and with oil, dirt, and Chief's blood. Going out with friends and coming back without them was getting very old, and very worrisome.

14

We returned to Dau Tieng too late in the day for hot food. It didn't matter though; we dropped our gear, stampeded to the shower, picked up our mail and were asleep shortly after dark. No one stirred for several hours but then we kept waking up every hour or so. I guess our bodies had been conditioned by weeks and months of little sleep in the field and felt as though we should be getting up for guard. Or, maybe we just couldn't believe the luxury of uninterrupted sleep and kept waking up to make sure it was true.

The next two days were to be spent resting, cleaning our gear, checking our weapons for repairs, and taking care of personal matters. Since there was no village entertainment of any kind, bars, or stores, we spent our time in the Company area. (In most of the news, films, and movies I've seen about Vietnam, Infantrymen seemed to have a lot of spare time to spend at bars, restaurants, a beach, or shopping. I don't know where they were stationed but we never saw any of these things, or had the time to enjoy them if we had.)

I divided my spare time between Jim and the men in the other platoons. In the field, you don't get to visit with anyone except the men in your own platoon, especially your squad. There were faces I had never seen before and there was a lot of information that hadn't made the rounds.

Jim told me he may have an M-14 for me in about a month. Somebody would be going home and he'd save it for me. Meantime, besides the frequent cleaning problems, he said the M-16 magazine was flimsy and the spring was kind of weak. He said to put eighteen rounds in the magazine instead of twenty. That way, the spring wouldn't weaken and cause feeding and seating failure of the last two rounds.

Unfortunately, there was a shortage of cleaning equipment and new magazines, so we just had to do the best we could. Our M-60 machine guns were old and very worn too. The gunners would be having their problems because no new guns, and not very many parts, were available.

The M-72 LAW had a history of failures. It was suspected that moisture in the trigger mechanism caused misfires.

Lt. Young would be leaving soon and no Officers were available to replace him. We were to have an E-5 Sergeant as our Platoon Leader.

Our Medic was due to leave the field. Again, there would be no replacement for a while.

With all the personnel in country, maybe half a million(?), we thought the fighting units should at least get some priority on men and weapons. We felt as though the whole war effort was falling apart at the most basic and important level, the Infantry. If you're going to be in a war, don't short the fighting units. After a while in county, you have to give up taking everything seriously. You take what comes, and do your best. You can't control anything, you can't change anything. You accept the realities of war. You'll find that either you are steady and confident right from the beginning, or you never will be.

The only good news was that on Thanksgiving Day, every soldier would have a hot turkey dinner, no matter where he was, by order of the Commanding General.

One of the new faces in the Company was one of Jim's and my Drill Instructors from Advanced Training, Sgt. Thoms. He was a hard-nosed instructor, tough, but fair. We didn't particularly like him, so it felt good to see him get a taste of the good life. We were anxious to see how he coped with the real thing. Even though he was in the Army by choice, it must have been extra difficult for him at this point because he had become a father during the past month.

Many people have asked if a lot of fighting went on in base camp, the tough soldier not getting enough thrill from combat, and picking fights to show how tough he is. This is one of the lies promoted by movies and books, along with drugs and sex, among other things, and it's not even close to the way it was. Not only were combat troops too tired to even consider such unnecessary strenuous activities, they had seen enough blood and pain, and just wanted to get away from anything that resembled fighting, to forget. Any fighting to prove macho prowess was carried on by base camp personnel, if at all. But, this misses a very important feature of a fighting unit; they had to depend on each other with their lives, to work together to survive. There certainly was not an environment of hostility between GI's. They did not work as an individual member, but worked together in teamwork. Bill Mauldin wrote in his WWII book, *Up Front*, "The surest way to become a pacifist is to join the Infantry." That sums it up very well, in base camp and for years to come.

The two days in camp passed very quickly and it was time to go back out to the boonies again, back to our home. This operation would be around the Dau Tieng area, mostly in the Rubber Plantation. There was a lot of VC movement in the area, especially near the villages and hamlets. The VC frequently stole food from the villagers because they didn't have a steady supply from the North. Special Forces and Recon patrols, affectionately known as Sneaky Pete, had detected movement of small units, all moving in the direction of Saigon and other large cities. Even so, we spent virtually one hundred percent of our time looking for VC. They were always around us but we couldn't find them, because they weren't ready for us to find them. They were under us in tunnels, mixed in with villagers, and hiding in the bush. Even when we fought, many times we couldn't see them.

On this operation, the walking would be easy through the Rubber trees. The area wouldn't be too bad for ambushes or booby traps, but it would be deadly for snipers.

A Scout Dog and Tracker Team would join us for a week or so. These teams, one man and one dog, usually a German Shepherd, had fairly good success sniffing out hiding places such as tunnels, and hearing movement, but the heat was harsh on the dogs. One thing we were told to be sure of was, never, ever get between the dog and his handler. The dogs were very protective.

This operation, I would travel light again. Between the heat and the long patrols walking in the Rubber, I didn't want any spare baggage. My gear and uniform had become more casual, less conventional. There weren't any gear requirements, except to be completely functional in your duties. In this heat and humidity, it would be very exhausting to carry all of it, or even most of it; it affected your maneuverability and quickly became litter the VC could use. It didn't take long to live happily without a gas mask, most of your grenades, half your canteens, bayonet, and your flak jacket. The only extra weight I would carry this time was an air mattress Jim had gotten for me. I'd have to blow it up every night, and deflate it every morning, but it would be softer than the sticks and rocks I had been sleeping on.

Waiting at the LZ for the choppers, everyone was quiet. I tried to think of something funny to say, or light talk about anything. What can you say at a time like this? Everybody knows what's coming. There's no humor that can lighten our feelings.

I asked Sgt. Bauer if he thought the LZ would be hot. He said, "I hope not. I may not be able to let go of the chopper door this time." His answer was unexpected, but I knew it was sincere. Things were starting to get to him. I could understand how he felt, but it shook my confidence and raised questions about how stable someone really would be when you get into a tight spot together.

The LZ wasn't hot. We took off into the Rubber trees, on our own again, back to the grind. It was all there, unchanging, waiting for us. We moved quietly through trees that were very old, almost ancient, as if they were the first Rubber trees planted in Vietnam. I didn't know exactly where we were, except that we were close to the Cambodian border. Charlie is here somewhere, we just haven't found him. After eight or nine kilometers, and no contact, the CO called a halt to set up our night perimeter.

The resupply chopper wouldn't come out until the second night, so we wouldn't be firing the mortar. I thought that would mean a good night's rest, but instead, I had to go out on LP. I don't know which is worse, flank or LP; both have high casualty rates.

Shortly after sunset, Wes and I took rifles, ammo, water, slap flares, and a radio and took off. Since the Rubber trees are wide open, not dense and bushy, we had to go about three hundred meters out, operating on the same principle as flank distance. Three hundred meters from safety, in the dark, we might as well have been three hundred miles. We did have a bright, full moon in our favor. We could see a long way. The gnarled trees and shadows made the area look like an evil, sinister place. It was not a place for someone who isn't stable.

Every hour, the Company RTO radioed us for a SITREP, requesting we break squelch twice for negative enemy movement, instead of talking and making noise. The call to us seemed loud enough to give our position away, even though we had the volume turned very low. There were stories in the Company about GI's who had OP but were afraid of being so far out there by themselves that they would sneak back toward the perimeter. Since they had to be quiet anyway, their position would not be given away to the perimeter, and they would spend the night a little more safely. Anyway, I believed the stories because it definitely was not an adventure being out there, isolated and alone.

Here we were again, watching, waiting, listening, mashing mosquitoes, and trying to stay awake. About 1 A.M., I thought I saw movement way off in the distance; no sound, just movement. I nudged Wes and pointed. We watched together but didn't see anything. I passed it off as tired eyes. We hadn't seen anything all day so there seemed to be no VC around. I knew better than to believe that, though. As the Officer at booby trap school said, "Don't think you were never in his sights..."

Since the radio volume was turned low, I was holding the handset to my ear. Soon, I heard another LP radio the CP that they had movement. There was definitely someone out there. The other LP pulled back to the perimeter. The VC fired and received a storm of return fire. We were told to stay in place in case the VC worked toward us around the perimeter. If there were just a few, we could ambush them. We got behind a tree for cover, in case any firing came in our direction.

The firing stopped, and it became deathly quiet. Now every shadow looked like a VC in black pajamas. The little guys are no bigger than a shadow, anyway. I wasn't sure if I wanted to see them and know where they were, or not see them and wonder if they are nearby.

A large cloud passed in front of the moon and it got so dark I couldn't see Wes sitting next to me.

We waited some more. The only sounds we heard were mosquitoes and the distant mutter of artillery.

After about an hour, we relaxed. I told Wes to get some sleep. That I'd stay awake. Tomorrow would be another long day. In minutes I would hear the regular breathing of his sleep.

POOP. POOP. In the distance I heard a mortar. Wesley popped upright as though he had been sleeping on a spring. I called the CP and they said they'd heard it, too. The VC probe must have been to find our perimeter so they could mortar us. Now what? There was no place to take cover and running back to the perimeter was definitely not healthy. More mortar rounds were fired. The first round hit way off target. They had the distance right but the direction was off. No DEFCON's had been set and by the time artillery could be called in the VC would be gone.

The mortar stopped and the CP said to stay out. So we tried to sleep, one-up, one-down, for the few hours until dawn. Maybe in the morning the dog could track the VC.

At dawn, we returned to the perimeter and had a quick can of rations as we moved out for the day.

We found the site where the mortar had been fired. The dog picked up a scent but lost it at a stream. After searching the area, we gave up and moved on.

Back to the grind, the same old stuff. We covered several kilometers with negative contact.

We set up a night position, carried supplies and the mortar in from the LZ, and started the nightly routine. I was too tired to blow up the mattress. It didn't matter anyway because I found a hole in it. I slept on the kind of ground cover that made the hole in the first place; sticks, rocks, thorns, whatever. So much for the comforts. We slept for an hour while another squad fired the mortar, then changed off. We totaled maybe four hours of sleep.

In the morning, we tore everything down, carried it to the LZ and took off.

Day after day, the pattern continued; start the day tired, hump mile after mile, dragging along. Quite often I thought it would be nice to make contact, just a sniper, so we could lie down, get off our feet, and rest. After Loc Ninh, I realized that killing was really the easy part of the war, and everything else was the hard part. Lying down and shooting was easy. This daily grind and nightly routine was killing us. It's kind of sad when you can honestly say something like that, and mean it sincerely.

Several more days of the same and we moved to another area. Waiting in the LZ, I could hear the pulsing, thrumming sound of the approaching Hueys, coming to take us out of here. To this day, my heart quickens when I hear the unmistakable sound of the Huey helicopter; not any helicopter, just the Huey. To some people, all helicopters sound alike. But, if you hear that special sound, for a year, the sound that means help, safety, or food, you'll never forget it.

The chopper I got on was a patched-up thing. It had body panels that were scavenged from at least five other helicopters. You could tell because there were different shades of green on different panels. Everything in this war seemed to be worn out and patched up; men, guns, and helicopters.

The overloaded, worn-out chopper lifted off the ground and started flying forward. The other choppers began to climb, but we didn't. We just kept going forward. At the end of the LZ were very tall trees, maybe two hundred feet tall. We kept flying straight at them, not climbing. The co-pilot pointed to a gauge that was labeled "Torque", and the dial indicated zero. The co-pilot tapped the gauge but it didn't change, staying at zero. I didn't know what that meant, but it was obvious we may be in some deep trouble. Unless something changed, and soon, we would either hit the trees or land back in the LZ, alone. We just kept going toward that tree. I thought about throwing gear overboard, to lighten the load, but I knew it wouldn't help. We just kept going toward that tree. Finally, the chopper slowly, ever so slowly, began to climb. I was sitting in the open door with my feet hanging out, the way I usually did, but I pulled my feet in because I could tell they would have been hit by the tree limbs as we finally passed just over the tree. That was the second time we almost hit tree limbs during take-off, if you count the C-130 take-off at Dau Tieng. I hoped there wouldn't be any more of those.

The area we flew to was around some villages where Rubber tree workers lived. We had covered the area before, the same villages, and found nothing. The Scout Dog and Tracker stayed on the chopper and returned to base. We entered the first village and encountered some females. They said, "No VC here. No VC here." It seemed as though they met us at the edge of the village to deliver their message so maybe we would go elsewhere; not a good sign. Nobody paid much attention to them, but they insisted, "No VC here. VC numbah ten." We searched a few of the hooches and found nothing, the females following close behind. For all we knew, the females could be the VC.

The CO told us to spread out and sweep the village, checking everything. My platoon spread out and, with me the end man, I joined up with Sgt. Thoms and his platoon. He either didn't recognize me, or didn't want to, because he said nothing. Perhaps my eyes and face had changed to what I saw when I was new in country. Maybe I looked like every other GI, another rubber stamp image. It really didn't matter though, because we had work to do.

This village had more trees and bushes than usual, so there were more suspicious areas. This caused me to walk slowly from spot to spot, and often forced us to walk single file. At one of the narrow spots, I was walking in front of Sgt. Thoms. I was uneasy in this area and was walking very slowly, causing Sgt. Thoms to step on my heels occasionally. When I came to an open area at the edge of the trees, I stopped to look around before stepping out. I had that feeling. Sgt. Thoms bumped into me from the rear and said, "All right, Specialist. Step it up or step aside." This was my cue to hop to, which I would have done if we were in the states; act gung ho. Not here, though. That "sixth sense" wouldn't let me, so I stepped aside. As Sgt. Thoms walked by, I said, "I don't like it, Sarge. Bad feeling, bad news. I can feel it." I should have saved my breath. Sgt. Thoms walked past me, maybe ten feet, and POP. He fell dead, half his head blown away by one AK-47 round, hit in the face. That was almost me. Almost, again. While I looked at him and tried to find the sniper, I thought to myself, "I knew something was going to happen. I could feel it. I told you of my intuition and you didn't believe me. That bullet would have gotten me if you hadn't been in a hurry. But, I'm going to carry you to the LZ myself. It's the least I can do for you.

We looked for the sniper, maneuvering through banana trees and bushes, radios crackling here and there as we moved along. Nothing. He must have crawled into a tunnel somewhere, or he was a she. There were females still in the village. Some were the ones who had said, "No VC here." They returned our stares as though they were watching a television; no emotion. They acted disinterested, but they weren't going away, or hiding from the firing that might result on discovery of the sniper. Something was wrong here, something was going to happen.

A platoon of men was split off to take our KIA to an LZ about a quarter mile away. A helicopter was on his way to pick him up. Several men offered to help me carry Sgt. Thoms' body but I wanted to do this myself, for him. That was a long quarter mile, and I didn't think I was going to make it. But, I did. Somebody helped me lay his body on the floor of the chopper, and then he was gone. Somehow, I felt as though a part of my own life was gone, too. I wiped my bloody hands on my pants and we took off for the village.

BOOM. A huge explosion came from the edge of the village, followed shortly by screams, yells, and a cloud of dust and smoke.

Somebody had hit a booby trap. Then a firefight broke out; rifles and machine guns fired, and it was over in less than a minute.

We ran back. On the ground by a fresh crater, where a trail entered brush, were several GI casualties. Near a hooch were Vietnamese bodies. We suspected what happened, just didn't know details.

I asked and a guy named Dyer from Third Platoon told us. "We came this way to search. There was a noise in the bush and a team broke off to check it out, and they hit a trap. They were baited, and she just watched." He pointed to one of the bodies. "She knew and said nothing. She just watched while GI's died." Dyer pointed his rifle again. "That kid and another female came running out of that hooch with rifles." He pointed to more bodies. "They fired and hit Louis. He opened up and got all of them. Somebody fired at us from that hooch and got another one. Some of the rounds went through the hooch and killed a kid. We didn't know." His voice broke a little from emotion. "We couldn't see it. They shouldn't have been shooting with a kid in there. It all happened so fast. They must have been crazy. A young kid. We didn't know."

I said, "Yeah, but if you had known there was a kid in the hooch, would you have let them shoot all of you anyway? Besides, how do you know it wasn't one of them that shot the youngster? Their bullets were flying around, too. They may have even done it on purpose. Or, that kid may have been firing a weapon."

We had no instructions for encounters like this, "When to shoot and when not to shoot." The book we learned from, and were to go by, assumed the enemy was not only a man, but known to us to be the enemy. That, and nothing else. So we just had to do the best we could in any situation. The shock of such an incident was worse than shooting a man because you haven't mentally prepared yourself for such a thing.

He settled down after realizing they had been forced into a position where they had no choice. It was a question of survival. Who was guilty? The women who said, "No VC here"? If they knew anything, they would probably deny it. The women who knew there was a booby trap here? Most likely, they were all guilty. We knew the VC used children as pawns, and they also trained women and children to kill because GI's drop their guard when confronted by them. They can't believe women and children are killers, and that has cost many GI's their lives. The obvious results were that the GI's would be labeled war criminals by their own country, the number one goal of North Vietnam, for killing a female or a child, or that GI's would be shamed because a mere child had killed one of them, a trained soldier. The residual effects in the GI's daily lives were that they knew they could not trust women or children, desensitization, callousness, and the silent anger within that keeps building, an anger which is fueled by frustration, horror, and now insecurity. Insecurity is felt because you don't know if you can trust any Vietnamese, and because you have this doubt forming whether or not we belong here, whether or not the people really want us here.

I was glad there were no news people around. We would have been crucified by a picture of the child's body.

It was strange that these people had sacrificed themselves so openly. A thorough search of the village failed to turn up anything big so we guessed they were covering the hasty exit of some VC unit of soldiers, or maybe wounded. The delay in our movement was evidently successful.

We finally left the village and continued on our sweep. The routine continued; humping all day, searching villages, ambush patrols, and, dog tired, firing the mortar at night.

At night, we were mortared occasionally. The following day we would search a nearby village and usually find nothing. We didn't trust any of the people anymore, we never knew what to expect from them.

An ambush scored several VC killed and wounded, but the mortar attacks at night continued. The VC were watching us, or were getting their intelligence from the villagers, or they were the villagers, because they always knew where we were going.

Heat, exhaustion, long patrols by day, and sleepless nights were wearing us thin. The only break we had was for about two hours on Thanksgiving Day. A chopper brought a hot Turkey meal with all the trimmings. We even had ice cream, which melted before we could eat it. It didn't matter because the sight of ice cream, the fact that it still existed somewhere in the world, was enough. The meal filled two paper plates per man, more food than we had seen in a long time.

An Army photographer also came out on the chopper and took some pictures of us eating. I realized that anyone looking at these pictures would undoubtedly think it wasn't too bad in the field. It just shows an isolated moment though, not the bigger picture.

We continued working the area for several more days. Except for another successful ambush which gave us an operational total of eight VC KIA and ten WIA, we turned up nothing.

We flew to another area to see if we could stir up something. This time we were back in the jungle with its smothering heat, humidity, bugs and dense foliage. Salt tablets disappeared like candy. Skin problems multiplied, diarrhea got worse, self-inflicted wounds, called accidents, became disturbingly common. We had a rash of mysteriously broken eye glasses, which Army Regulations said disqualified the person from combat until replacements were made and delivered.

Every night we had movement outside the perimeter. It was dark under the jungle canopy and imagination made you think the enemy was about to hit. Nerves and imagination made you try to put sleep off as long as you could. At the slightest sound, you woke up thinking of Loc Ninh and ground attacks. Having to sleep is bad enough, but sleeping at night, in complete darkness, is very uneasy. You know your buddy on guard is tired and fighting to stay awake. There's nothing between you and whatever is out there, when anything is out there.

One night around 2 A.M., a new guy was sitting up on guard and dozed off. He was suddenly awakened by noise just a few feet in front of him. In the complete darkness, he lost his rifle and panicked when something large jumped at him and hit him. The GI jumped up and ran down the perimeter yelling and stepping on everybody. Someone tackled him and he calmed down. The thing that jumped at him turned out to be a wild pig rooting in the leaves for something to eat. The GI never did live that down.

Day after day, we fought our way through hostile country, searching for the VC, with negative contact. We passed through another defoliated area, bleak and withered. It was supposed to help, but you couldn't prove it by our experiences.

In the mornings, we often encountered ground fog, an ideal place to be ambushed. Moving into it we were blind.

In the evenings, soaked in sweat and covered with scratches, we tried to find old bomb craters. They almost always had water in them and a quick dip in the stagnant water, clothes and all, was a morale booster.

After being in firefights, and spending countless days humping the boonies, everybody definitely agreed that killing was the easy part of everything, and all the rest was the hard part of combat. But, no matter what we did on any given day, we always felt as bad as a day in Vietnam.

On our next to last day out, we saw an American fighter plane crash. There was no trail of smoke, no parachute, and no explosion. He just went down. It looked to be less than a mile away. We set out to rescue the pilot, spending most of the day traveling the short distance through the dense growth. The plane was still largely intact, the crash softened by the tall trees and dense foliage. We searched the wreckage, and a large area around it, but found no sign of the pilot. We never heard what happened to him but we suspected the VC beat us to him and took him across the Cambodian border.

Charlie was around us, no doubt about it. He just wasn't ready to fight again, not yet. Not in this area, anyway.

After several weeks, this operation ended and we returned to Dau Tieng a little more bitter, more insecure, and a lot more tired.

15

Something called Operation Diamondhead was now over. None of us heard about it at the time, except probably at Brigade and Division levels. My Brigade, the Third, got credit for over 200 VC KIA and nearly 500 POW's. The Second Brigade destroyed many kilometers of tunnels, thousands of acres of jungle, nearly 200 tons of rice, and recovered VC documents of achievements, awards, and promotions. They also helped the South Vietnamese people by giving them ten tons of clothing, eight tons of food, 17,000 bars of soap, and two sewing machines. I saw some of the people wearing their donated clothing. It was kind of sad, and kind of humorous, to see the little kids wearing a dress shirt which hung below their knees, and no pants or shoes, or a shirt that said, "Disneyland" above a picture of the castle there, a place they probably had never heard of but would give anything to see. They didn't care; they were proud of every item.

The Second Brigade also painted the maternity ward and a school classroom at Hoc Mon, and rebuilt and painted the entrance to Bao Trai. They had only one color of paint so almost the entire town was the same color, but the villagers weren't worried about airs. At the Division level, 75 million leaflets had been dropped in our area, over 100 VC had defected (Hoi Chanh) and 5000 more GI's had gone through the school at Cu Chi. We were, and would continue, working at the war effort from both sides; fighting the VC and helping the South Vietnamese. Every effort showed progress. More of the enemy were being killed than were Americans. I have no doubt we could have won the war using the strategy employed, if we had been willing to make a long-term commitment; very long term. But, a long term commitment was never our intention. Proper wartime military strategy was never employed either, so the GI just continued to pour out his heart and blood until the conscience of the American public could no longer allow it.

This trip to base camp coincided with the one quarter mark of my one-year tour. If I can just handle doing all that three more times then I'll have to go home because my "All Expenses Paid" are for only one year.

This trip also marked the first time I looked in a mirror and saw a stranger with that look in his eyes; the sunken eyes and the distant, ice cold stare that slices right through you. When you realize that you are looking at yourself, it's frightening. You could call it a symptom of combat *dinky dau*, crazy from combat.

For the next few days, we made daily Combat Assaults out of Dau Tieng. It was nice to look forward to sleeping on a cot every night, instead of mud, but not so great to risk hot LZ's every day.

I didn't have to go on the first assault. I was told to go on a MEDCAP (Medical Civil Action Program – providing medical care for the villagers, such as inoculation for smallpox and cholera). In two choppers, we had one Doctor, a couple of medics, and eight Grunts for security in the village while the Doctor was working. I'm sure the village was supposed to be safe from VC, but I didn't like the feel of the whole thing.

The chopper dropped us off at about ten in the morning, and would come back for us about three in the afternoon.

We spent those hours "Winning Hearts and Minds" through medical care, sharing our rations, talking with the people, and playing with the children. Once in a while, we would ask the Vietnamese what their word is for something, for example water, or tree, and they would ask us. We had a back and forth time of laughter and good times. These kids were too young to have been indoctrinated by the VC, so all was innocent visiting. There were no problems with VC, but we felt relief when boarding the choppers in a field next to the village. As the choppers were climbing over the village, the engine on my chopper stopped and we started falling. Someone in the village where we had just won hearts and minds shot us down. The chopper felt as though it was falling out from under me. My rear end was trying to hold onto the floor. There was no engine noise, just the wind. There are no atheists in foxholes, or in falling helicopters. I thought of the pilot that crashed in the jungle and disappeared. Damn. After everything I have survived on the ground, I'm going to die in the air. This is it, it's over. I'm going to be splattered all over some village by one of the villagers we just tried to help.

I looked at the pilot. He was fighting with the controls and my first thought was., "The stupid SOB doesn't even know yet." We fell some more and then I felt some lift. Of course. The pilot was doing auto rotation; the air rushing through the falling helicopter's blades was providing lift and the pilot was manipulating the blades. I hoped he knew what he was doing and that the chopper didn't go to pieces before I had a chance to get out. He did and it didn't. We landed with a thud, bounced and almost tipped over. We Grunts ran outward to form security around the helicopter, happy that we could get off. The second chopper landed, dropped off the Grunts, picked up our passengers and pilots, and left us with a useless chopper, a radio, sore butts, and an unfriendly village nearby.

Nothing like this was ever mentioned in training so we weren't sure exactly what we were supposed to do. None of the villagers came out to see if they could help. We weren't surprised, but it convinced us that the entire village was sympathetic to the VC.

In about an hour, a Huey dropped a team of GI's. They rigged the downed chopper so it could be slung under a Chinook and taken back to base for repairs, or used for spare parts. Finally, after waiting four or five hours, the Chinook came back with a Huey and we all left. We had no more sniper fire, but every one of us wanted to burn that damned village to the ground.

For this mission, and a few others, the Republic of Vietnam awarded us a citation, a medal for Civil Action, the Cross of Gallantry, and the Fourragere.

Back at Dau Tieng, we were told that Military Intelligence had warned of a mortar attack that night on Dau Tieng. I never did figure out how they knew these things were going to happen but couldn't do anything about it. Sure enough, about two in the morning, mortars started falling. I was sharing Jim's hooch with him and we heard the rounds in our sleep. They were falling at the other end of the base camp so we kept sleeping. The rounds kept coming in and walking closer and closer to us. When they started hitting about two hundred meters from us, Jim said, "They're starting to get close. Guess we better get up." Just as we gave up our sleep, the attack stopped. From our Company area, we could see the fuel dump had been hit and the sky was bright orange from the flames. Damage was already done to communication equipment, trucks, tents, and American lives. It was another example of how a few VC could take pot shots at large American installations and not miss. We, on the other hand, never had the luxury of large, fixed targets. We had to hunt for ours, and they were usually small, and not fixed.

The next day, I went on an Eagle Flight to some area that looked vaguely familiar. We were looking for VC movement near the border area. It was a wasted day except two new guys on flank in Charlie Company were wounded by a booby trap. They decided to follow a trail instead of cut through the brush; looking for the path of least resistance, the easy way. Otherwise, negative contact.

We would eventually learn that all the VC movement in this area was toward Saigon for their Tet '68 offensive. The VC were moving in small units and hiding to prevent contact to ensure a sizable number had made it to their objective.

The next day, I rode shotgun on a truck going to a large base to pick up items for our Supply Sergeant. I thought it would be kind of fun for a change and get a break from the war. The truck I was assigned to had a driver with goggles and a scarf hanging around his neck. I thought, "Great. Looks like some kind of gung ho, hot dog weirdo." The driver put on his goggles and the scarf over his nose and mouth, and we took off on the dustiest ride I have ever had. We were in a thick, choking cloud of dust the entire trip, and the dust stuck to our sweat soaked skin and fatigues, changing us to the reddish-brown color of the dirt. After that trip, I dug dirt out of my ears and nose for a week. The ride was uneventful otherwise; no ambushes, no scenery through the dust, and no radio to listen to.

After we took care of business, the driver suggested we wet our whistle, and he got no argument from me. It was then that I got my first look at life in a big base camp. This wasn't the best base in the country, but it wasn't the worst by a long way. I saw a movie screen, hot showers, a big PX, ice, air conditioners, ice cream and other things I had forgotten existed. I could spend the war at a place like this, very easily. It was probably better duty than in the States because there wasn't as much of the petty harassment. We went into a small Enlisted Men's club to get something to drink. It wasn't fancy by any means. It was just a wooden shack, with a makeshift bar, and large floor-type ice chests with soda and beer. But, it was the fanciest thing I had seen in a long time. Feeling conspicuously out of place, I took off my helmet as we entered, an Army Regulation learned Stateside. The driver forgot, and we were greeted by a bartender ringing a bell, smiling from ear to ear, and pointing to a sign that said, "He who enters covered here, buys the house a round of cheer." So, my friend bought ice cold drinks for me and eight guys in the club. I have often wondered what those eight guys did for the war that allowed them time to sit in a club in the middle of the day. We didn't stay long because someone had to fight the war.

The driver made one last stop before we took off. He picked up something called a SP pack (Sundry Pack), something I in the field had never seen or heard of since my time in country. It was a large box filled with every kind of thing you could think of for use by the GI's in the field; candy, gum, cigarettes, razor blades, stationery, pencils and more. I wondered why we, the soldiers in the jungles and paddies, weren't getting these goodies, and who was getting our share. Were they even getting out of base camp?

I looked back as we left and decided that was the only way to fight a war, if you can get away with it, and maybe that was part of the reason why the war kept dragging on; so many GI's in a comfortable camp and always short-handed in the field? Seems like we in the field were in a war, and in base camps they were just here, enjoying a good life. Are we at war, or are we not at war? Where in the Military chain of Command

and responsibility was it decided that we in the field, the one in ten, are the only ones carrying our fair share of the war and everybody else was just pooping around? There is just that much more bitterness and frustration building in the combat troops.

We got back to Dau Tieng without any problems. I couldn't see much scenery because of the dust, but I had seen all of the country I wanted to see by now anyway.

We stopped at Battalion Headquarters to check into camp. While the driver was inside, a fight broke out across the road. A group of mercenaries from various countries was spending a day or two in Dau Tieng and, not surprisingly, a disagreement led to a fight. I watched as the group formed a circle around the two fighting men, cheering them on. No GI's went over there because the mercenaries were not subject to our rules, and if there was trouble it could get sticky. One of the mercenaries was getting the better of his opponent until a shot rang out from a concealed pistol. The cheering stopped, the circle broke up and a body was left lying on the ground. In fact, it stayed there for a couple of days because the group had no leader; each man operated independently, responsible only to himself. When the group finally left Dau Tieng, somebody buried the body to keep down the smell and the bugs.

From Headquarters, we drove toward Bravo Company area and passed Vietnamese workers on their way home. The American Government provided jobs for many Vietnamese on American military installations. They worked for different amounts, usually one hundred piasters per day (about one dollar). They performed menial tasks, such as sweeping and filling sandbags, but a few were skilled, such as barbers. Rumor had it that one of the barbers working on base was a VC and was killed trying to infiltrate the camp perimeter at night. There was no doubt that some of them were VC, or sympathizers. It was an ideal way for the enemy to locate strategic points for a mortar attack or overhear useful information. The idea was to help the South Vietnamese, but I think the program did us more harm than good.

We arrived at the Company area at the same time as a truck from the helipad. On the truck was a guy wounded during our operation in the Ho Bo Woods. He was being returned to duty even though he couldn't lift his arm above shoulder height because of pain and healing muscles. I heard of wounded being sent back to their units even though they weren't fit for duty, and now I was seeing the first of many in our Battalion that would be returned too early; unfit. I talked to him and he was bitter. He said the medical personnel had orders to return everyone as quickly as possible because unit strength was way below requirements. So the Grunts would have to pay for the manpower shortage. He showed me the large red scar on his shoulder and I hurt for him. I was glad it wasn't me trying to hump a load and have that pain to live with. He handed me a pair of boots before he left. Somebody from Bravo had been hit on today's Eagle Flight and all that was being returned by the hospital was one dog tag inside one of the boots. I read the name; it was a new guy. He probably hit a booby trap following the path of least resistance.

The next day, Delta Company sent out an ambush patrol. They spotted three VC digging in and called for artillery. The result was three VC killed and two bicycles captured. The combat assaults continued for a few more days, mostly with no contact. It was evident that Charlie was hiding so we would have to move to another area to look for him and carry on the war.

16

In camp the night before going out on an operation, it was often a solemn affair. No one wanted to go back out to the boonies, the jungle and the paddies, and no one could think of anything to say to get our minds off tomorrow. After several months in country, the gripes slowed down and things were accepted with numbed silence. Nothing can be done about any of it, short of self-inflicted wounds, and there a few of those.

There was a little hope, flickering, like a small candle; rumors of Peace Talks. They were supposed to start soon and everyone was silently hoping they would be short so we could go home.

Meantime, it's back to the field. This time we'll go to LZ Gold, near Soui Tre. We will work with the ARVN's and sweep the area on the Cambodian border again.

Weapons Platoon was to carry a flame thrower. I'm glad it wasn't me. The thing weighed over 40 pounds, was very clumsy, and if the tank was hit by a tracer the bearer would become a crispy critter.

Waiting at the helipad the next day, I was more than a little surprised to see the ARVN's carrying medical stretchers to the field, and not just a few. There seemed to be one stretcher for about every twelve to fifteen men. I wasn't sure if they were trying to be prepared of if the litters represented knowledge based on past experience.

Back to the grind. We started our long sweeps through jungle, brush, heat, thorns, bugs, and diarrhea, looking for Charlie. He was nowhere to be seen but booby traps and punji pits told us he had been around recently. We lost men due to those booby traps, and due to the heat. We pushed on even though our ranks were slowly dwindling.

Patrolling from sunrise to sunset, setting up a night position, firing the mortar, the back-breaking, mind numbing routine was always our daily fare. We looked for any excuse to stop and rest, to get off our feet, and get the heavy gear off our backs. We walked to the point of paralysis, losing alertness, concentrating on the effort needed for that next step, our eyes on the ground in front of us, not paying much attention to much else. Our sphere of awareness shrunk to the effort required to take the next step, to get through this and survive. We passed a Montagnard walled city. (Montagnards are a primitive, smallish tribal people who live mostly in the highlands. The name is supposedly derived from a French word meaning Mountaineer. The city looked like something out of medieval history. It was out in the middle of nowhere, nothing nearby. It was almost circular, maybe 700 to 800 feet across. The wall around the city was almost thirty feet tall, was made of logs sunk vertically into the ground. The logs were about two feet in diameter and fastened together, no space between them. We couldn't see into the city; there were no windows in the wall, and only one gate, which was closed. The wall must have required monumental effort to build, especially by the smallish Montagnard people. Not a single person was to be seen. There was no sound coming from the city. I could feel eyes watching us as we walked part way around it. It was an eerie experience.

As we continued walking, there was a B-52 bomb attack some miles away. It's an awesome thing to hear and see. It sounds like the Earth is exploding, smoke and dust billow high, and dense. We walked through the bombed area two days later and I couldn't believe the total devastation. Nothing was standing. Nothing. The ground was marked by huge craters and there was only dirt between them; no standing trees, no grass, nothing.

We set up for the night, and Muleskinner brought the mortar, and the mail, which had two one-pound canned hams from my sister. Real ham, it was like gold. I knew my shrunken stomach couldn't hold a whole ham so I shared one with Wesley. I told him I would share the second one with him in a few days if he carried the extra weight. He agreed. I made sure nothing happened to him for those few days, as best as I could.

That night the FO set the DEFCON's with air bursts of (Willie Peter) white phosphorus shells. The second shell burst directly overhead and burning phosphorus ash showered down on us. Phosphorus will eat its way through your body, unless you flush the area with water to rinse it off, not to extinguish it because it can't be put out like a regular fire. If you try to brush it off like dirt, it spreads and burns a larger area. Much precious water was wasted and many burn scars were received that night.

As with almost every previous day in country, we spent the night in a different place than before. We had to familiarize ourselves with our surroundings so when we were awakened by firing, or for guard, we could find our way around in the dark. It's not an easy thing to wake up befuddled from a sleep of exhaustion, which is not enough to recover all your wits, and know where everything is, and exactly what to do immediately, and even more so when everything is different every night. It was not unusual to hear a GI groping around in the dark until he woke his brain and got his bearings.

The next morning, we choppered to base, and then flew immediately to Katum by plane. Katum was a large fire support base being built near the Cambodian border. This would be our first operation with an armored unit (basically Armor is Armored Personnel Carriers (APC) and tanks; any vehicle with tracks). The terrain we usually worked in was too difficult for Armor to negotiate. It had to be done on foot and by sweat. The terrain here was fairly open. We were to provide security for them, protection. The Armored units did pretty much the same thing we did, but instead of being afoot, they rode and carried many of the "luxury" items with them, the items we left in camp because of weight. It was a nice step up from the Infantry.

We thought we would see some action here as VC units crossed the border. Their Central Office in South Vietnam, or COSVN, was thought to be nearby in Cambodia. But, it turned out to be more of the same old grind. Endless days on foot, searching. The Infantry got the brushy areas; the armored units got the open areas. We found many trenches and fortifications, and even slipped across the border into Cambodia to look around. Since we weren't supposed to be in Cambodia, we had orders not to shoot, but to reconnoiter and gather intelligence. We found an abandoned barracks and quite a few graves.

Sunburn was a severe problem. Many GI's burned pretty bad and some became heat casualties.

A large camp with many men has a garbage problem. The accumulation of trash at Katum drew rats, roaches, flies, and every other creature you could think of.

Aside from booby traps, the ten days we spent there had only two incidents which were signs of enemy presence.

The first was when someone in another company was checking their Claymores. One of the mines had been turned around so it would kill GI's when it was detonated. Another mine had the detonation wires cut. Some VC had evidently crawled out to the perimeter at night and decided to play a good joke on us.

The second incident involved my Company. We were fortunate enough to have hot food in the evening for a few days. Some VC must have been watching us from a distant tree line when we gathered for food, and decided a few mortar rounds might get some of us. When we heard the mortar fire, we dove for cover. They fired just a few rounds and came pretty close. The next day, the same thing happened at the same time. We were caught unprepared after a long day. The third day we set up our mortar about an hour before chow, then continued with our routine. When we heard the first round fired, we estimated the range and direction and sent out a barrage of our own. As we fired, I did a search of the impact area by using Search and Traverse, and that was the last we heard from them.

Search is distance from you, and Traverse is left to right, or right to left, at a set distance. For example, you might start at 900 meters out, and fire 4 rounds going from left to right every fifty meters. Then increase the distance to 1,000 meters and fire rounds 4 rounds from right to left. Then continue this pattern to cover the suspected area.

Otherwise, it was the usual mind-numbing, back breaking routine of humping from dawn to dusk, and firing the mortar all night. We were pushed hard all day, all night, every day, and every night. We never gave up, we kept trying, but it was frustrating.

The human body can take only so much of this physical abuse; lack of sleep, strenuous days and nights, and poor living conditions. The effects showed up every so often, and in different ways. One of the most common was falling asleep on guard. Whenever someone woke up and realized there was no guard awake in our position, the culprit could be determined by looking to see who had my watch on, which was the only watch in the squad. Whoever had it on was the guilty party. Some of the guys took advantage of this and, if they were on guard but wanted to sleep, they would slip the watch on the arm of someone sleeping and then lie down and get a little sleep themselves. This would only happen when we were in an area that was relatively secure, having had no contact or movement by the enemy, and our night camp was large.

We choppered to the Ho Bo Woods-Boi Loi Woods area which we had worked before, but that didn't mean a thing because the VC were constantly moving in. We had to return to areas again and again. If we stayed away too long, the VC took advantage of that, and built camps and dug tunnels. This time, we were to prevent the VC from stealing the rice harvest from the South Vietnamese farmers.

It was still more of the grind, with occasional firefights. We killed over a hundred VC in about a week and lost twenty seven GI's.

In one fight, my company was moving through brush when we came to a hamlet. The South Vietnamese ignored us, except for the children. As we moved around the village, the point man hit a booby trap. The Vietnamese surely knew it was there but didn't try to warn us. We spread out around the casualty to protect him and the Medic, and started receiving heavy rifle fire. Two more GI's were hit. We tried to get to the wounded and pull them back for medical attention, and a squad was pinned down. We couldn't get to them and they couldn't move back. The VC brought in a machine gun and we thought we'd never see that squad again. We tried to maneuver around the VC but the machine gun hit several more GI's. We tried to flank the machine gun on both sides and almost reached the squad; we could see their faces clearly. They had been hit real hard and had run low on ammo. One of the men was cracking up. We had watched while his friends were cut to pieces and he couldn't do anything but watch. The guy was shaking and had a wild look in his eyes. He couldn't move, or even crawl back to safety. After a while, lying in the heat of the day, and running out of water, he was going to go into shock soon. Wesley and I found a way to crawl up to them and told the guy suffering from stress to follow us back to safety. Our platoon was covering us as we dragged some wounded back. Our position was weak and the machine gun opened up again. A second machine gun joined the first. Rounds were hitting everywhere as we crawled and dragged the wounded back to safety. The wounded were in bad shape and couldn't move themselves. The shaken GI didn't follow us. He was hugging the ground and couldn't move, frozen with fear. He would be the last man taken out because he wasn't wounded. Two more GI's joined us and made a trip dragging wounded out. One of the two was hit by the VC. GI's were being wounded faster than we could get them out. The other one, the one not wounded, said that was all, no more were in there. Wesley and I looked but couldn't see the shaken man. We said there was one more and he answered again that there wasn't. Realizing that he was too scared to go back for another trip, we crawled back in. The VC fire was getting heavier and closer, and our platoon was starting to fall back. We needed more firepower. If we didn't hurry, we'd get pinned down and cut to ribbons. When we got to him, all hell broke loose. The VC knew we were falling back, and they started firing more heavily. They threw everything they had. The brush was being chewed up by the hail of fire, just like a chain saw. Limbs and leaves were flying everywhere, broken off close to the ground. We knew we couldn't move because there was no place to go. Wesley and I looked at each other with that "What the hell have we gotten into?" look of realization in our eyes. We couldn't move. Bullets were raking the area. Dirt geysers were dancing all around us. We both thought this was it; it's all over for us. There's no way we'll get out of this alive. I'll tell you for sure, there are no Atheists in combat.

Then, return fire got heavier. We looked back and saw Zipper. Next to him was another machine gunner. Next to them were two thumpers. Behind them was the flame thrower. They were firing as fast as they could and moving up slowly. Wesley and I hugged the ground. Rounds were heavy above our heads, going both ways. When they finally got up to us, the VC firing had stopped. The flame thrower came forward and started burning everything. A wall of flame and smoke went up in front of us. Wesley and I dragged the shaken back. All firing stopped. The VC just took off. The fighting and killing had built to a feverish peak, and then, very suddenly, all was quiet. Those who were still alive returned to normal activities of eating a tin of rations, reloading magazines, and quietly going about their business. A sweep of the area later found three dead VC and blood trails. The rest got away, probably in tunnels.

The guys who rescued Wes and me considered their act of bravery as just another day, but also a chance to take out some of their hostility on the VC. They enjoyed that; finally, a chance to do some damage. And, a chance to get it taken care of, so they could rest.

The villagers could have warned us of the danger, but they didn't. Some of them were probably VC, or VC sympathizers. So, do you kill them? Which ones? All of them? How do you prevent them from causing more GI's to die? Wasn't it enough that we had to fight the VC, without worrying about the South Vietnamese too? But, we kept trying. We never gave up. We lived in the dirt, with death and pain, every day, and became more frustrated and bitter.

We moved to a LZ for extraction and the first flight requested a colored smoke grenade to locate and identify us. The CO told them to look for yellow smoke. We threw out a yellow smoke grenade, and the flight leader saw yellow smoke, but from two different places. The VC was trying to lure the choppers into an ambush in a different LZ; they had been monitoring our radio transmissions. The flight leader requested a second color, and we were soon on our way to camp. The smoke trick worked for the VC once in a while, and they shot down some of our helicopters. Tricks were the only hope the VC had of winning the war.

It was Christmas Eve, and we felt sure we would get several days off, or at least that one day, since it was Sunday also. Not that we ever got Sundays off, but it was the day before Christmas. We didn't. As soon as we hit base camp, we were choppered out on another operation. We were to intercept the flow of rice across the border, rice stolen by the VC. We dropped into an LZ next to a village and struck out for the trees. At the tree line we found shallow punji pits in a trail. Further along were deep punji pits, maybe ten or twelve feet deep, with punji stakes maybe three feet tall sticking up from the bottom. As we walked, I kept wondering what it would be like to fall ten feet and be impaled on those stakes, which probably had septic buffalo dung on them. That had to be a nasty way to go.

We ran into a VC who was trying to crawl down into a tunnel. The VC stopped, held up his hands, and said, *"Chieu Hoi"*, saying he wanted to surrender. When the GI closest to the VC moved closer to tie him up, the VC produced a grenade from nowhere and dropped it at their feet. The grenade exploded and killed both of them.

A GI volunteered to go down into the tunnel and see what he could find. A tunnel rat is a person who has to be small, he has to be gutsy, and it helps if he's a little crazy. You can imagine crawling into a narrow, dark tunnel and not knowing what you'll run into. You might hit a booby trap, get stuck, get lost, get claustrophobia, or run into a VC just waiting for you. The VC even hung scorpions and poisonous snakes from tunnel ceilings to bite intruders.

This time, the tunnel rat found only a place for a few VC to live.

We did find a large rice cache. After killing a few VC guards first, we extracted almost forty tons of rice.

After another week in the boonies, we returned to Dau Tieng. While we were out, there had been a Civic Action program which had distributed more than a ton of candy and over fifteen thousand toys to children. That must have been tough duty passing out all those Christmas goodies. Meantime, we had several men killed or wounded, and one missing in action. No one knew what happened to that one missing man, he just disappeared.

That's how we ended 1967, because it was New Year's Eve.

Soon it would be Tet, the Vietnamese Lunar New Year of 1968, the Year of the Monkey.

17

New Year's Eve wasn't a night off, either. There was a large movement of enemy troops near Fire Support Base Burt, near Soui Cut, and we had to sit up all night with our gear in hand, ready to go fast, in case the VC attacked there. The entire situation was uncomfortable. First of all, January 1 and 2 was supposed to be a cease fire in honor of the Holiday. The VC never honored any cease fire agreements. Only Americans were sucker enough to do that. Second, a favorite VC tactic was to attack a base with overwhelming numbers so help would be called for, and then ambush the American relief forces rushing in to the rescue. We were the relief force for Burt.

The VC, true to form, used the cease fire to move two regiments (three to four thousand men) toward Burt. Their plan was to slow down U.S. clearing operations so they would have cover of trees and brush while moving to Saigon for Tet '68. They didn't attack New Year's Eve, but their movement was detected.

On January 1, I was one of the men chosen to go to Burt to stay there and help them build up their defenses. Of course, we weren't told about the true military situation, if it was known, only that we were a detail to help.

Happy New Year.

We choppered out in the morning and started building bunkers. Little did we suspect that some of these bunkers would be the place of death for the men building them.

I was in a perimeter position with strangers. My friends were back at Dau Tieng and I was here with guys I had never seen before, and probably never would again. It didn't matter though, because everyone was a comrade in arms. There was no distinction by race, or acquaintance. When the firing started, everyone shared the danger and did his part for group survival.

The dust was terrible. Every time a chopper came in, we held our shirts over our noses and faces to filter the air.

After working in the heat all day, and being awake all night, we were hoping for a little sleep. But, we had to keep working long after sunset.

About 10:30 P.M., word was passed that ambushes and LP's had detected movement around the entire perimeter. Just what we needed to get the year started right was to be surrounded by the enemy. Another eyeball-to-eyeball confrontation promised itself. And I was supposed to be here only to help build up the perimeter. I was beginning to wonder why I have been sent on so many special missions, like this one. I never have figured that one out.

We waited in our bunkers, watching, listening, wondering when it would happen, how many there would be, and who would be dead before morning.

About 11:30 it hit the fan. Mortars started falling all around the perimeter. We hunkered down in our bunkers, waiting for the wave of humans that was sure to follow. Whatever was next just had to be dealt with as it happened. We had to be flexible, adapt to the unexpected. If you had to know what was next, you wouldn't last long because the enemy will try to outguess you.

I didn't have my mortar, but it was just as well. Until we could see them, or received direct fire, it would do little good to shoot it.

The incoming mortars eased up and trip flares began igniting around the perimeter. Claymores exploded. Rifles, machine guns, and grenades went off everywhere. The air was electrified. Everywhere you looked. Tracers were screaming by. Explosions, flashes of light, muzzle flashes and fires caused a deathly glow of light. Slap flares went off. It didn't matter what color, because they produced light.

Artillery thundered behind us. HE (High Explosive) rounds exploded in the trees to our front; point blank artillery. Artillery flares went off overhead. The world seemed to be exploding, and we were right in the middle of it. Death was waking and rearing its ugly head.

In the dim light, I could see hundreds of VC running toward us through the trees and firing. I fired my rifle, threw grenades and blew Claymores, and fired my rifle some more. There was no shortage of visible targets. VC were falling to their death everywhere. In the massive horde of attacking humans, you could shoot in any direction you wanted and hit someone. VC were running, crawling, falling, and shooting in every direction. Around me were screams of pain, yells of anger, and curses. Several men near me had been hit and were lying on the ground at my feet. I felt frustrated because my duty was to continue firing, and let the medics tend to the casualties; if all of us stopped firing and dropped our defenses, we would all be killed. But, here at my feet were Americans bleeding and dying, and maybe I could … No, the choice had to be to keep firing and maybe help us all survive.

A brief backward glance gave me a glimpse of:

A short distance along the perimeter I could see Armored Personnel Carriers (APC's) burning from RPG's, GI's burning to death inside. Behind them, artillerymen were working around their cannons feverishly, firing beehive canisters rounds and HE rounds point blank at the VC, scattering bodies like shards from a shattered pane of glass.

A tank turret gun fired, turned a little, fired, turned, fired, ...

A machine gunner on the perimeter was firing a constant stream of tracers, and VC bodies were all around him, even on top of his bunker.

Men were running inside the perimeter; some were Medics, some were carrying ammo, some were reinforcing weak spots in the perimeter, some were VC. I almost couldn't tell if the VC were inside the perimeter, or we were outside.

The firing, explosions and yells continued on, and on, ... I was so busy that I was aware of them only now and then, concentrating on the mess to my front. Part of the perimeter had obviously been overrun. I doubt if any of us expected to get out alive. The VC plan was to attack with men faster than we could kill them, overwhelm us with sheer volume, and then overrun FSB Burt. The VC kept coming. Streams of tracers reached out to the nearest VC, then swung to the next, then to the next. A RPG shooshed in and hit a GI. He disappeared. Bodies littered the area, inside and outside the perimeter. Every time a flare popped, there were more bodies lying around.

After several hours, men started crawling, and running low, back to the supply sites for more ammo. Somebody returned to our bunker and yelled above the noise, "They're running low on ammo."

Helicopter gunships appeared and started shooting up the area. The noise of battle was even louder than before. VC grenades were exploding around us. We kept firing; it was a frenzied reaction. We threw grenades, reloaded, and fired. The gunships fired all around the perimeter, moving from here to there, then another place. I guess they were zeroing in on sources of green tracers.

Fast movers came overhead and dropped bombs everywhere. Some were right up near the perimeter. Incoming slowed for a minute until more VC moved up. The jets swooped in again, and one cluster of bombs exploded so close to me that it knocked my helmet off. It didn't matter; we mentally cheered them on between curses. The bombs had to be close or they wouldn't do any good.

Another man in my position was hit. We were running low on men, as well as very low on ammo. I ran back to get more ammo and glimpsed more results of the fight. The perimeter was lit up like a Christmas wreath by the firing, explosions, and flames. Burning hulks of APC's had been abandoned. Men were running here and there, on what must be important missions to be out in this mess. Bodies were scattered around, some with bandages. Wounded men were crawling to safety. There were tracers flying everywhere, green and red. Artillery was firing point blank, empty shell casings paving the area around the cannons. Bombs were exploding. Trees were falling over. Merry Christmas, everyone.

I had no idea what was going on. Are we winning or losing? If this is winning, then the losers must be going through hell. Whatever the case, the only thing I could do was to keep doing what I was doing.

As I reached the center of the perimeter, a Huey settled in among a group of waiting men. Little Bear had flown in through all this crap, in the dark, to bring in ammo, and take out wounded. The men worked fast and he was gone in less than a minute. Another chopper came in and someone yelled, "He's just in time. We're out of ammo. Take this to the line." My skin crawled when I heard that we were that close to being out. The chopper lifted off and drew heavy enemy fire as he flew low leaving the perimeter. Another came in through the firing. He must have been hit, but he flew out somehow. Those pilots probably saved the lives of us on the ground, as well as the wounded they evacuated. They made many trips that night.

The battle raged on, no less intense than before. The VC seemed to be advancing in an endless wave. Now I knew how General Custer felt at his Famous Last Stand. "WHERE did they all come from?" Will they ever stop? The intensity of the battle didn't slacken but our inner rush did. We just weren't panicked anymore because we were tiring from the physical and emotional strain. Those of us not wounded kept firing, kept pushing, though the wounded tried to help. Everyone was hanging in there until the bitter end, too tired to be panicky.

Air attacks, machine guns, blood, exhaustion, fires, bodies, smoke, and noise kept straining and tearing at our sanity, our soul.

Long after we had stopped looking for the end, the firing lessened, and then sputtered to an end. About 5:30 A.M., dawn was near and, since they were nowhere near a victory, the VC withdrew. The silence, the absence of the bombs, screaming aircraft, cannons firing, and explosions was strange. My ears felt numbed from all the noise. My body hurt from being pushed. I sat with my back against the bunker, waiting for my heart to start working again, waiting to see how many casualties we had, how many VC we had to bury, and how much cleaning up we had to do. It would be another long day.

I realized I hadn't had much to drink for almost eight hours, and I thought that was why I couldn't swallow, why I couldn't get my tongue unstuck from the roof of my mouth. A whole canteen later, my tongue was still dry. In fact, I couldn't spit for the rest of the day. I guessed I was too busy to notice how scared I was.

Sunrise came and I looked around me. The whole area had become a wasteland, all shot to pieces, and a junkyard of bodies and gear. You can't imagine what it looks like because you have nothing to compare, or relate, it to. You want to close your eyes and make it all disappear; it can't be real.

My bunker had sustained a direct hit on top from a mortar, and an RPG in front. Some of the sandbags were missing, and the ones left were pretty raggedy. But, the bunker was still solid. The roof had been made with PSP (Perforated Steel Plate) and heavy logs.

Craters were all around, bushes were uprooted or gone, trees had splintered or fallen, tree limbs were all over the ground. The tree line outside the perimeter had been blown down for over a hundred meters by the artillery and air strikes.

There were bodies hanging on the concertina wire (barbed wire, fashioned to collapse in one "wreath-like" bundle, or strung out like a Slinky toy, to form a fence along the perimeter). Twisted and mangled bodies, pieces of bodies, and gear littered the area in every direction. Hulks of APC's, bunkers and gear were charred black from fires and explosions. Curls of smoke rose above the smoldering debris.

Within a thirty-meter radius of me, I counted fourteen bodies, or groups of pieces, that looked like they came from one body. Next to me were two dead GI's, and one wounded. We all were splattered with blood.

Around the area, men were involved in various kinds of activities. There's no rule to follow after a fight, you just kind of do things. What could be a normal activity after you almost were killed many times over, some of your friends did get killed, and all of you killed a bunch of humans? A few men were mourning the death of a close friend, kneeling over a body. Medics were moving around tending wounded. GI's were carrying casualties to the LZ, and a DUSTOFF was there being loaded. Artillerymen were cleaning up around their guns. Some were repairing their bunkers, cleaning their weapons, setting out new trip flares and Claymores. There was little talk.

I went to the supply area near the LZ to get some rations for breakfast before I started rebuilding. When I arrived, there was a group of men already there. Some were waiting for a MEDEVAC, some were eating C's, and some were just there. I couldn't help but think of the Statue of Liberty – "Give me your tired…, your huddled masses…"

I saw faces that no longer had the shine and color of youth. It was mostly quiet, just occasional eye movement. The eyes, always the eyes. Eyes can tell a story. These told of terror, sadness, anger, hate, bitterness, and exhaustion. They told of being tired beyond physical exhaustion, beyond physical rest. They told of being so tired that you forget where you are, of being tired of the whole thing, down into the depths of your soul. The eyes look back at you and tell you that they don't want to go through another day. They are close enough to reach out and touch, but they look back at you from some place you can't reach.

I asked one of the guys sitting at the LZ if I could use his P-38. He just sat there, staring straight ahead. A wounded man next to him said, "Here's mine. I won't need it anymore." Nodding toward the speechless GI next to him, he continued, "He lost it last night. His position was wiped out when he went to get some ammo. Lost three friends at one time. Don't know what hit 'em. Could have been one of those new Chi-Com rockets. There were chunks scattered everywhere; mangled, twisted, dripping. Everywhere. Probably find their dog tags out in the bushes, if you can find the bushes." Absolutely crazy.

Walking back to the perimeter, I felt sorry for the guys that were emotional casualties, as well as those that were physical casualties. Most GI's seemed to be able to handle the strain of combat, at the moment. But, some couldn't handle it from the moment they hit the bush, and times like these pushed them over the edge.

It isn't possible to relieve the constant physical and psychological strain of men in combat. This stress was relentless, building and building, all the while weakening their psyche, often showing signs in their behavior. Then something like Soui Cut happened, and they snapped. They couldn't help it; couldn't control it, prevent it. They just go to pieces.

We killed a lot of VC that night, and the following night. The war wasn't any shorter for it. We didn't get any time off to rest because of it. And, the next day it was back to the grind.

The whole thing was crazy, a nightmare scenario you can't dream up unless you see it firsthand. Just like the end of the Earth; you just have to see it to believe it.

18

Occasionally, something out of the ordinary happened. One day, we sunk a Sampan. It was leaving the area where we lost a man to a sniper. The Sampan wouldn't stop when we signaled it, and somebody on board shot at us. That was his last mistake. We had a thumper that could land a grenade on a dime at two hundred meters. The Sampan had something explosive on board, and went up in flames. That did a lot more for our morale than it did for the war.

On another day, we set into an LZ late in the evening. We had only enough time to dig holes in the ground for our positions. The CP hole, maybe four feet deep and ten feet in diameter, where the CO and the HQ section would be, had a hole in a wall, three or four feet below ground level. The basketball sized hole was sort of shrugged off as some kind of air bubble in the dirt, and maybe would be looked at in the morning light. So, the CO and HQ section stayed there that night, with the opening just feet from them. In the morning, when it was light enough to make the position larger, digging resumed. As the fighting position got larger in diameter, the hole in the wall got larger, until it was obvious that it was part of a tunnel. A tunnel rat shined his flashlight in the tunnel and saw a VC. The VC had been right there all night. We threw a CS gas grenade (like tear gas but much stronger) into the tunnel and out came five VC. One of them was a paymaster who was carrying 20,000 Piasters. Five POW's and not a shot fired.

Another time, we had an IG (Inspector General) Inspection during my tour. Generally speaking, in the States these were to make sure units, and personnel, were by the book. They would normally check everything. Everything. Paperwork, dog tags, rifles, pots and pans, you name it. Everyone complained bitterly that in a combat zone, you just can't go by the book. It just can't work that way. We were assured that the inspections were only going to make sure that we had everything we needed to fight the war. That sounded reasonable, but turned out not to be true. It so happened that on the day of the inspection, I rode shotgun on a convoy. When I returned, filthy, I went straight to the shower, leaving my dirty gear out to clean afterward. An Inspector saw my dirty rifle and wrote it up as a deficiency against my friend, Jim, the Company Armorer. I couldn't help but feel they were trying to justify their existence: a dirty rifle in a combat zone; blame placed on the Armorer, who had nothing to do with it. They never said anything to me. As if we didn't have enough to worry about, we had to put up with petty harassment.

While these things happened, the war was still dragging on. As if to remind us, we were informed by a South Vietnamese in Dau Tieng that he was teaching his son the family trade because it would be needed for many more years. His trade was coffin making. He said he was making a lot of money because so many of his people were being killed by the VC. He told me the VC attacked a village in this district, had assassinated the village council chairman, and had driven away the Vietnamese Government personnel. The VC had also attacked Bao Trai (where we painted some buildings for the villagers), had killed many people and left hundreds homeless. There were also rumors of slave labor by the VC using captured villagers. He said all those people would soon die and he would be very busy.

We were busy too, fighting with understrength units, looking for that light at the end of the tunnel, trying to hang on until the shape of the table at the Peace Talks could be decided and peace could follow. That time was being bought by the lives of friends we were loading in DUSTOFF helicopters, fiends who had soldiered their guts out as part of the peace effort.

We continued fighting the symptoms of Communistic activities in South Vietnam, instead of the source in North Vietnam, with no plan or goal to win the war. The U.S. was completely fooled into chasing the carrot that North Vietnam dangled in front of us. The South Vietnamese wouldn't fight the war against Communism so the U.S. decided to fight it for them. The Grunts struggled on alone in this no-win war.

The grind we met with our very first day in the field never ended. We choppered to Location A for a day or a week, then to Location B for a while, and then to C, or maybe back to A. Kill a few VC here, lose a few friends there. Combat Assault to a hot LZ. Dig up some VC graves. Night position gets mortared, lose a few more friends. Firefight, destroy tunnels, walk into a minefield, search more tunnels, battles with air strikes, and carry more friends to a DUSTOFF. As time passed, the number of familiar faces grew less as the war took its toll.

All the while, we lived in the elements, thinking that the war was the same, no matter where you happened to be in Vietnam. It wasn't though, but we didn't find out until we were pulled back to Saigon/Tan Son Nhut during Tet '68. We spent most of that time just outside the city and airfield for security, but Jim and I had a chance to go into the city. The first thing I saw was the tens of thousands of Vietnamese villagers that had come to Saigon for safety. Since they had no houses, and no money, they built hovels for their families from anything they could scavenge; wooden crates, pieces of boards and cardboard. Some were no more than large cardboard boxes. These makeshift dwellings were everywhere, throughout the entire city. Block after block, the city was jammed with these people who chose to be free in the South, rather than be Communist and live in the North, which meant war and living in boxes. There were severe problems with space, sanitation, food, and medical arrangement, but they were a little safer here.

Further into town, we passed ARVN's. There were more ARVN's here than there ever were in the field. They wore starched fatigues and seemed to be doing little, if anything, for the war effort. They were walking around the streets laughing and shopping, protected from the war which was not very far away. We were supposed to be helping these people, but it seemed they had withdrawn completely and let us carry on alone.

Then we came to the American Sector and I really couldn't believe what I saw. The sun was just setting and night life was beginning. There were paved streets with curbs and sidewalks, electrical powerlines, motorcycles, humming air conditioners, flower gardens, restaurants, gift shops, and more electric lights than I had seen in what seemed years. The smell of food cooking in restaurants drifted by, as did long forgotten smells and sounds. These guys were almost tourists. The only difference was our government was paying for this. And, no guns. No one was carrying a gun. This is the U.S. Army in Vietnam? What the hell am I, busting my butt all day every day, so these guys can live like this? Everyone had clean starched fatigues, clean shaves and haircuts, and smelling like after shave. Jim and I had rumpled, sour smelling, mildew fatigues, shaggy haircuts, and smelled like we should smell after no shower in several weeks. We stood there for a long time, not saying a word, just looking and watching. Are we still in Vietnam? GI's were hurrying down sidewalks talking about which restaurant to eat in, which club had the best entertainment that night, and griping because there was a power failure earlier and they had no hot water for a shower. Poor guys really had a rough time of it. Can you imagine, no hot water? It was very difficult for Jim and me to accept what was happening here when just a short distance down the road we live in the dirt, like animals, spilling blood, and were overjoyed when we got a tin of cookies from home.

We decided to try a night spot since we were here so we selected the swanky looking club we happened to be standing in front of. The outside was traditional French/Vietnamese architecture, neat as a pin, and could have passed as the Country Club. We went inside and saw carpets, mirrors, uniformed Vietnamese waiters, and a long well-stocked bar. We got a lot of stares at our pitiful fatigues, as though we were ruining somebody's war. We continued walking, and down a long hallway saw a club room, a restaurant, and finally the room with live entertainment. We felt very out of place but we plopped down at a table right next to the stage because we weren't about to leave all this. Somebody had been holding out on us, big time.

The show was a rock group from the Philippines and they were good. Of course, any music would have sounded good to us.

After a couple of drinks, a few guys came to our table and started talking. When they found out we were from an Infantry unit, they started asking questions. Then they started buying our drinks so we would tell them war stories, about the war they were "fighting." These guys didn't know what was going on; not a clue. War news here had to be brought in from the field.

The last time I remember seeing Jim that night, he had about ten guys huddled around him listening to his stories (and he was just the base camp Armorer). I turned back to my ten listeners, who were buying me drink after drink, and continued telling them about the great Battle of Shooey Cuth, No, Swee Cot. Whatever. At the bottom of the war was the Grunt.

V

Physical and Emotional Effects

19

There is no "lived happily ever after.'" Only, the harsh life of combat, except in the movies and in the minds of those who have never been there.

The memories are there for a long time, some even permanently, some suddenly brought back by little triggers; the sight of blood; the sound of a helicopter; stepping in mud; the smell of diesel exhaust fumes or sour, damp cloth; or just walking at night, in the dark.

The effects are more scarring. Some are permanent. The variety and severity of effects certainly must vary somewhat, depending on each GI'S emotional make-up and the specific events during his tour. Some are very pronounced and, I believe, some are subtle, latent; there, though often you may not even realize it. To this day, fifty years later, I have a strong compulsion to travel light, every day, always checking for spare baggage or hindrances. I also still have a need to keep noise levels down so I can hear if anything threatening is happening around me, though I know nothing is. I also feel that I have a nerve problem, problem feet, skin problems, spine problem, and other physical problems caused by my year in Vietnam. None are bad enough for me to qualify for disability, but are bothersome on a daily basis. The point is I, and no doubt countless other combat veterans, just have to live with these things which weren't there before we went.

Some effects were short-lived, beginning to fade after returning home. For instance, the effects from the discomfort of having to live in the elements day and night; jungle rot from weeks of not being able to bathe; mud, bugs, thorns, sleeping in the mud and rain, and the drudge in the hostile, wet, green hell. Soap, hot meals, a clean change of clothes, and even dry feet were luxuries we had to do without. It was a harsh life where you had to worry about having enough food, water, even toilet paper, while trying to preserve your human dignity as well as your sanity. It was a life where mail from home was the only thread linking you to civilization, sanity; the only assurance that there was still a normal life out there somewhere.

There were physical effects, many of which, if not all, that were not experienced by noncombat personnel; the exhaustion of pushing, night and day, carrying a heavy load of gear through the relentless grind; tired from little or no sleep; no occasional afternoon off to escape for a short rest, to forget for a while and regenerate; the monotony of daily life, including the cold, greasy canned meals and the diarrhea from the filthy living conditions and nervous strain. Then there was the nagging worry of the little things that accompany such a Spartan life where you never have proper weapon cleaning equipment or not enough gear, or the fear of running out of ammo. This was life where joy was gotten from finding a small piece of paper and a stub of a pencil to write a note home, and having the time to write the note, of finding a bomb crater full of stagnant water to rinse off a little stink.

There were constant emotional strains like separation from family and friends, wondering if your M-16 would fire when you need it, and wondering if your buddies would crack in a tight spot. There was the bitterness spurred by the realization that the South Vietnamese didn't carry their full share of the war effort. We were fighting their fight for them, bleeding our blood, and dying our deaths.

Finally, there was the frustration of not being able to fight a conventional war, which is what we were trained to do. We couldn't find the enemy, or see him. We tried to force direct confrontation, exposing him by clearing land, burning vegetation, and using defoliant. The enemy then hid among the people. Then we could hear the voices and see the people, but we couldn't tell if they were allies or enemies. It was a hide and seek war. This caused the frustration of impatience with a long drawn out war. America demands fast solutions, quick results. We expected, and were expected, to win the war in short order and go home. North Vietnam substituted a protracted engagement knowing America would lose interest. North Vietnam couldn't confront our military strength in a conventional war so they wanted to drain our patience, reduce our will to resist. America never lost a battle, or ran from one. But it did us little good since we controlled nothing, and had no plan for victory. Since we had no plan, and knew we could still die, for nothing, there's little reason for surprise that the frustration and bitterness manifested itself, in the later years, in marijuana and drugs, and even an incident like My Lai.

It was difficult for the people back home, and for many in Vietnam, to realize these things could be so constant, because they were living in comfort. They would turn the TV war off and naturally assumed the Grunts could, too. But, we couldn't; that was our life, 24/7. These things were only part of a larger picture, because the whole situation was frustrating. It not only had the feel of never ending, but we knew from intuition that we weren't fighting the war to win, only to keep the country from collapsing. We also knew the ARVN's would never be able to hold on by themselves, and let us go home. It was a defensive war, not an offensive war. No matter how conscientious a soldier we were, the course of the war was unchanged, so the outcome was predetermined, as witnessed by the endless stream of casualties going home. The effects of all these things begin to lose their edge soon after returning home.

Then there are the longer lasting effects, some of which become permanent scars on your soul. Some of these effects are caused by the relentless exposure to the elements of combat; the killing, gore and rage; the brutality and terror; the pain and suffering; the danger and fear; the constant physical and emotional strain. You are exposed only to the down side of life, nothing from the good side. It's very lonely facing death but you have no choice, and your only duty is to kill while trying to survive. When you lose a friend you don't just see a body but enough pieces to look like a jig saw puzzle, or his remains drip from trees. He isn't just dead. That isn't enough in war. He's mangled, mutilated. A few deaths sadden you, but you can't recover because there's a constant stream of bodies until you either break, or it takes the edge off your emotion, allowing you self-preservation. Combat is very different in person than in a picture. A picture shows one or two dead, for example, but not the endless stream of bodies that numbs your senses. A picture can show the strain of the moment on a GI's face, but not the fact that it is just one of a relentless flood of moments that keeps grinding you down. A picture can show the reaction of the moment, of anxiety and danger, but not the fact that for months, even years after the war, loud noises, sudden noises, and sudden movement cause a phobic reaction, as one example. I sincerely believe that to appreciate the scarring effects of combat, you have to live in it twenty four hours a day for months, until you can't remember what it was like; to sleep without a rifle in your hand; to wake up and not smell like garbage; to not worry about getting shot by a sniper, or in an ambush, at any second; to walk without worrying about stepping on a booby trap; to just do something because you feel like it; or to know that tomorrow wouldn't bring more killing. Then, after you reach the point when you don't think you can take anymore, and thoughts of right versus wrong have long been replaced by the struggle for survival, and you have nothing to look forward to but more of the same, and you focus on something else except killing the enemy, and it continues to get worse, not better or less, then you are ready to measure your scars.

It seemed as though America was shocked to see death and killing on their television screens, that this just shouldn't be allowed, that they didn't realize that's what war is all about. This is exactly the purpose and the result of war.

Then there was the lack of support from our own country as well as the Vietnamese. Someone sent us, and someone wanted us in their country, but no one seemed to appreciate our efforts. We were no different than the people who sent us. We were just doing our best to win an unwinnable war, but we only heard about the bad effects of our efforts, not the good. We were fired on from "friendly villages" and found that the people we thought we were helping were really VC, or at least helping the VC.

What of the Americans who demonstrated, who labeled us with unfair names, while we were doing our best? They may as well have stabbed us in the back. What of the people who ran off to Canada, but now have been excused from treason, and now enjoy citizenship without paying the dues asked of them? The difference now between them and we who served? We both have citizenship; they at no risk and no cost, we at great risk and, for some, the ultimate cost.

What of the Americans who went to North Vietnam, the enemy, to console them and speak against GI's and U.S. policy? If we GI's had done this, we would have been convicted of treason.

The feeling of abandonment by our own country, the very ones who sent us, was very strong; resentment of being alone in the war effort, of being misused, of wasted lives. I don't wonder that some GI's seemed alienated, some perhaps even hostile, after they returned.

The Grunt fared worse than the other GI's. Grunt life was at the bottom. He could endure all the hardships, but for all his soldiering, it could end any day, any minute, and there was no respite. He could only hang on, wondering what would happen next. The final test of training should have been killing the enemy in an offensive war. Because of the restrictions placed on the military, the war was a defensive war and the final test became survival. Since there was no plan for victory, the U.S. was wasting Grunt lives for nothing. Every U.S. policy seemed to affect the Grunt the most. Because we couldn't cross the Cambodian border, the enemy had a free zone in the midst of the war. When the U.S. honored a ceasefire for various holidays, the enemy was busy building his strength, or infiltrating for an attack. Then to try and understand how base camp life could be so unnecessarily comfortable, even in some places so luxurious, just a few miles down the road from where the Grunts were sleeping and dying in the mud, it was difficult to accept the war as a serious military effort at times.

All these things are not easily forgotten. Some will never be forgotten. The results, callousness, desensitization, phobias, numbing, and rage of combat, are scars caused by something most people will never understand because they will never have to experience it. The Combat Infantrymen were no different than the people at home who sent him, but he changed. He had to become callous to the value of life so that it was easy to kill and have no regrets. He didn't want to see the killing and suffering, but he had no choice. He had to take life before his was taken. He was forced to change to survive. His soul was burned out of him leaving a hollow shell.

It's difficult to explain why, for years afterward, you don't want to go to sleep, and try to stay awake as long as possible. Or, why you walk silently, as though you are sneaking around someone. It's more difficult to explain the rage awakened by training and deeply ingrained by combat. It's impossible to explain how you can still, years later, know you can look someone in the face and mechanically shoot him, and sleep well that night. Like learning to ride a bicycle, you never forget. Today you can still turn off your emotions the same way you learned to do to ensure personal survival, to cover yourself with that callousness.

If it's shocking to talk about these things, then try to imagine how it felt to be forced to make these changes to survive, for self-defense. These weren't just part of life, they were life. They were burned into our subconscious, like a scar, and became part of us.

Finally, in twenty-four hours, the Infantryman was taken from the jungles and rice paddies, flopped into the middle of society and expected to flip a switch from "War, kill. No rules" to "Society. Don't kill. Follow the rules." Imagine the fear of walking down the sidewalk in a city, hearing fireworks, a car backfire, or any sudden, loud noise, and having the instinctive reaction to kill.

This extreme 180 degree change not only can't be done in twenty-four hours but the short period of time served to contrast the extreme in which we had been living for so long. After a few months, we adjusted to combat life so that it seemed normal. The return in twenty-four hours was a jolting reminder that our life had not been normal.

Imagine landing at the airport and being greet by a hostile, name-calling crowd.

The instinctive reaction to hostility is to attack. It's a wonder there weren't more serious incidents when GI's returned home and were met by the jeering groups of people calling them murderers and baby killers.

It's no wonder alcoholism, drug abuse, divorce, post-traumatic stress syndrome, and suicide were so common among combat vets.

Confusion in learned instincts caused severe readjustment problems. I had my problems, too, but they did pass and I attribute the success in dealing with them to the same ability I used to develop that protective callousness. Support also came from a loving and patient family.

No doubt all vets thought they'd return home unchanged, to a society that was unchanged, but neither was. It was a sad thing to be in a crowd of people you fought in behalf of, and be very alone, even shunned. You've had to build up the energy of your youth on survival in the rice paddies and jungles, risking death for nothing, and no one gave a damn.

That's what made Vietnam different.

What did we accomplish? Nothing.

What did it cost the U.S.? Estimated $168 Billion. But the tax dollars can be replaced.

Then there are the permanent effects, and the real cost of the war:

Of the 2,594,000 who served in-country:
58,267 were killed.
153,303 were wounded.
16,413 Missing in Action.
48% of the deaths occurred in 1967 and 1968.
28% occurred in one year, 1968. (one every 32 minutes)
2,415 in one month, May, 1968.
69% were 22 years old or younger.
57% were 18 years old.
20% were teenagers.
32% were Infantry, MOS 11B.
382 suicides.
Permanently disabled ?
Agent Orange ?
PTSD ?

VI

Looking Back

20

I have decided that a description of combat life requires more than a few words. It requires a story, a recount of events, because there is nothing else in life that it can be equated with. The events in combat can be found nowhere else, only in combat.

This was a brief look at a few typical, actual events, covering only a short period of time. There were many other things that happened during that period, and many more during the balance of my tour. Some were more vicious and bloody. Some were more tense and painful. But, to mention all of these other things would take a book of considerable length. I know you would be interested in the other events, and reading about everything that was experienced during that year would impress on you all the more the relentless exposure of a Grunt to combat.

After writing, reading, rewriting, and rereading this manuscript, I feel that it falls short of conveying the complete effect of that year In Vietnam. The words focus on a string of events that are a small part of the scenario unfolding around them, and their weight is fully meaningful only when experience can fill in the rest of the picture; the intensity, fear, and horror. But, it does give you a small taste of what Grunts experienced.

Further, I think that news pictures seen by Americans on TV could not be very informative, maybe even misleading, because they were only an isolated moment in a string of events. Thus, you have an isolated moment offered to describe the war when in fact it may not describe the event.

It's easy for me to look back and say, "Yes, I'd do it all again", because I returned safely, no wounds. The truth is, I would. I feel the cause was a good one, but the means were self-defeating.

I've looked for the silver lining on my experience in Vietnam, and have found only one; a deeper appreciation of Freedom, or, Democracy. In a sense, my feelings toward Freedom had come full circle. At first, I knew it was wonderful, but I wasn't aware of the cost. When I became aware of the great cost, my feelings became ambivalent. Next, I became hostile toward the war and, by extension, Democracy. Then I realized it wasn't the reason for this war that deserved the hostility, but the way we fought the war. Finally, I realized how wonderful Freedom is. And I was fully aware of its cost. Because it is so wonderful, people all over the world dream of coming to America to enjoy our freedom. Freedom, Democracy, does not exist naturally. It must be fought for and constantly protected, and that is why Vietnam happened.

God bless America.

"Freedom never yet was given to nations as a gift,
but only as a reward, bravely earned by one's own exertions."
             -Lajos Kossuth, Hungarian Revolutionary Patriot

"All Expenses Paid"
Highlights of my year-long visit to Vietnam (Combat Infantry)
Review: One star – Would Not Recommend
Come healthy, leave a medical mess.

Accommodations: Muddy ground, with bugs.
Dining: All meals from cans, cold.
Travel: Walking, or helicopter with feet hanging out the door (Our choice).
Dress: We provide, all green, your size not available.
Souvenirs: Unlimited, but you need to use your ingenuity.
Hunting: VC, NVA, Chinese Advisors. (Caution, they shoot back).
Photo spots: Occasional, usually not rated G.
Things to see and do:
I saw: Pain and lots of blood.
  Rain and lots of mud.
  Held my friends as they took their last breath, before their death.
  The enemy who killed my friends.
  Jungles, with tangles and tunnels.
  Days and moonless nights, both seemed to have no end.
  Always wet, from rain and sweat, in the green hell.
  Always smelled sour because we had no way to shower.
  Tired, stink, and stress.
  Oppressed villagers.

ABOUT THE AUTHOR

All Expenses Paid is John Launer's initial published offering. He is proud to be the first to present the true story of how combat Infantrymen in the Vietnam conflict were misrepresented to the American public by the media. While in Vietnam, he earned many awards, including the Combat Infantry Badge and Bronze Star, but was denied the Purple Heart for political reasons. He holds an MBA from the University of Texas. John is now retired and lives in McAllen, Texas with his wife Jan, and daughter Lisa. He enjoys spending his time with family, college football, and trying to help others along the "right" path in life.

www.ingramcontent.com/pod-product-compliance
Lightning Source LLC
Chambersburg PA
CBHW061758110426
42742CB00012BB/2006